THE LANGUAGE LIBRARY

EDITED BY ERIC PARTRIDGE AND SIMEON POTTER

★

ALREADY PUBLISHED

ALAN S. C. ROSS

ETYMOLOGY

WITH ESPECIAL REFERENCE TO ENGLISH

unte ƕarjatoh waurde at mannam
innuman maht ist anþarleikein inmaidjan

SKEIREINS VI

ANDRE DEUTSCH

FIRST PUBLISHED 1958 BY
ANDRE DEUTSCH LIMITED
105 GREAT RUSSELL STREET
LONDON WC1
© ALAN S. C. ROSS 1958
SECOND IMPRESSION JUNE 1962
THIRD IMPRESSION JULY 1964
FOURTH IMPRESSION NOVEMBER 1969
ALL RIGHTS RESERVED
PRINTED IN GREAT BRITAIN BY
STEPHEN AUSTIN AND SONS LTD
HERTFORD

233 95552 6

CONTENTS

PREFACE

AN UNOFFICIAL directive informed me that the terms of reference of the present book were that it was primarily to be addressed to the Second Year student at the University. I find these terms of reference very agreeable. The book is thus essentially elementary; nevertheless, many of its readers will have acquired some knowledge of Anglo-Saxon, of its sound-changes, and, thus, of the nature of Sound-Change—all important matters for the English etymologist. At the same time there need be—and is—nothing in the book to make it unsuitable for the non-academic public, a body of persons among whom I have long observed a very considerable interest in etymological questions. I hope also that a third group of persons— my colleagues and fellow-workers—may find the Methodology and Theory of Language of the book not altogether without interest.

The elementary character of the book is the excuse for a certain old-fashionedness of presentation; essentially, I have presented matters rather as I myself learnt them in the Honours School of English Language and Literature of the University of Oxford during the years 1927–9 under the excellent tuition of such etymological enthusiasts as Dr C. T. Onions, the late Professor H. C. Wyld, Professor J. R. R. Tolkien, and Professor C. L. Wrenn. The cognoscenti will notice this old-fashionedness most in my attitude towards Ablaut—for they will find here no mention of Laryngeal Theory. This means, in effect, that what I have said about Ablaut cannot be entirely true. My untruthful attitude has a twofold cause. First, as I write, Laryngeal Theory is somewhat in a state of controversy [1] so that, although what I say about Ablaut is partly false, it would be difficult, perhaps impossible, for anyone yet to say about it that which is wholly true. Second—and perhaps the more important—it is certainly quite impossible for anyone to understand Laryngeal

---

[1] Cf., for instance, E. Polomé, Zum heutigen stand der laryngaltheorie, *Revue belge de Philologie et d'Histoire* xxx, 444 ff.; R. A. Crossland, A reconsideration of the Hittite evidence for the existence of " Laryngeals " in Primitive Indoeuropean, *TPS* 1951, pp. 88–130; W. P. Lehmann, *Proto-Indo-European phonology*.

Theory without being thoroughly familiar with junggrammatisch Ablaut—and it is, essentially, the Ablaut of Brugmann that I present.

I may take this opportunity of explaining the technique with regard to the giving of the meanings of words that I have adopted here. In Indoeuropean Etymology the practice has, in the main, been one of renaguing upon the meanings, giving only just sufficient to enable words to be identified. This is undoubtedly hard upon the elementary student. The opposed technique, which is probably methodologically ideal, is to give the meaning of every word which is not a word of the language in which the book is written. This is, however, a laborious process and one which takes up much space. In the present book I have adopted a compromise, one which I hope may be thought useful : I give the meaning of every non-English word unless it is a word of a language belonging to one of the three following Sets :—(A) Latin and Greek ; (B) the " great " modern languages (*weltsprachen*), French, German, Italian, Portuguese Russian and Spanish [1] ; (C) the Germanic Languages.[2][3] The giving of meanings in any reasonably concise form is a hazardous business ; I hope the fact that I have not followed the sound Finno-Ugrian practice of giving all meanings by citation from and in the original language of the source-works will not have led me into all too much error.[4]

In conclusion I must express my most sincere gratitude to Mr R. Burchfield (Oxford) for all the care and hard work he has lavished upon this book ; further to Mr E. G. Stanley (Birmingham) and to my wife for advice upon the most diverse points.

ALAN S. C. ROSS

---

[1] Of the other two weltsprachen, Arabic and Chinese, the former finds little mention in the present work, the latter but one ; I exclude Arabic from my Set B.
[2] See p. 74.
[3] Because of German, Sets (B) and (C) are not mutually exclusive.
[4] Cf. also p. 37, note 2.

ABBREVIATIONS

Grammatical Terms

a. *or* acc. = accusative ; adj. = adjective ; adv. = adverb ; aor. = aorist ; ἄπ.λεγ. = ἅπαξ λεγόμενον ; ba. = borrowed as ; comp. = comparative ; d. = dative *or* dialect ; def.art. = definite article ; dial. = dialect ; encl. = enclitic ; f. = feminine ; g. = genitive ; i. = instrumental ; imp. = imperative ; impf. = imperfect ; intr. = intransitive ; lw(f). = loan-word (from) ; m. = masculine ; n. = neuter *or* nominative ; p. = plural ; part. = partitive ; pass. = passive ; pf. = perfect ; pl. = plural ; ppart. = past (preterite) participle ; pres. = present ; pret. = preterite [1] ; s. *or* sg. = singular ; sup. = superlative ; tr. = transitive ; voc. = vocative.[2][3]

Languages (and English dialects) [4]

A = Anglian ; AFr = Anglo-Frisian ; AN = Anglo-Norman ; Arm = Armenian ; Av = Avestic ; Bg = Bulgarian ; E = English ; EMids = East Midlands dialect ; Fr = Frisian ; HG = High German ; Ic = Icelandic ; IndE = Indoeuropean ; It = Italian ; K = Kentish ; Lith = Lithuanian ; MLG = Middle Low German ; N = Norse [5] ; Norw = Norwegian ; nsorb = " niedersorbisch " ; Nth = Northumbrian ; oberd = " oberdeutsch " ; OPR = Old Prussian ; OS = Old Saxon ; osorb = " obersorbisch " ; Port

---

[1] sg.pret. = 1st and 3rd sg.pret. (in some Germanic languages).

[2] In the case of verbs, absence of indication denotes that the main mood and/or voice is intended ; thus 3rd sg.pres. = 3rd sg.pres. indicative (Germanic), 3rd sg.pres. indicative active (Latin).

[3] These abbreviations are frequently combined without intervening stop, as ds. = dative singular.

[4] The abbreviations E (*Early*), L (*Late*), M (*Middle*), Mn (*Modern*), O (*Old*), Pr (*Primitive*) are used before these names, as OFrench = Old French, MHG = Middle High German.

[5] Note the abbreviation (following an English word) " N lw. : Ic . . ." ; this means that the English word is a Scandinavian loan-word and that the Icelandic word is a congruent of the etymon.

9

= Portuguese ; PrGmc = Primitive Germanic ; Prov = Provençal ; PrSlav = Primitive Slavonic ; S-Cr = Serbo-Croatian ; Skt = Sanskrit ; Sp = Spanish ; Sw = Swedish ; Ukr = Ukrainian ; WG = West Germanic ; WMerc = West Mercian ; WMids = West Midlands dialect ; WS = West Saxon.

Texts

AR = Ancrene Riwle (ed. M. Day, EETS 225) ; A. Wisse = Ancrene Wisse ; Ayen = Ayenbite (ed. R. Morris, EETS 23) ; CM = Cursor Mundi (ed. R. Morris, EETS 57, 59, 62, 66, 68, 69, 101) ; Hav = Havelok (ed. W. W. Skeat and K. Sisam) ; KathGr = Katherine Group ; KG1 = Kentish Glosses (ed. J. Zupitza, *Zeitschrift für deutsches altertum* xxi, 1 ff. ; xxii, 223 ff.) ; LambHom = Lambeth Homilies (ed. R. Morris, EETS 29, 34) ; Laȝ = Layamon (ed. F. Madden) ; Lind = Lindisfarne Gospels (Urs Graf ed.) ; PP1 = Piers Plowman (ed. W. W. Skeat) ; PromptP = Promptorium Parvulorum (ed. A. L. Mayhew, EETS*ES* 102) ; RG1 = Robert of Gloucester (ed. A. Wright) ; Rit = Durham Ritual (ed. A. Hamilton Thompson and U. Lindelöf) ; Ru¹, Ru² = the first and second portions of the Rushworth Gospels (ed. in W. W. Skeat, *The Holy Gospels in Anglo-Saxon, Northumbrian, and Old Mercian versions*) ; VPs = Vespasian Psalter (ed. in Sweet *OET*).[1]

Books [2]

d'Ardenne = S.T.R.O. d'Ardenne, *An edition of þe liflade ant te passiun of Seinte Iuliene* ; BB = *Beiträge zur kunde der indogermanischen sprachen* ; EAGS = *English and Germanic Studies* ;

[1] I mention here certain texts which I refer to without abbreviation :—Beowulf (ed. F. Klaeber) ; Chaucer (ed. W. W. Skeat) ; Chronicle = Peterborough Chronicle (ed. C. Plummer) ; Corpus = Corpus Glossary (ed. in Sweet *OET*) ; Epinal = Epinal Glossary (ed. in Sweet *OET*) ; Gawain = Sir Gawain and the Green Knight (ed. J. R. R. Tolkien and E. V. Gordon) ; Leiden Riddle (ed. in A. H. Smith, *Three Northumbrian poems*) ; Morte Arthure (ed. E. Björkman) ; Orm (ed. R. M. White and R. Holt) ; Ruthwell Cross (ed. in B. Dickins and A. S. C. Ross, *The Dream of the Rood*). The text of the Gothic Bible is cited from W. Streitberg, *Die gotische bibel* (for Crimean Gothic see W. Streitberg, *Gotisches elementarbuch*, pp. 280–2) ; for Runic Norse forms see A. Jóhannesson, *Grammatik der urnordischen runeninschriften*.

[2] This section is not to be taken as, in any sense, a bibliography ; the works enumerated are simply those whose frequent citation in the present book renders abbreviation of their titles economic.

EETS = Early English Text Society (*ES* = Extra Series); *JEGP* = *Journal of English and Germanic Philology*; *JRAS* == *Journal of the Royal Asiatic Society*; *KZ* = *Zeitschrift für vergleichende sprachforschung*; *LSE* = *Leeds Studies in English and kindred languages*; Luick = K.L., *Historische grammatik der englischen sprache*; *MSL* = *Mémoires de la Société de Linguistique de Paris*; *NED* = J. A. H. Murray et al., *A new English dictionary*; *PBB* = *Beiträge zur geschichte der deutschen sprache und literatur*; Pedersen = H.P., *Vergleichende grammatik der keltischen sprachen*; Persson = P.P., *Beiträge zur indogermanischen wortforschung*; Pokorny = J.P., *Indogermanisches etymologisches wörterbuch*; Sweet = H.S., *Anglo-Saxon Reader*; Sweet *OET* = H.S., *The oldest English texts* (EETS 83); *Tables* = A. S. C. Ross, *Tables for Old English Sound-Changes*; *TPS* = *Transactions of the Philological Society*; Trautmann = R.T., *Die altpreussischen sprachdenkmäler*; Walde-Hofmann = A.W. and J.B.H., *Lateinisches etymologisches wörterbuch*; WP = A. Walde and J. Pokorny, *Vergleichendes wörterbuch der indogermanischen sprachen*.

ETYMOLOGY

CHAPTER ONE

ETYMOLOGY

ETYMOLOGY [1] is an esoteric subject and it is therefore not possible to define its scope in a few words ; nor, indeed, would this be desirable. Etymology is a branch, and an important one, of the subject called *Philology* or, alternatively, and synonymously, *Linguistics*. Before the subject of Etymology can even be approached, it is therefore necessary for a reader to be very clear as to the true nature of Philology. Since Philology is not taught in the schools of English-speaking countries, or in those of many [2] other countries, and, since it is not at all a self-evident subject but, rather, one highly esoteric, the general reader, approaching it as a beginner, must expect to have to devote a good deal of hard reading and hard work to its understanding—just as he would have this expectation if he were to start the subject of Algebra *ab initio*. I therefore begin the present work with some account of the nature of Philology (or Linguistics) ; in the course of this account the definition— and the explanation of the nature of—Etymology will be reached.

PHILOLOGY (or *Linguistics*) falls into two parts. The First Part is called either *Descriptive Linguistics* or *Synchronic Philology*, the Second Part either *Historical Philology* or *Comparative Philology* or *Diachronic Philology*. It is possible to indicate the scope of Descriptive Linguistics in a short and non-esoteric manner, but it is not possible to do this for Comparative Philology. This is not to say, however, that Descriptive Linguistics is " easier " than Comparative Philology ; in fact the reverse is true.

Descriptive Linguistics seeks the Answers to two Questions, each of which is a question very simple to state. The First Question

---

[1] The English word *etymology* is a borrowing of French *étymologie*, which is a borrowing of Latin *etymologia*, which is a borrowing of Greek ἐτυμολογία, which is a compound of ἔτυμος ' true ' and λόγος ' word '.

[2] But in some countries (e.g. Finland and pre-War Czecho-Slovakia) a little Philology is/was taught in the schools.

may be cast in the form " What is the best way to describe Language, or to describe a given language ? " Or even, " What is a good way of doing this ? " When the term *a given language* is used here, I mean, of course, a language at a given period of time ; as it might be, the present-day English of an English reader of this book, or the Anglo-Saxon of King Alfred. The Second Question may be put very shortly indeed : it is, " Unto what is Language like ? " Of these two Questions, it may be said, first, that neither has been answered and, second, that they are both " proper " questions, that is, questions to which it is reasonable to expect an answer. As to the propriety of the First Question [" What is the best way to describe Language ? "], I may say that the practical necessity of doing just this is a sufficient (but by no means the only) justification for it. The propriety of the Second Question [" Unto what is Language like ? "] is a little more abstruse. The matter may perhaps best be put thus : living in the kind of universe in which we do live, we expect almost everything to be like something else. To many people, it would therefore be most disquieting to have to admit that there was in fact nothing unto which Language was like ; indeed only those (very few) philologists who maintain that Language is a Divine Gift to Man [1] could reasonably remain unsurprised if no parallel to Language could be found.

I have said that both our Questions are at present without an Answer. It would, however, not be true to say that both are without hope of answer. But—oddly enough, it may seem—the hope of solution is much greater for the Second Question [" Unto what is Language like ? "] than for the First Question [" How to describe it ? "].

It is the recently-developed, and now very fashionable subject called *Communication Theory* or *Information Theory* which, it seems, may one day produce the Answer to our Second Question, " Unto what is Language like ? ".

But, at this point of the discussion, we encounter a major difficulty of treatment. Communication Theory is a highly technical subject ;

[1] Despite the " oddity " of intermingling Theology and Philology, this has been done and not so very long ago : I have in mind the large work, *El lenguaje,* of the well-known Spanish philologist J. Cejador y Frauca, of which the first volume appeared in 1901.

even to understand its nature requires the ability to appreciate complicated mathematical notations (an ability only rarely to be found among Arts Students), its real understanding a considerable knowledge of certain branches of Mathematics and Physics (particularly, of current trends in Electrical Engineering). Under these circumstances, I feel that it is impossible to give any account here of the place of Language in Communication Theory ; this, not only because such an account could not but fail to be incomprehensible to most (though not, of course, to all) readers of this book, but, also, because Communication Theory does lie rather far from the proper subject of this book which, after all, is Etymology and not Philology. It must therefore suffice if I here refer the reader to some standard works.[1] This difficulty of treatment (and its rather unsatisfactory solution of merely referring the reader to standard works), first encountered here, will recur in the pages immediately following. It is a difficulty with which the philologist of to-day is becoming all too familiar, as ever more branches of Philology are seen in fact to have intimate liaison with esoteric, highly technical (and, to the Arts Student, impossibly " difficult ") branches of Mathematics, Physics and Medicine.

Reverting now to our Second Question, " Unto what is Language like ? ". In the first place, it will be convenient—and, I think, legitimate—to transform it by substituting in it the words *the typical linguistic act* for the word *Language*. It does, indeed, seem possible that we should be justified in considering a typical linguistic act as made up of the following things in this order :—

1) An encoding.
2) The production of a phonetic effect.
3) The production of an acoustic effect.
4) A hearing.
5) A decoding.

That is, suppose that there are two English-speakers, A and B,

---

[1] Viz. :—C. E. Shannon and W. Weaver, *The mathematical theory of Communication* ; S. Goldman, *Information Theory* ; N. Wiener, *Cybernetics* ; W. Jackson, *Communication Theory : Papers read at a Symposium on " Applications of Communication Theory "* held at the Institution of Electrical Engineers, London, September *22nd–26th 1952* (especially the paper by my colleague Dr D. A. Bell, *The ' internal information ' of English words*, at pp. 383–91) ; C. E. Shannon, Prediction and entropy of printed English, *Bell System technical journal* xxx, 50 ff.

B

in a normal room, and that A says to B *I'll come to tea to-morrow*, then this linguistic act consists in A's giving linguistic effect to his " thought " by some mental process combined with, or followed by, appropriate acts of his vocal and other organs, acts which produce sound ; this sound is heard and interpreted by B.

It must at once be admitted that little or nothing is yet known of Links 1, 3, 4 and 5 of the chain which constitutes the Linguistic Act, though very much is known of the second link. Regarding the matter in a manner slightly different, it would be true to say that each Link is a vast subject on which very much research-work has been, and is being carried out.

It is obvious that, in this book, I must be forced to treat all the Links save the second in the manner in which I have just treated Communication Theory, and for precisely the same kind of reasons. The study of Link 2 essentially constitutes the subject called *Phonetics* and, in works on Linguistics, it has very long been customary to treat of Phonetics in detail without at all mentioning the detail of any of the other Links. For the student, this has practical advantages, for Phonetics is, for the average philologist, not a particularly " difficult " or esoteric subject, whereas the subjects relevant to the other Links are all both these things. But the inclusion of Phonetics as the sole link-subject discussed can hardly be justified methodologically or logically because this particular Link is no more important than any of the others ; moreover its inclusion is not nearly as necessary as it once was, since the advent of the fundamental and useful concept, *phoneme* (see pp. 23–5), which is essentially a non-phonetic concept. It is abundantly clear that the things philologists are concerned with are phonemes, not speech-sounds ; it is only if we are dealing with the philology of a language of which we do not know the phonemes (such as Ostyak) that it is necessary to discuss its phonetics and, in such a case, it might be argued that it was equally necessary to discuss its speech-acoustics. The inclusion of Phonetics within Philology is, in fact, purely traditional and conventional. So conventional is it that it is impossible to read philological literature without some understanding of the main phonetic terms. After careful consideration, I have decided to adopt the logical course here and, in this book, to treat Phonetics in precisely the manner I treat the other link-subjects (that is, by virtual exclusion and by reference to standard works). At the same time, in consequence of the frequent use of simple phonetic terms and notations in philological literature (in contradistinction to the lack of use of such terms and notations arising out of the disciplines relevant to the other Links), I should wish to impress upon the student the fact that it is greatly more important—and far " easier "—for him to familiarise himself with some simple standard work on Phonetics than it is for him to do likewise in the case of any of the other subjects here treated by me in this manner.

I thus limit myself to the briefest remarks upon the five links— the five may conveniently be reduced to four, for it is difficult to separate the processes of encoding and decoding, they are better regarded jointly under the title *coding*.

Phonetics, the subject arising from the second Link, the production of a phonetic effect, is, in reality, a branch of Medicine, though it is not usually so regarded ; it deals with the Anatomy and Physiology of the vocal organs and classifies speech-sounds with reference to the position of various organs.[1]

Speech-acoustics, the subject arising from a consideration of Link 3—the acoustic effect—is, naturally, a branch of Theory of Sound, which subject is, in turn, a sub-section of Physics. Unfortunately, from the point of view of Acoustics (that is, Theory of Sound) the sounds and noises occurring in Speech are immeasurably more difficult to study than are some of the sounds occurring in Music (as, for instance, sounds arising from the vibration of stretched strings, as of violins). Physicists are, of course, in complete agreement as to the physical origination of the sound of a violin-string but there is not yet complete agreement as to the physical origination of all speech-sounds.[2]

Theory of Hearing, the subject to which the hearing of speech-sound—as of other sound—belongs, is a branch of Medicine, though it may be noted that the Mechanics of Hearing demands rather specialised mathematical treatment. In this field we are most markedly in a realm of conflicting theories.[3]

[1] See D. Jones, *Outline of English phonetics* ; K. L. Pike, *Phonetics* ; V. E. Negus, *The mechanism of the larynx*.

[2] See A. Wood, *Acoustics* ; G. W. Stewart and R. B. Lindsay, *Acoustics* ; H. Fletcher, *Speech and Hearing in communication* ; R. Jakobson, C. G. M. Fant and M. Halle, *Preliminaries to Speech Analysis*.

[3] See E. G. Wever, *Theory of Hearing* ; S. S. Stevens and H. Davis, *Hearing*.

The Links that I have called *Coding* have, at first sight, a much more direct application to Etymology than have the others. For it is here that, for the first time in this book, we have encountered the vast problems connected with the concept *Meaning*. The subject of Meaning is associated with very profound and quite unsolved problems. It has connections with a whole range of different subjects—with Medicine, with Psychology, with Philosophy, with Cybernetics and with Symbolic Logic, to mention only a few. I take two examples.

In the medical field, it is at least safe to say that patients afflicted with those disorders of speech grouped under the head of *Aphasia*, which are caused by physical change within the brain (as from an injury, or a tumour), may suffer alteration of their processes of encoding and/or decoding. What actually happens is, however, very far from clear.[1]

Second, with regard to Symbolic Logic. It is, of course, theoretically possible to make up a symbolism of thought quite divorced from any actual language. Such symbolisms are especially useful for expressing "complicated ideas" very shortly. I take an example; I, (1) write the statement in a standard system of symbolic logic, (2) "translate" each symbol in turn, (3) write out the whole statement, and, (4) add a commentary.

$$(1)$$
$$(x)\,(a)\,[(x \in N\ .\ a \in x) \supset (\hat{\beta}\,(\beta \subset a) \in 2^x)]$$

$$(2)$$

(x)	*read* " For all x " ;	
(a)	,, " For all classes a " ;	
[(	the brackets act as punctuation-marks ;	
x	*read* " x " ;	
$\in$	,, " is " ;	
N	,, " a member of the ' Class ' of Natural Numbers " ;	
.	,, " and " ;	
a	,, " a " ;	
x	,, " x " ;	
)	the bracket acts as a punctuation-mark ;	

[1] See H. Head, *Aphasia and kindred disorders of speech* ; A. Ombredane, *L'Aphasie et l'élaboration de la pensée explicite.*

∋   *read* " if . . . then ", the *then* being in its written place but
        the *if* transposed so as to follow the term (a) ;

(the bracket acts as a punctuation-mark ;

$\hat{\beta}$ *read* " the class of all classes β, such that " ;

(the bracket acts as a punctuation-mark ;

β *read* " β " ;

⊂   „   " is a ' subset ' of " ;

a „   " a " ;

)   the bracket acts as a punctuation-mark ;

ϵ *read* " is " ;

2^x „   " 2^x " ;

)]   the brackets act as punctuation-marks.

(3)

" For all x, and for all classes a : if x is a Natural Number and the Class a is x-in-number, then the Class of all Classes β, such that β is a subset of a, is 2^x-in-number ".

(4)

For the purposes of the present example, a *class* may be defined by saying that it is a set of all-different things (if there are n things, the class is said to be " n-in-number "). A class γ is said to be a *subset* of another class δ if every member of γ is also a member of δ (though every member of δ need not be a member of γ). The *class of classes* here mentioned consists of the totality of subsets of the Class a. The statement now becomes clear, as may be seen from an example. Suppose $x = 3$ (a Natural Number) and that the Class a consists of three balls, one red, one white and one black ; then, by the Statement, the number of possible subsets is $2^3 = 8$—and this is true ; for, from the Class a, it is possible to select the following classes :—(1) no balls at all ; (2) a red ball ; (3) a white ball ; (4) a black ball ; (5) a red ball and a white ball ; (6) a red ball and a black ball ; (7) a white ball and a black ball ; (8) all three balls.

There is, perhaps, no reason to suppose that this kind of thing has much to do with the Linguistic Act. Most writers who try to make liaison between Logic and Language seem to assume that Language is, of necessity, meaningful. But this seems not to be entirely true ; at all events, some language is more meaningful than other language. Thus, if A says to B (two English-speakers)

I'll come to tea to-morrow, that remark is fully meaningful. But if
A says *Good-morning*, that remark is so little meaningful as to be
almost meaningless.[1]

It may perhaps be thought that the Five Links set out above
should have been seven in that the Chain should have included
What is encoded at the beginning and *What is decoded* at the end.
But here we strike against a major difficulty in this difficult field
for some have held that, in the case of a monoglot speaker, *What
is encoded by him* is one thing with *His encoding*. But, at this point,
I must leave the subject of Meaning (so important for Etymology)
in an undefined, chaotic and nebulous condition and, furthermore,
in a condition not showing promise of amelioration. From the
practical point of view the state of affairs is not as bad as my
preceding statement may have led the reader to believe ; after all,
most of us understand very well the meaning of the statement " The
French for *dog* is *chien* ".

I turn now to our First Question, " What is the best (*or* a good) way
to describe Language (*or* a given language) ? ". Two things are quite
clear. First, no one has yet answered this Question in a manner
agreeable to all, or nearly all philologists. And, second, what may
be called the " standard " Answer, that is, " Language may best
be described in the terms in which Latin and Greek are conven-
tionally described " is now rejected by nearly all philologists.
Moreover, it seems reasonable to say that no answer can be satisfactory unless it applies equally to all languages. Examples of how
unsuitable, inconvenient and indefinable are concepts such as
Sentence, Word, Ending and *Part of Speech* in application to all
except some Indoeuropean languages are so easy to find that it will
suffice if only a few are here mentioned.

(1) If, when motoring, the word SLOW is encountered on
approaching a corner, what part of speech is this ?

(2) Probably few would deny that, in the English compound
'sponge-'cake, *sponge* is an adjective ; would more deny it if the
word were pronounced *'spongecake* (as it often is) ?

(3) In Hungarian, *ház-unk* ' our house ' beside *vár-unk* ' we are
waiting ' shows that the distinction between verb and noun has

---

[1] On Symbolic Logic see W. V. O. Quine, *Methods of Logic* ; the same, *Mathematical Logic* ; A. N. Whitehead and B. A. W. R. Russell, *Principia mathematica*.

not always been as clearcut in Hungarian as it is in Latin (*ház*
means ' house ', *vár* is the verb ' to wait ' and *-unk* is the suffix
of the first person plural).

(4) In standard school-grammar, v/e are used to conjugating
verbs and comparing adjectives—but, of course, we may equally
well conjugate prepositions, as Welsh *at* ' to ', *at-af* ' to me ', *at-at*
' to thee ', etc. ; or nouns, as Finnish *kirja* ' book ', *kirja-ni* ' my
book ', *kirja-si* ' thy book ', etc. Indeed, some of the " neatest "
Finnish constructions are effected by declining and conjugating a
verbal noun at the same time, as *sanoa-kse-si* ' that thou mightest
say ', which is the First Infinitive of *sanoa* ' to say ', in the translative case and the second person singular. In Finnish, too, a noun
may be compared ; thus *se on pohjalla laatikossa* means ' it is in
the box, at the bottom ', whereas *se on pohjemalla laatikossa*
means ' it is in the box, *more* at the bottom ' ; here *pohjemalla*
is the adessive case of the comparative of the noun *pohja* ' bottom '.

(5) By all the rules of school-grammar we must consider Eskimo
aulisautissarsiniarpuŋa as a word ; it means, approximately, " I
wish I had something that would do for a fishing-line " and it may
seem questionable whether it is really convenient to have to regard
it as a word and not as a sentence.

(6) It could certainly well be maintained that the only reason
that the *'s* of *the President of Colombia's daughter* is an " ending "
and not a " word " is—that we are acquainted with the History of
the English Language.

(7) A " sentence " is supposed to be " complete ", but the whole
virtue of elliptical sentences such as *If I catch you doing that again,
I'll— !* " is, surely, precisely that they are not complete.

It is however possible to define certain linguistic concepts in a
manner which makes them equally applicable to all languages. Of
these concepts, the most important for our present purposes is
undoubtedly the *Phoneme*. The definition of the Phoneme is, however, long and difficult, and it would be out of place to attempt here
either this definition or any other of the universal definitions of
Language.[1]

But, although it is difficult to define a phoneme, it is not at all

---

[1] I may refer the reader to my article " Theory of Language " *EAGS* iv, 1–12.

difficult to explain the nature of phonemes by means of examples. Thus, the difference between the two [k]-sounds of the English word *kingcup* is appreciable both phonetically and acoustically— given suitable apparatus, of course. This difference is *not* a difference between phonemes in English because no pair of English words is distinguished solely by it. On the other hand, the difference [k]/[t] is a difference between phonemes in English, because at least one pair of English words (*kin : tin*) is distinguished solely by it. Again, the *h* of Japanese *hana* ' flower ' is different from the *h* of Japanese *hito* ' human being '—the first *h* is approximately that of English *house*, the second approximately German *ch* of *chemie* or *ich* (phonetically, [h] and [ç], respectively). No two Japanese words are distinguished solely by this difference [h]/[ç] and we therefore say that the difference [h]/[ç] is *not* a difference between phonemes in Japanese. But this same difference [h]/[ç] does occur as a phone- matic difference in Norwegian, for at least one pair of Norwegian words is distinguished solely by it, namely the pair *høre* ' to hear ' (with [h]) : *kjøre* ' to drive ' (with [ç]). So we observe that a difference that is non-phonematic in one language may be phonematic in another. A curious psychological point may be mentioned in the context of phonemes : normally, speakers of a language (1) do not hear differences in speech-sound which are not differences between phonemes in their own language ; and, (2) expect differences between phonemes which exist in their own language to exist in all other languages. Thus, speakers of English (1) do not normally hear the difference between the two [k]-sounds of *kingcup* and, (2) are surprised to learn that, in Ainu, the difference [n]/[d] is not a difference between phonemes (i.e. that an Ainu can no more hear the difference between [n] and [d] than an Englishman can hear the difference between the two [k]-sounds of *kingcup*). If we denote the two [k]-sounds of *kingcup* by K and k respectively, then the state of affairs existing may best be set out by the statement : " In English the relevant phoneme is, at the least, two-part (or ' bipartite '), that is, the phoneme K^k materialises, at the least, as K and k." Phonemes are often multipartite (cf. pp. 91, 95–6).

The concept *phoneme*—the fundamental concept in Theory of Language—might at first sight appear to be a purely theoretical and " useless " kind of concept. In fact, this is very far from being the case, for Phonematology has one extremely practical application, that is, in the construction of alphabets for languages hitherto unwritten. An alphabet is said to be *perfect* if there is a one-one correspondence between phoneme and letter i.e. if each phoneme is represented by one and only one letter and each letter represents one and only one phoneme. The goodness of an alphabet is, naturally, measured by how near it is to perfection. Thus the English alphabet is one of the worst in the world—*thought* has seven letters but only three phonemes ($[\theta]$, $[\mathrm{ɔ:}]$, $[\mathrm{t}]$) whereas the alphabets of Welsh and Finnish are very nearly perfect. At this point in the discussion it will be well to emphasise something that is doubtless obvious *viz.* the difference between *sound* and *symbol* in written languages ; it is always the philologist's duty to strip away the written symbol, leaving the phoneme exposed, for it is with the latter that he is mainly concerned.

I have said above that the First Question of Descriptive Linguistics, " How to describe Language ? " is without an answer and I have demonstrated that School-Grammar is certainly not its answer. The establishment of the important concept *Phoneme* is, of course, the beginning of an answer, but it does no more than cover a small fraction of the Question. What, then, are we to do in practice and, in especial, in the practice of the present book ?

The obvious thing to do—what indeed always is done—is to compromise. If my *Etymology* had been mainly concerned with languages very " different " from English (such as many of the American Indian languages), no compromise would have been possible. But, in fact, I shall be almost entirely concerned with Indoeuropean languages. School-grammar was designed by the Greeks, passed on by them to Latin-speakers, and it thus became part of the cultural tradition of Europe. The " grammar " of most of the Indoeuropean languages differs but little from that of Greek, and School-grammar therefore " fits " them quite well, though these are the only languages which it does fit. Our compromise is then fairly straightforward : we shall accept School-grammar, thoroughly realising, however, that its terms cannot be defined in any rigid and watertight manner ; they can however usually be explained, in a rather vague kind of way.

I now proceed to give some very brief notes on Grammar. It would not be desirable for these to be more than notes. To take an example : it is very clear from what has gone before that, apropos the distinction between noun and verb, we are never going to get beyond some such statement as " Everyone knows what is meant by this distinction " and there is clearly no virtue in the setting-out of statements of this kind.

1) An English *word*, then, may be defined—trivially—as a " Head-Word " of the *New English Dictionary* (that is, an entry in black, clarendon type)—and similarly for the words of other languages.

2) In the English genitive *dog's*, the *s* is an *Ending*.

3) That branch of Philology which is called *Morphology* is concerned with *Endings* and *Affixes* ; Morphology, like Philology itself, can, of course, be either Descriptive or Historical.

4) An *Affix* is either a *Prefix*, an *Infix* or a *Suffix* ; *be-* of MnE *becalm* is a prefix ; *n* of MnE *stand* (as against pret. *stood*) is an infix ; *-ness* of MnE *goodness* is a suffix.

5) MnE *goodness* is said to be " derived from *good* by means of the suffix *-ness* ". MnE *goodness* therefore stands in a certain relation to MnE *good* ; we may then say that MnE *goodness* is " related to " (better, *cognate with*) MnE *good*. It is clear, also, that we are then entitled to say that MnE pres. *sing* is, somehow, cognate with MnE ppart. *sung*. This cognateness clearly exists, equally clearly it cannot be held to be a cognateness of derivation, as is that of *goodness* to *good*. It is common parlance to say that " *sing* changes into *sung* in the past participle " or that " *sing* makes its past participle by changing *i* into *u* ". This use of the word *change* is better avoided, for reasons which will appear below (pp. 30–5). We may however appropriately say that " *sing* alternates (better, *varies*) with *sung* " or that " *sing* is in variation (better, *alternation*) with *sung* " and we may write this as " *sing* ∼ *sung* ".

6) *Ablaut*. This term does not at all rest upon School-Grammar and it is therefore possible to define it rigidly. Using *variation* as above, *Ablaut* may be defined as a variation for which we have no explanation. In Modern English there is a variation sg. *foot* ∼ pl. *feet* ; this is *not* Ablaut because the reason for it is known (though the notation of the setting-out of this reason demands a forestalling of a later section of this book—pp. 31 ff.). We have, in fact, MnE sg. *foot* < OE nas. *fōt* < PrGmc ns. **fōt*, as. **fōtu* < IndE ns. **pōd-s* as. **pōd-m̥* ; MnE pl. *feet* < OE nap. *fēt* < PrGmc np.

*fōtiz < IndE np. *pōd-es. In the language called Yenisei-Ostyak (or, alternatively, Ket) a variation of a kind very similar to MnE sg. foot ～ pl. feet is found, as, for instance, sg. şes ' stream ' ～ pl. şas. This is Ablaut because, here, there is no explanation of the variation. The reason for this lack of explanation is clearly to be sought in the fact that Ket is a language virtually without a history. On examination, the case with which we started, MnE sing ～ sung, does, in fact, prove to be Ablaut. It thus follows that, if we were omniscient and possessed of a full history of every language, Ablaut would cease to exist. We never can be this so that Ablaut always will exist.[1] The concept Ablaut first [2] came into being apropos the variation of one vowel with another in certain Indoeuropean languages (thus, of type sing ～ sang ～ sung). The definition I have given above is, of course, a generalisation of the original concept. For there is clearly nothing in my definition to prevent its application to consonants as well as vowels and to multiple units instead of single ones. Such cases do occur in practice. Thus, in Finnish, we have a consonantal ablaut (usually called Stufenwechsel) e.g. part. sg. kät-tä ～ gs. käd-en ' hand ' [t ～ d], ns. kukka ' flower ' ～ gs. kukan [long k ～ short k]. One of the most complicated ablauts known is to be found in Lappish e.g. Norwegian Lappish čiekkâ ' corner ' ～ gs. ciegâ ～ illative sg. čikkii.

I have now, in some sort, dealt with the first side of Philology, Descriptive Linguistics, and I turn now to its other side, Comparative Philology, also called Historical (or Diachronic) Philology (or Linguistics).

The nature of Comparative Philology may best be indicated by saying that it is all consequences arising from a consideration of the following two Axioms.

---

[1] It is interesting to speculate upon the existential status of the concept Ablaut. Clearly, it has much in common with that of a much better-known concept, Chance. When a coin is tossed, we say that it is evens whether it falls Heads or Tails, meaning thereby only that no reason is known to us why it should fall Heads rather than Tails. But, were we possessed of a full knowledge of the mechanics of the throwing, we should of course know whether the coin would fall Heads or Tails. It is from such considerations that there develops the regarding of Chance as " a multitude of unknown causes ". So Chance, just like Ablaut, would vanish in the face of omniscience which is not, of course, the case with all concepts (e.g. Primality).

[2] In this use the term Ablaut is due to J. Grimm (Deutsche grammatik i [1819], 10).

Axiom I. " Two languages are *related* if, and only if, they were once one language ". Thus, French and Spanish are related because, and only because, they were both once Latin.

Axiom II. " The word *congruence* in application to parts of two related languages is to be understood in precisely the sense in which the word *relationship* is applied as a consequence of Axiom I to the two languages themselves ". Thus, English *stone* and German *stein* are congruent because, and only because, they were both one word in the language which English and German both once were—that is, they were Primitive Germanic **stae^ina-*.

Above, I have expressed these Axioms in a rigid and carefully-worded manner. I now go on to examine them in more detail and, at the outset, I may note that Axiom I is much easier to understand than Axiom II. The statement " French and Spanish were Latin " is readily intelligible ; it can of course be put in a variety of ways. We may say " In Spain, that which was Latin has become (*or* has changed into *or* is) Spanish " ; or, again, " Spanish is descended [1] from (*or* is a descendant of) Latin ". The simplest way of expressing linguistic relationship is graphically, by means of a drawing which is, essentially, comparable to family trees of the male line (i.e., those not showing marriages). Thus, in such genealogies, the drawing (or *Pattern of Descent* as it may better be called)

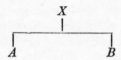

means that *X* is the father of *A* and *B* (and we are not interested in *X*'s wife). The Pattern of Descent

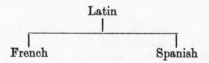

has now an obvious meaning.

In the case of Latin, French and Spanish, all three members

---

[1] The term *derives from*, though both frequently-used and innocuous-seeming, is better avoided (I have used this term in quite another sense, p. 26 above).

of the Pattern of Descent actually exist—father and two children ; in the case of most linguistic patterns of descent we are not so fortunate in this respect, for usually the " father " no longer exists. Thus English and German are related, but we must write

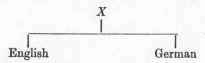

for virtually nothing of the father now remains.

The fact that linguistic patterns of descent are so similar to, and are modelled on, genealogical systems has naturally given rise to a whole terminology ; and it is a convenient terminology provided that we never quite lose sight of the essential character of the state of affairs actually obtaining. Thus, an arrangement such as

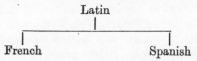

is called a " Family " of languages. Linguistic families, like human ones, may be large or small (the smallest kind being, of course, that containing just one son). French, Spanish, Portuguese, Italian and some other languages belong to the family which has Latin as its father :—

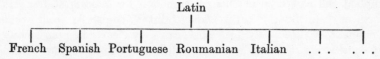

Linguistic families are usually given names ; French, Spanish, etc. are members of the *Romance* family, English and German of the *Germanic* family. In the case (the usual one) where the father of a family no longer exists, it is normal to call him by the name of the family with the word *Primitive* prefixed, so the *X* of

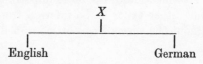

is called *Primitive Germanic*.

Like human families, linguistic families proliferate into sub-families, sub-sub-families, etc. So, for instance, we have the Pattern of Descent :—

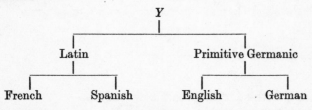

This whole family is called the *Indoeuropean* (often, *Indogermanic*) family so that *Y* is called *Primitive Indoeuropean*.[1] Naturally, the terms of human relationship have penetrated deeply into linguistic terminology. We may say, for instance, that English and German are sister-languages, that English is a cousin of Spanish and—more important—that English is more closely related to German than it is to Spanish. In concluding this Section, I may note that, naturally, the use of terms such as *sub-sub-sub-family* is felt as unbearably cumbrous ; philologists tend to use *family* meaning either ' family ', or ' sub-family ', or ' sub-sub-family ', etc., leaving the number of *sub*s to be inferred from the context.

Before attempting a proper consideration of Axiom II, it will be necessary to say something of *Linguistic Change*. I have already implied the existence of this phenomenon by making statements such as "In Spain, Latin *changed* into Spanish " ; and, that Linguistic Change really does exist, can very clearly be seen merely by considering the same language at different periods of time. Thus, present-day English, the language of Shakespeare, the language of Chaucer, and Anglo-Saxon are, very obviously, four different stages of one and the same language, English ; it is clear, too, that, here, each stage has changed into the one succeeding it.

Linguistic Change is multifarious. Here, I can do no more than attempt a rough classification of the more important types, leaving the nature of some other types to be inferred from the examples appearing throughout the succeeding portion of the book.

---

[1] In this name the word *Primitive* is frequently dropped and the abbreviation is usually (and always in this book) *IndE* instead of *PrIndE*.

In my attempt at a classification, I first distinguish between (A) Changes due to the influence of one language upon another and (B) Changes not due to this cause. Taking (B) first, for convenience of treatment, I might suggest a subdivision into three broad classes : B.1 Sound-Change ; B.2 Semantic Change ; B.3 Analogy.

B.1 Sound-Change.[1] There are many different kinds of Sound-Change ; the following are some examples.

The nature of the most important kind of Sound-Change (that often called *isolative*) is best seen from an example. Consider the Set :—

OE	*stān*	*rād*	*bāt*	*hām* . . .
ME	*stǭn*	*rǭd*	*bǫt*	*hǭm* . . .
MnE	*stone*	*road*	*boat*	*home* . . .

(we can find many more similar examples). On the evidence of this Set we formulate the " Sound-Laws " :—" OE *ā* changed into ME *ǭ* " ; " ME *ǭ* changed into MnE [ou] "[2] which we write " OE *ā* > ME *ǭ* > MnE [ou] "—cf. also the statement " MnE [ou] < [read as " derives from ", *better*[3] " descends, is descended from "] ME *ǭ* < OE *ā* "[4]. This Sound-Law has a Corollary : Every OE *ā* must give MnE [ou] unless special circumstances prevent it doing so. Thus OE *hālig* > MnE *holy*, correctly, but OE *hālig dæg* > MnE *holiday* (not *holy day*) because, in Middle English, the *ǭ* of the (correctly developed) ME *hǭli* was shortened to *o* (> MnE [ɔ]).

Some sound-changes are of a character much more " obvious " than the preceding one as, for instance, the Anglo-Saxon change which is called " Breaking ". We assume that, just before this change took place, the consonants *h, l, r* had, or acquired, a

---

[1] The totality of the sound-changes of a language is called its *Phonology* ; a little reflection will convince the reader that, by the nature of sound-changes, there can hardly be a *General Phonology* (that is, a subject consisting of the study of sound-changes in general), but only phonologies of individual languages. The term *phonology* is, unfortunately, subject to ambiguity, for it is used by many writers to mean the study of the phonemes of a language (in this sense, then, a *Genera Phonology* does exist). It is, however, better to use *phonology* in the sense I have defined it above, using *phonematology* for the second sense of *phonology*. (*Phonology* is, then, purely Historical, *phonematology* purely Descriptive).

[2] Written in various ways.

[3] For I have used *derive* in quite a different sense at p. 26.

[4] The notation with > < is used for whole words as well as for phonemes ; thus we write OE *stān* > MnE *stone* ; MnE *stone* < OE *stān* ; meaning that OE *stān* has become MnE *stone* and that MnE *stone* once was OE *stān*, respectively.

back pronunciation (*h* as *ch* of MnHG *nacht*, *l* as *l* of Russian *loshad'*, *r* as *r* of MnHG *reiten*, or the like). It is difficult to pronounce a front vowel before such a consonant, but the difficulty can obviously be avoided by either (*a*) changing the front vowel into a back one, or (*b*) inserting a back vowel between the front vowel and the back consonant. Hence PrE **æld* (< PrGmc **alþa/ō-*, > MnHG *alt*), (*a*) > Mercian *ald* (> *āld* [1] > ME *ǫld* > MnE *old*), (*b*) > PrE **æold* > WS *eald*.[2] The kind of sound-change just described is called *combinative*—because it involves two or more phonemes (it is thus in contradistinction to the first type described— the isolative type—which involves only one phoneme). There is, naturally, an immense variety of combinative sound-changes. Here I may mention some types of combinative change which are of very frequent occurrence and which have, therefore, received definite names.

Umlaut [3] is generally applied to a sound-change whereby a vowel of one syllable is " affected " by the vowel of the next ; e.g. PrGmc np. **mūsiz* > OE *mȳs* [> MnE *mice*] ("*i*-umlaut") ; Ic *saga*, as. *sǫgu* ("*u*-umlaut") ; Greek βαίνω < **βανι̯ω* is a rather similar umlaut, so is Welsh *mab* ' son ', pl. *meibion*.

Loss is a self-evident term : OE *beran* > ME *bere* (loss of final consonant) > MnE *bear* (loss of final vowel).

Intrusion is often used of consonants, but the same phenomenon in the case of vowels is usually described by saying that the vowel is a *svarabhakti* ; thus OE gs. *punres* > ME *þundres* (cf. MnE *thunder*) ; PrGmc **fugla-* (> Gothic *fugls*) > PrE **fugl̥* > **fugul* (the second *u* is a svarabhakti) > OE *fugol* (> MnE *fowl*).

Assimilation and *Dissimilation* are used, rather loosely, of the making of two consonants like or unlike, respectively. Thus OE dsf. *þisre* is assimilated to *þisse*, PrE pl. pret. **lerutun* (> **leurutun* > OA *leorton*) is dissimilated from **lelutun* < **lelōtun* (> Gothic 3rd pl. pret. *laílotun*).

Metathesis, used of the interchange of consonants ; OE *wæps*

---

[1] *a* lengthened before *ld*.

[2] With *ea* written for *aea*.

[3] Also called *Mutation*, but the term is better avoided, because *mutation* has for long been applied to a Celtic variation (not a change, and not an ablaut (for its explanation is known)) ; thus, in Welsh, *cadair* is ' chair ' and *y* is the definite article but ' the chair ' is *y gadair* and we say that, in the latter case, we have the *soft mutation* of *c*, viz. *g*.

> MnE *wasp* (one metathesis), but MnE dial. [wɔps] (another metathesis) ; OE *weler,* cf. Gothic *wairilo.*

B. 2. Semantic Change may best be described by saying that it comprises all those linguistic changes in which the attention of the philological observer is focussed upon the meaning, rather than upon the form.[1] Like Sound-Change, Semantic Change is very multifarious, so that, here, I can do no more than give a few examples.

Perhaps the most obvious type of semantic change is one not usually considered as appertaining to Linguistics at all, that is, the dying out, or the introduction of an " idea " in a language. Thus, the concept expressed by OE *gold-wine* ' a friend connected in some way with gold ' i.e. ' a friend who distributes gold ' i.e. a retainer's " lord " (because the good lord gives gold to his retainers) no longer exists in Modern English.[2] Again, the concept ' aeroplane ' did not exist among the Anglo-Saxons.

An idea, expressed in one way at a certain period of a language, is expressed in a way not descended from this way at another period of the language. Thus, the Anglo-Saxon for ' dog ' was *hund* ; again, the phrase *I can go* was expressed in Anglo-Saxon by means of another auxiliary (*ic mæg gān*).

The most familiar type of semantic change—and the one most useful to the etymologist—is that whereby a word, or other part of a language (e.g. ending, or construction), has " changed its meaning " ; thus OE *hund* > MnE *hound,* OE *mæg* > MnE *may,* and, from what has just been said, it is clear that, in both these cases, there has been a change of meaning.

B. 3. Analogy. The nature of analogical change is easily seen from examples. In Gothic, the dative plural of *dags* ' day ' is *dagam* ; *nahts* ' night ' " should have " dp. **nahtim,* but, in fact, it forms *nahtam* because night is " associated with " day. Again, in the OE Lindisfarne Gospels, we have *seofa* ' seven ' beside the " correct " *seofo,* " by analogy with " **æhta* ' eight '. Analogical change is

---

[1] The study of Semantic Change is a branch of *Semantics* (the term *Semasiology* is probably better avoided, *Semology* certainly so). Though it would theoretically be possible to study the semantic changes of a particular language *per se,* there would be very little virtue in so doing ; so, in sharp contradistinction to *Phonology,* it is always *General Semantics* (i.e. the Semantics of all languages) that is the subject of study.

[2] Except among those familiar with Anglo-Saxon literature.

frequently very potent in determining the fates of morphologies ;
thus the *s*-plural and *s*-genitive of Modern English (*dogs*, *dog's*)
derive from OE *-as* and *-es*, respectively ; in Anglo-Saxon, these
endings were confined to certain classes of nouns (*stān*, *stānas*,
stānes but *nama*, *naman*, *naman*) ; from these classes these endings
(and their descendants) " spread " to *all* classes. Analogy often
disrupts sound-change ; thus (due ultimately to a seventeenth-
century sound-change) we have the rule that *wa* is pronounced
[wɔ] in Modern English (*was*), save before gutturals (*wag*) ; pret.
swam is thus " irregular " from the phonological point of view and
its irregularity is due to association with other preterites—" *sit* :
sat : : *swim* : X, ∴ X = *swam* ", to use a very convenient German
notation for this kind of analogy.

A. Loan-effects. We have next to consider linguistic changes
which are due to the effect of one language upon another. By far
the commonest kind is simple borrowing ; that is, a word (or other
linguistic element) belonging to the giving language may enter the
receiving language, sometimes replacing a word (or element) already
existing in the receiving language. Thus the Scandinavian expression for the third personal pronoun (: Ic npm. *þeir*, apm. *þá*, gp.
þeirra, dp. *þeim*, etc.) has replaced the English one (OE nap. *hīe*,
gp. *hiera*, dp. *him*), hence MnE *they*, *their*, *them*. Or, to take a
syntactical example : in Welsh, the genitive is expressed by simple
juxtaposition (*y mab y tad* ' the father's son '—*mab* ' son ', *tad*
' father ', *y* def. art.) and this expression of the genitive has come
to be used in the English dialects of certain parts of Wales (e.g.
Breconshire) ; thus *Jones Pytin-du* meaning ' Jones *of* Pytin-du '.
Sometimes a " word-for-word " translation is made ; thus MnE
that goes without saying is *a translation-loan of* (better, *is calqued on*)
MnFrench *cela va sans dire*. Naturally, it rarely happens that the
phonemes of two languages are phonetically identical and this fact
cannot fail to be without effect on borrowings. If a difference is
slight, or non-existent, the effect is trivial and not worthy of note ;
thus the French word *chef* has been borrowed into Modern English
as [šεf] ; it may well be that there are slight differences between
the French phonemes *š*, *e*, *f* and their English representatives,
š, *ε*, *f*, but, even if there are, the representation is still an "obvious"
one. It is only when there are considerable differences that the point
becomes philologically interesting. Thus Russian has no *h*-sound

other than [x] (as the initial sound of *khoroshii*) but this sound is so unlike the *h* of many other European languages that Russian *g* is "nearer" to it, so we get Russian *gigiena* 'hygiene' and the like. This phenomenon of replacing a foreign phoneme by the native one(s felt nearest to it is called *lautersatz* and sometimes its effects are complicated. Thus OE *rōda* 'the red' is a borrowing of ON *rǫuðr* (> Ic *rauðr*), only the first element of the diphthong having been heard by the English; ME *gōk* (: Ic *gaukr*) shows the same effect, whereas ME *gowk* preserves the diphthong more accurately. PrGmc *gulþǫ, gs. *gulþas (or, perhaps, *ʒulþǫ, *ʒulþas) (Gothic *gulþ*) was early borrowed into Finnish. Finnish had neither *g* nor *ʒ* in the initial position, nor had it [θ]; at the period of the borrowing it did however have an ablaut *lt* ∽ *lð* (> MnFinnish *lt* ∽ *ll*, as *valta* 'power', gs. *vallan*); hence, making the appropriate lautersatzes, MnFinnish *kulta* 'gold', gs. *kullan*.[1]

Consider next the two Patterns of Descent :—

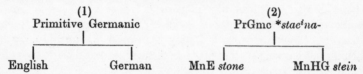

(1)		(2)	
Primitive Germanic		PrGmc *stae^ina-	
English	German	MnE *stone*	MnHG *stein*

We may now appreciate the full significance of Axiom II, for it is indeed clear that the mutual relationships of MnE *stone*, MnHG *stein* and PrGmc *stae^ina-* in (2) are identical with the mutual

---

[1] English affords exceptionally rare types of linguistic interconnection by reason of the fact that its Scandinavian loan-words were borrowed (*a*) from a very closely-related language (we must suppose that, at the time of the borrowings, English and Norwegian (or, in the event, Danish) were closer than are German and Dutch to-day) and (*b*) in a bilingual community (we must suppose that this community in the main spoke both Anglo-Norse (the form of Scandinavian spoken in England) and English). For instance, OE *drēam* means 'joy', Ic *draumr*, 'dream'; MnE *dream* has the Scandinavian meaning but the English form (OE *drēam* > MnE [drijm] by normal sound-change). Again, PrGmc *sk* remains in Scandinavian but gives [š] in MnE, cf. MnE *short* = Ic *skortr*—it is, of course, for this reason, that most English words beginning with *sk* are Scandinavian loan-words (e.g. *skin* : Ic *skinn*); frequently, therefore, the native English word and the Scandinavian congruent exist side-by-side in English (e.g. *shirt*, *skirt* : Ic *skyrta*); now, in Old English, there existed a word *scīr* 'shire' which has no congruent in Scandinavian; the Leeds local name *Skyrack* essentially represents an OE *scīr-āc* 'shire-oak' but a Scandinavian *sk* has been substituted for an English [š]—presumably because, in the bilingual subconscious of the borrowing-period, *sk* and [š] were felt as one and the same thing, by reason of the Set whose typical modern member is *shirt* : *skirt*.

relationships of English, German and Primitive Germanic in (1). There is, however, one small point of terminology : in the case of Axiom II it is convenient to avoid the use of the words *related, relation(ship)* and to substitute for them the words *congruent, congruence.* The reason for this is clear if we consider the two following Patterns of Descent :—

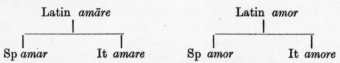

As I have said above (p. 26), it is common philological parlance to say that Latin *amor* is related to Latin *amāre*, or that Sp *amor* is related to Latin *amāre*. I have rejected the use of *related* in the first case for good reason ; it will be advisable to reject it in the second also. Further, I suggested that *cognate* was the correct word in the first case ; it may well be used in the second also (there is little danger of ambiguity as between these two cases). Introducing the written symbols = [meaning ' congruent to '] and : [meaning ' cognate with '], I may epitomise my terminology by writing the following statements ; in some cases I add the " spoken " version by way of example.

1. Latin *amāre* > Sp *amar.*
2. Latin *amāre* > It *amare.*
3. [Combining (1) and (2)], Latin *amāre* > Sp *amar* It *amare.*
4. Sp *amar* < Latin *amāre.*
5. Sp *amar* It *amare* < Latin *amāre.*
6. Sp *amar* = [is congruent to] It *amare.*
7. Sp *amar* : [is cognate with] It *amore.*
8. Sp *amar* : [is cognate with] Latin *amor.*
9. Sp *amar* : It *amore* (< Latin *amor*).
10. Sp *amor* : Latin *amāre* (> It *amare*)

—and so on.

I am now, at last, in a position to define *Etymology* and it will be convenient to give the definition in a rigid, symbolic, algebra-like form, then to add clarifying examples.

There is a language A_0 and we are concerned with the etymology of one of its words, x_0. A_0 has related languages A_1, A_2, . . . A_n and parent, A :—

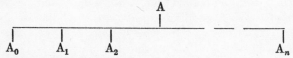

I next distinguish two cases.

Case I. Suppose x_0 of A_0 to be a loan-word and, precisely, a borrowing of a word y of a language B [1]; then the necessary and sufficient etymology of the word x_0 is the statement

$$A_0 x_0 \ [\text{'} z_0 \text{'}] \ ; \ \textbf{lwf. } B \ y \ [\text{'} \zeta \text{'}] \ —$$

where z_0 is the meaning of x_0 of A_0, ζ that of y of B (in the event, to give the meanings z_0 and ζ may be supererogatory—hence the square brackets [ ] in the formula).[2]

Examples

    (i) MnE *coach* ; lwf. Hungarian *kocsi* [3] ' do.'

    (ii) MnE *catch* < ME *cachen*, lwf. AN *cachier*.[4]

Case II. Suppose x_0 of A_0 not to be a loan-word ; then the necessary and sufficient etymology of the word x_0 is one of a Set of statements of which the following are typical examples :—

    (i) $A_0 \ x_0 \ [\text{'} z_0 \text{'}] < A \ x \ (> A_{i_1} \ x_{i_1} \ [\text{'} z_{i_1} \text{'}]$
$A_{i_2} \ x_{i_2} \ [\text{'} z_{i_2} \text{'}] \ \ldots \ A_{i_m} \ x_{i_m} \ [\text{'} z_{i_m} \text{'}]) —$

where x is the word in the parent language, A, from which x_0 of A_0 descends ; $A_{i_1}, A_{i_2}, \ldots A_{i_m}$ are a selection of m languages of the $\overline{n+1}$ members of A's family ; $x_{i_1}, x_{i_2}, \ldots x_{i_m}$ the descendants of x of A in these languages ; $z_{i_1}, z_{i_2} \ldots z_{i_m}$ the meanings of these m words.

    Example. MnE **wolf** < OE *wulf* < PrGmc *$wo^ul\bar{o}a$-* (> Gothic *wulfs* Ic *ulfr* MnNorw *ulv* OSw *ulver* MnSw *ulv* ODanish *ulf* MnDanish *ulv* OHG *wolf* MHG *wolf* MnHG *wolf* OS *wulf* MLG *wulf* MDutch *wolf wulf* MnDutch *wolf* OFr *wolf* MnFr *wulf*) < IndE *ulk^uo-*

---

[1] B may or may not be one of the set $A_1, A_2, \ldots A_n$.

[2] If z_0 has been given and $\zeta = z_0$, *do.* is often written for ζ. As stated in the Preface, the meaning of every word is not given in the present work ; " *do.* " is to be interpreted as indicating that the meaning is the same as that of the last word whose meaning is given. I may note here that the meanings of nouns and verbs are distinguished as ' love ' ∞ ' to love '. Hyphens are used to separate the parts of words for the sake of lucidity and without regard to the normal printing of the words.

[3] Hungarian *kocsi* is a shortened form of *kocsi szekér* ' cart from the town of Kocs '.

[4] Old Central French *chacier* (ba. MnE *chase*) > MnFrench *chasser*.

(> Skt $vŕka$- ' wolf ' Pāli $vako$ ' do.' Prakrit via ' do.' Gypsy ruv
' do.' Av $vəhrka$- ' do.' Sogdian $wyrky$ ' do.' Khotanese $birgga$-
' do.' Ossete (West) $bēräγ$, (East) $bīräγ$ ' do.' Paračī $γurγ$ ' do.'
Yidgha $wurγ$ ' do.' Sarīkolī $wərk$ ' do.' Shughnī $wūrǰ$ ' do.' Zoro-
astrian Pahlavī $gurg$ ' do.' MnPersian $gurg$ ' do.' Arm $gayl$ ' do.'
Albanian $ul'k$ ' do.' Greek $λύκος$ Latin $lupus$ (> Roumanian lup
' do.' It $lupo$ Rhaeto-Romance luf ' do.' OFrench leu MnFrench
$loup$ Prov lop ' do.' Catalan $llop$ ' do.' Sp $lobo$ Port $lobo$) OPR
$wilkis$ ' wulf ' [1] Lith $vilḱas$ ' wolf ' Lettish $vilks$ ' do.' OBg $vlьkъ$
' do.' MnBg $vĭlk$ ' do.' Russian $volk$ ' do.' Ukr $voṷk$ ' do.' S-Cr
$vûk$ ' do.' Slovene $vôlk$ ' do.' Polish $wilk$ ' do.' Czech vlk ' do.'
Slovak vlk ' do.' osorb $wjelk$ ' do.' nsorb $wel'k$ ' do.').

(ii) $A_0\ x_0\ [\,'\,z_0\,'] = A_{i_1}\ x_{i_1}\ [\,'\,z_{i_1}\,']\ A_{i_2}\ x_{i_2}\ [\,'\,z_{i_2}\,']\ \ldots\ A_{i_m}$
$x_{i_m}\ [\,'\,z_{i_m}\,']$—
the notation as defined immediately above.

Example. This kind of statement is chiefly used in the case of
language-families where the reconstruction of the proto-forms is
uncertain, though the congruences are not. It is well-exemplified
in Finno-Ugrian where, in general, the consonants of the parent
language can be reconstructed but the vowels cannot. The Finno-
Ugrian word for ' three ' will serve as an example :—

Lappish $gǫl'bmâ$ Finnish $kolme$ Mordvin (Erz'a) $kolmo$, (Moksha)
$kolmă$ Cheremyss (West) $kə̑m$, (East) kum Syryane $kujim$ Votyak
$kuiń$ Vogul $hurum$ Ostyak $həlьm$ Hungarian $három$.

(iii) $A_0\ x_0\ [\,'\,z_0\,']: A\ \bar{x}\ (> A_{i_1}\ \bar{x}_{i_1}\ [\,'\,\bar{z}_{i_1}\,']\ A_{i_2}\ \bar{x}_{i_2}\ [\,'\,\bar{z}_{i_2}\,']\ \ldots$
$A_{i_m}\ \bar{x}_{i_m}\ [\,'\,\bar{z}_{i_m}\,'])$—
where $\bar{x}$ of A is a cognate of x of A and $\bar{x}_{i_j}\ [\,'\,\bar{z}_{i_j}\,']$ is the typical
descendant of $\bar{x}$ of A.

Example. This type of statement is rather rare. OE $teagor$
' tear ', recorded only at v. 1340 of the poem Guthlac [2], does, however,
essentially afford an example. The parent form of the word is far
from clear but, nevertheless, the word is certainly cognate with
a large number of Germanic and other Indoeuropean words for
' tear '. Hence we may write, for instance :—

---

[1] i.e. MnHG $wolf$.
[2] Ed. in G. P. Krapp and E. van K. Dobbie, *The Exeter Book*.

OE *teagor* : PrGmc **traxani-* (> OHG *trahan* MHG *trahen* OS nap. *trahni* MLG *trân* MDutch *traen* MnDutch *traan* MnFr *trien*) —or again :—

OE *teagor* : IndE **dakróm* n. (> OIrish *dér* ' tear, drop ' Gothic *tagr*).[1]

(iv) $A_0\ x_0\ ['z_0']:A_{i_1}\ \bar{x}_{i_1}\ ['\bar{z}_{i_1}']\ A_{i_2}\ \bar{x}_{i_2}\ ['\bar{z}_{i_2}']\ \ldots\ A_{i_m}\ \bar{x}_{i_m}$ $['\bar{z}_{i_m}']$.

Example. Like the second type of statement above, this fourth type, too, is not usual in Indoeuropean etymologies. The following will serve as a Finno-Ugrian example :—

Hungarian *egy* ' one ' : Finnish *ensi* ' first '.

(v) $A_0\ x_0\ ['z_0'] < A\ x\ (> A_{i_1}\ x_{i_1}\ ['z_{i_1}']\ A_{i_2}\ x_{i_2}\ ['z_{i_2}']\ \ldots$ $A_{i_m}\ x_{i_m}\ ['z_{i_m}']):$[2] $A\ \bar{x}\ (> A_{k_1}\ \bar{x}_{k_1}\ ['\bar{z}_{k_1}']\ A_{k_2}\ \bar{x}_{k_2}\ ['\bar{z}_{k_2}']\ \ldots$ $A_{k_\mu}\ \bar{x}_{k_\mu}\ ['\bar{z}_{k_\mu}'])-$

where A_{k_1}, A_{k_2}, ... A_{k_μ} are a selection of μ languages of A's family and the k-set may or may not overlap with the i-set (notation otherwise self-evident).

Example. MnE *tough* < OE *tōh* < PrGmc **tanxu-* (> MLG *tâ tei(e* OHG *zâhi* MHG *zæhe* MnHG *zähe* MDutch *taey* MnDutch *taai*) : PrGmc **tangu-* (> OE *ge-tang ge-tenge* OS *bi-tengi* OHG *gi-zengi*).[3]

From the formulae and examples given above, the nature of Etymology will now be clear to the reader. Two points may be added.

(i) Not every word has an etymology ; thus MnE *girl* and much of the Hungarian vocabulary are totally without one.

(ii) In the foregoing it has tacitly been assumed that each word has only one meaning, which is, of course, only rarely the case. It is, perhaps, rather a criticism of present-day Etymology that too little notice is taken of the meanings of words ; the convention of etymological dictionaries may perhaps be summed up by saying that semantic discussion only takes place in the case of widely-divergent meanings. Lack of space would, indeed, render any

---

[1] On " tear " see my full discussion, *TPS* 1954, pp. 87–91.

[2] In such a position the colon of cognateness is often replaced by *cf.*

[3] See further A. S. C. Ross, *TPS* 1952, pp. 140–1.

other procedure impossible, as is well-seen from the following example.

In Spanish, there is a word *baladí* (sometimes spelt *valadí* in earlier Spanish). It has the following meanings :—

1 (*a*) ' worthless, inferior, of little value ' ; (*b*) ' ersatz ' ; (*c*) ' trivial, light ' ; (*d*) ' futile ' ; (*e*) ' frail, feeble ' ; (*f*) ' cowardly '.

2 (*a*) ' indigenous, local ' ; (*b*) ' rustic '.

3 It is used to denote special kinds of vines, grapes and wine.

4 In Spanish practice a distinction was (is ?) made between the type of shoeing animals called *baladí* and that called *hechiza*, the sense of the latter word being ' made-to-measure ', i.e. the opposite of ' ready-made '.

5 In the Kingdom of Granada there seems to have obtained a distinction between the coins called *doblas moriscas* ' Moorish doubles ' and those called *doblas moriscas valadíes*.

6 *gengibre valadí* was a special kind of ginger.

In Arabic, there is a word *balad* which is of very general meaning ; essentially, it denotes a dwelling-place of any kind ; thus E. W. Lane, *An Arabic-English Lexicon* s.v. بلد glosses it ' a country, land, region, province, district or territory ; and a city, town, or village ' ; its derived adjective *baladī* has ' indigenous ' as its best-attested meaning ; among its uses, this adjective commonly occurs in the names of plants and products to distinguish the native from the exotic, sometimes, indeed, almost with the sense ' ersatz '.

Sp *baladí* is certainly a borrowing of Arabic *baladī* and (cf. Case I, above) this is a sufficient statement of its etymology if we disregard the meanings. Actually, however, the matter is far more complicated than this.

The Spanish Sense numbered (2) above is clearly to be derived directly from the main Arabic sense ' indigenous '. So also is Sense 5, the application to Moorish doubles, because these were in fact doubles which the Sultan ordered to be struck in Granada, in contradistinction to the ordinary Moroccan doubles which were struck in Africa. The Arabic connotation ' ersatz ' was also taken over into Spanish (Sense 1*b*) ; the emphasising of this connotation no doubt led to the main Spanish senses—Nos. 1*a* ' worthless, inferior ', 1*c* ' trivial, light ', 1*d* ' futile ', 1*e* ' frail, feeble '. The origin of the application of the word in Spanish to vines, grapes and wine (No. 3) and to the shoes of animals (No. 4) is not so certain.

But it seems possible that both these applications develop out of Sense 1*e* ' frail, feeble '. The *baladí* grape has a thin skin and, if the grape were thus so called, it would be natural to apply the word to the vine and wine as well. And the main difference between the *hechiza* and *baladí* shoeing lies in the comparative smallness and lightness evidenced in the latter. Sp *baladí* as applied to ginger is, in all probability, distinct from Sp *baladí* in all its other senses. In its application to ginger the word is merely the name for a particular sort of ginger and, therefore, it is probably not a direct borrowing from Arabic into Spanish ; doubtless it came with the ginger itself and, in all probability, from Italy. The word exists in medieval Italian (*beledi*, etc.) as in other western European languages (e.g. ME *belendyn*,[1] *valadyne*) and appears to have originated in the Arabic spoken on the West Coast of India, a great ginger-producing area. Its meaning in this context is not entirely clear but it may plausibly be suggested that Arabic *baladī* here meant ' indigenous [*sc.* to some special part of the West Coast e.g. Calicut or Cannanore] '.[2]

It has now become clear that, implicit in any statement about a word's etymology, there lies, at the least, a number of statements about Sound-Change. Thus, to revert to our example MnE *stone* = MnHG *stein*, we are hereby implying the Set of statements :—

1) PrGmc initial *s* remains in OE and MnE.
2) PrGmc initial *s* > OHG *s* > MnHG [š], before *t*.
3) PrGmc *t* and *n* remain in English and German.
4) PrGmc *ae* > OE *ā* > ME $\bar{\rho}$ > MnE [ou].
5) PrGmc *ae* > OHG *ai* > MHG *ei* > MnHG *ei*.
6) In PrGmc, the ns. was *staen-az, the as. *staen-ą ; both in English and in German both these endings have vanished.

Even for this example, an extremely simple one, the implied statements underlying the etymology are thus numerous and esoteric and they cannot possibly be known to the student unless he is thoroughly familiar with the sound-changes of both English and German. And, naturally, the more languages concerned in the etymology, the more sound-changes it is necessary to know. Again, in this example, the sound-changes are from one phoneme into

---

[1] With intrusive *n* ; cf MnE *nightingale* < OE *nihte-gale*.
[2] On the whole question see A. S. C. Ross, *Ginger*, passim.

another rather " like " it. This must indeed, by the nature of sound-change, always be the actual case but it is often not the case presented to us ; it frequently happens that many intervening stages are unknown to us and we are left with a change from one phoneme into another most " unlike " it. Thus we have the equation : MnE *warm* = Latin *formus* = Greek θερμός = Skt *gharmá-* ' heat ' ($<$ IndE *$g^uhermo/\bar{a}$-* ∽ *$g^uhormo/\bar{a}$-*), a set showing widely different initial phonemes as a consequence of the sound-changes operative upon IndE *g^uh* in the four languages. Again, we are certainly entitled to say that the words MnE *cow* and MnE *beef* are identical, though two words could hardly be more unlike. For IndE ns. *$g^u\bar{o}us$* ' cow ' $>$ PrGmc *$kw\bar{o}z$* $>$ OE *cū* $>$ MnE *cow* ; and IndE ns. *$g^u\bar{o}us$* $>$ Oscan *bōs*, which was borrowed into Latin as *bōs*, as. *bōuem* ; the latter form gave Anglo-Norman *bǣf*, which was borrowed into English as ME *bǣf* $>$ *bēf* $>$ MnE *beef*.

Since the inception of true Comparative Philology, some one-hundred-and-fifty years ago, the sound-changes, and other changes, of almost all the languages of the Indoeuropean family (and of one or two other families) have, to a very large extent, been worked out by the philologists and are thus available to the student in print.[1] If a student is studying the history of a language at a university (there is always a fair number of such students), a main part—perhaps the main part—of his assignment will be the committing to memory of a large mass of detail of this kind ; and, at the end of his course, he will be examined therein. But it will probably not be until some further years of continued study that he will have sufficient detailed knowledge of the sound-changes, etc., to attempt much in the way of constructing etymologies for himself.

Philology is, however, in some ways, a rather advanced subject, and, in the case of many Indoeuropean languages (and some others) it is by no means necessary for the student to construct his own etymologies, for the great majority of such etymologies will already have been constructed by the patient labours of the philologists of the Past. In the main, these etymologies are to be found in the etymological dictionaries of the various languages and language-

---

[1] K. Luick, *Historische grammatik der englischen sprache* ; F. Sommer, *Handbuch der lateinischen laut- und formenlehre* and E. Schwyzer, *Griechische grammatik* are typical—and justly famous—examples of such settings-out.

families and in the etymological sections of the entries in the Essential Standard Dictionaries. The relevant dictionaries and parts of dictionaries are thus of three kinds : (1) Etymological dictionaries of individual languages such as A. Torp, *Nynorsk etymologisk ordbok* ; (2) Etymological dictionaries of whole families where the entry is made under words of the parent language such as W. Meyer-Lübke, *Romanisches etymologisches wörterbuch* (where the entry is, in the main, by Latin words) ; (3) Essential Standard Dictionaries of individual languages giving etymological information ; the *New English Dictionary* is the typical—and greatest—Essential Standard Dictionary and it gives etymological information.

The beginner will not find the consultation of these types of dictionary particularly easy and, in general, the method of using and understanding them is a definite technique which has to be acquired. In such dictionaries, it is naturally completely impossible even to attempt to indicate the sound-changes implicit in an etymology and standard sound-changes are always omitted ; only when the word shows some quite peculiar sound- or semantic change is mention made of it. Again, to save space, the entries are made in a highly-condensed, shorthand-like form, abounding in abbreviations, which (at least in dictionaries printed in Germany) are by no means always explained in a " Key ". I now give a selection of citations from standard etymological dictionaries and etymological sections of Essential Standard Dictionaries ; in the event, I follow the citation with a translation into English, tacitly expanding the abbreviations or glossing them in foot-notes ; in the English examples I add a commentary [1].[2]

1. *New English Dictionary* [*NED*] [3] :
Ten . . . [OE. *tien, -e* Anglian *tén, -e,* Comm. Teut., = OLG. **tehan,* OFris. *tian, tien,* OS. *tehan* (*tîan, tein*), (MDu., Du. *tien,* MLG. *tein,* LG. *tein, tien,* EFris. *tein, tian, tien*) ; OHG. *zehan* (MHG. *zehen, zên* Ger. *zehn*) ; Goth. *taihun* ; ON. *tíu, tío* (Norw. *tie, tio,* Sw. *tio,*

---

[1] The order of citation is intended to be one of ascending difficulty—obviously a rather subjective matter.
[2] Discrepancies between the English and foreign texts are due to my having (1) frequently put part of the foreign text into an English foot-note in order to make it clearer to the student and (2) always made use of the orthographies and methods of giving meaning standard in this present book.   [3] xi, 172.

Da. *ti*) :—OTeut. *teχan*, beside *teχun* = pre-Teut. *de·km*, L.
decem, Gr. δέκα, OSl. *desja(t^i)*, Skr. *daça(n-*. As final -*n* regularly fell
away in OTeut., the normal form for OE. would have been *teha*, *téa*
(as found in ONorthumbrian) ; but the actual form, as in OFris.,
OS., and OHG., had final -*n*, app. taken from the inflected form,
whence also the umlaut in *tien*, *týn*, *tén*. The inflected form, a
plural *i*-stem (: — *teχani^z*), in OE. *tiene*, etc. (neut. -*u*, -*o*, gen. -*a*,
dat. -*um*), ME. *tēne*, was used when the numeral stood absolutely . . . ;
the uninflected was used with a sb., and at length, in ME., in all
positions. (But see -TEEN, from -*tēne*.)]

Commentary. Comm. Teut. = common to the Germanic languages ;
EFris. = East Frisian ; *ON.* = OIc ; *OTeut.* = PrGmc ; *pre-Teut.*
= IndE ; *L.* = Latin ; *OSl.* = OBg ; *Skr.* = Skt.

2. M. de Vries and L. A. te Winkel, *Woordenboek der nederlandsche
taal* [1] :—

KRUIPEN, onz. st. ww. Mnl. *crupen* ; mnd. *krûpen* ; mdd. [sic !]
krûfen ; daarnaast met anderen klanktrap onfr. *criepan* ; ags.
créopan, meng. *creope*, *crepe*, neng. *to creep* ; on. *krjúpa*. *Kruipen*
komt van denzelfden wortel als *Kreupel* (verg. hetgeen ald. gezegd
is) ; volgens UHLENBECK (in *PBB* 26, 301) is 't o.a. verwant met lit.
grùblas. De verhouding van *kruipen* tot ohd. *kriohhan*, mhd. nhd.
kriechen is niet duidelijk.

Kruipen, strong verb (intr.) < MDutch *crûpen* = MLG *krûpen*
MHG *krûfen* ; cf. with differing ablaut, Old East Low Franconian
criepan = OE *crēopan* (> ME *creope*, *crēpe* MnE *creep*) Ic *krjúpa*.
Kruipen comes from the same root as MnDutch *kreupel* (cf. what
is said thereunder) ; according to Uhlenbeck, *PBB* xxvi, 301, it
is, inter alia, related to Lith *grùblas* ' hillocks '. The position of
MnDutch *kruipen* vis-à-vis OHG *kriochan* MHG *kriechen* MnHG
kriechen is not clear.

3. *Ordbok över Svenska Språket utgiven av Svenska Akademien* [2] :—

MJÖD . . . [fsv. *mioþer*, *miödher*, motsv. ä.d. *mioth*, *m(i)øth*, d.
mjød, isl. *mjǫðr*, honung, mjöd, mnt. o. ffris. *mede*, fht. *metu*, *mitu*,
honung, mjöd, feng. *meodo*, mjöd, av germ. *meðu*, motsv. gr. μέθυ,

vin, rusdryck, fslav. *medŭ*, honung, mjöd, lit. *medùs*, honung, fornir. *mid*, mjöd, sanskr. *madhu*, honung, söt dryck, av ieur. *medhu*, honung o. därav beredd dryck].

Mjöd < OSw *mioþer* = ODanish *mioth miøth møth* MnDanish *mjød* Ic *mjǫðr* MLG *mede* OFr *mede* OHG *metu* OE *meodo* < PrGmc **medu-* (= Greek μέθυ OBg *medъ* 'honey' Lith *medùs* 'do.' OIrish *mid* 'mead' Skt *mádhu-* 'honey, mead') < IndE* *medhu-* 'honey and the drink prepared from it'.

4. H. S. Falk and A. Torp, *Norwegisch-dänisches etymologisches wörterbuch* [1] :—

Tolk (dolmetsch), schw. *tolk*, anord. *tulkr*, von mnd. *tolk, tollik* (holl. *tolk*) = mhd. *tolc, tolke*, entlehnt von aslav. *tlŭkŭ* „interpretatio "; lit. *tùlkas* „dolmetsch " stammt wohl aus nd. oder russ. Dazu das vb. *t o l ke* (verdolmetschen) < mnd. *tolken* = mhd. *tolken*. Verwandt ist air. *tluchur* „rede " (von der wurzel *tluk). Mhd. *tolmetsch* (nhd. *Dolmetsch*) stammt von der ableitung aslav. *tlŭmači* und ist wohl durch das čech. entlehnt. Vielleicht ist anord. *þulr* „redner ", ags. *þyle* dass. (*geþyll* „brise ") verwandt.

Tolk = MnSw *tolk* Ic *tulkr* lwf. MLG *tolk tollik* (: MnDutch *tolk*) = MHG *tolc tolke* ; lwf. OBg *tlъkъ* 'interpretation' ; Lith *tùlkas* 'interpreter' is probably lwf. Low German or Russian. The verb MnDanish *tolke*, lwf. MLG *tolken* (= MHG *tolken*), also belongs here. OIr *tluchur* 'speech' is related (from the root **tluk-*). MHG *tolmetsche* (> MnHG *dolmetsch*) comes from the derivative, Church Slavonic *tъlmacь* 'interpreter', and was probably borrowed via Czech. Ic *þulr* (: OE *ge-þyll*) is possibly related.

5. M. Vasmer, *Russisches etymologisches wörterbuch* [2] :—

voкzál 'Bahnhof', zuerst *foksal* : St. Peterb. Vedomosti a. 1777, s. Grot FR. 2,480, auch poln. *woksał, wogzał*. Entlehnt aus engl. *Vauxhall*, einem Lustgarten und Vergnügungsort bei London, benannt nach der Besitzerin Jane Vaux (a. 1615), s. Heyse s.v., Karłowicz Archiv 3,665, Gorjajev EW. 53.

Vokzál,[3] at first *foksal* (recorded in *Sanktpeterburgskie Vedomosti* [a newspaper] in 1777 [4]) ; also Polish *wokzał, wogzał*. Borrowed from

---

[1] ii, 1269.   [2] i, 216.   [3] Vasmer gives also the Russian accentuation.
[4] See J. Grot, *Filologicheskiye razyskaniya* ii, 480.

MnE *Vauxhall*, a 'pleasure-garden and place of recreation near London, named after its proprietress, Jane Vaux (in 1615).[1]

6. A. Torp, *Nynorsk etymologisk ordbok* [2] :—
Snerka st. vb. 1 (stønne, sukke, pruste, snorke, Vo Ha Vestf), sv. di. *snärka* st. vb. snorke, pruste ; meng. *snerchen* sprute ut. Se de avlydende snarka og snurkla. Germ. rot *snerk*, hvortil svarer lett. *snirgōt* hulke, lit. *snarglȳs* snott. Egtl. vel « gi en skrapende lyd ». Til samme grundrot eng. *snore* snorke, *snort* pruste (nt. *snurten*). Bet. stunde, vente paa noget, ogsaa snylte (Sfj Nfj Snm) er vel utgaat fra « pruste » (sml. ana).

Snerka 1,[3] strong verb, ' to groan, sigh, snort, snore ' (Voss, Hallingdal, Vestfold) = MnSw d. *snärka*, strong verb, ' to snore, snort ' ME *snerchen* ; see **snarka** and **snurkla**, which are in ablaut. PrGmc *snerk-*, to which correspond Lettish *snirguôt* ' to sob ' Lith *snarglȳs* ' nasal mucus '. Essentially, probably ' to emit a scraping noise ' ; MnE *snore*, *snort* (= MLG *snurten*) are to the same root. The sense ' to yearn, wait for something ', also ' to sponge on ' (Sunnfjord, Nordfjord, Sunnmøre) is probably developed from ' to snort ' (cf. **ana**).

7. E. Hellquist, *Svensk etymologisk ordbok* [4] :—
kyss, Hels. 1587, liksom da. *kys* o. eng. *kiss* ombildat efter vb. kyssa osv., av ä. nsv. *kuss* Bib. 1541, fsv. *kus(s)*, *koss* = isl. *koss*, fsax. *kus*, *kos*, fhty. *kus* (ty. *kuss*), ags. *coss*, av germ. *kussa-*. Många tolkningsförslag, i allm. föga tilltalande ; se litter. hos Walde under *bāsium*, Olson Appell. sbst. s. 485, ävensom Heinertz Etym. Stud. zum ahd. s. 76 f. Säkerl. helt enkelt av onomatopoetisk karaktär liksom det naturl. obesl. *kus-* i grek. aoristen *ékyssa* Hom., ävensom p uss, ä. ty. *buss*, litau. *buczõ'ti*, kyssa, m.fl. En annan bildning är sv. dial. *muss*, kyss, jämte *myssa*, kyssa (jfr Wigforss S.Hall. folkm. s. 80), vartill *myss*. — Härtill: kyssa = fsv., isl. = ty. *küssen* osv. Jfr med annan slutkonsonant got. *kukjan*, östfris.

---

[1] See further J. C. A. Heyse, *Fremdwörterbuch* s.v. ; Karłowicz, *Archiv für slavische Philologie* iii, 665 ; N. Goryayev, *Etimologicheskii slovar' russkogo yazyka*, p. 53.
[2] p. 668.
[3] The first *snerka* listed.
[4] i, 541.

kükken. Likbetydande, men obesl. är grek. *kynéō.* — Ord med denna bet. innehålla vanl. vokalen *u*, men begynnelseljuden växla, vanl. dock läppljud, såsom *b*, *p* och *m*. — I ä. nsv. förekommer ngn gång *kyssår* i bet. ' smekmånad ' = ty. *kussjahr.* — Om andra ord för ' kyssa ' se under minnas i denna bet.

Kyss [1], like MnDanish *kys* and MnE *kiss*, is reformed on the verb *kyssa*, etc., formed from early MnSw *kuss* [2] OSw *kus(s koss* = Ic *koss* OS *kus kos* OHG *kus* (> MnHG *kuss*) OE *coss* < PrGmc **ko^ussa-*. There have been many attempts at interpretation but, on the whole, they are but little satisfactory [3]. The word is quite certainly of a simple onomatopoeic character, like *kus-* in Homeric Greek 1st sg. aor. ἔκυσσα, also **puss**, early MnHG *buss* Lith *bučuóti* ' to kiss ', etc. (all, of course, unrelated words). MnSw d. *muss* ' kiss ' (together with *myssa* ' to kiss ') [4] is another formation (to which also *myss* ' kiss '). To **kyss** there belongs the verb **kyssa** (< OSw *kyssa* = Ic *kyssa* = MnHG *küssen*, etc.). Cf., with a different final consonant, Gothic *kukjan*, East Frisian *kükken.* Greek κυνέω has the same meaning but is unrelated. Words of this meaning usually contain the vowel *u* but the initial varies—it is however usually a labial *b*, *p*, *m* [5][6].

8. F. Kluge and A. Götze, *Etymologisches wörterbuch der deutschen sprache* (16th ed.) [7] :—

Eimer M. Aus gr. ἀμ(φι)φορεύς ' Gefäss, das auf beiden Seiten einen Träger (Henkel) hat ' ist als Buchwort lat. *amphora* entlehnt. Daneben steht (mit der altlat. Aussprache des gr. φ, die im Volkslatein erhalten blieb, s. Elefant) lat. *ampora*, dessen Demin. *ampulla* ' Flasche ' fortlebt. Das Volkswort, das die Germanen mit der Sache kennenlernen, wird in einer roman. Form mit *b* und Wandel zum Mask. entlehnt und ergibt ahd. *ambar*, ags. *amber, ambor.* Bestätigt wird diese Form, die in österr. *amper*

---

[1] First occurrence : E. P. Helsingius, *Synonymorum libellus* (1587).
[2] First occurrence : *Bible* of 1541.
[3] For literature see Walde-Hofmann s.v. *bāsium* ; E. Olson, *De appellativa substantivens bildning i fornsvenskan*, p. 485 ; further, N. O. Heinertz, *Etymologische studien zum althochdeutschen*, p. 76 f.
[4] E. Wigforss, *Södra Hallands folkmål* : *ljudlära*, p. 80.
[5] In early MnSw there occasionally occurs the word *kyss-år* ' honeymoon ' = MnHG *kuss-jahr.*
[6] For other words for ' to kiss ' see minnas in this sense.   [7] p. 162.

fortwirkt, durch die gleichbed. Ableitungen ahd. *amprī* N., ags.
* embren* sowie durch die aus dem Germ. entlehnten aslav. *ǫborŭ*,
aruss. *uborŭk*, poln. *węborek* und das aus dem Slav. stammende
apreuss. *wumbaris*. Die jüngeren Formen ahd. *eim-, einbar*, asächs.
ēmbar beruhen auf volksetym. Anlehnung an ein und bëran
'tragen', vollzogen, nachdem sich die zweiohrige Kruke zum
Kübel mit Henkel gewandelt hatte (s. Zuber). Weiterhin ist *mb*
zu *mm* assimiliert (mnd. mnl. *emmer*) und (wegen des vorausge-
henden Diphth.) zu *m* vereinfacht worden. Dän. *ember*, schwed.
ämbar sind vor jener Assimilation aus dem Mnd. entlehnt. Wie
lat. *amphora* war Eimer von vornherein auch Flüssigkeitsmass;
in den Alpenländern ist diese Bed. heute die wichtigste. Umgangs-
sprachlich wird das Gebiet des Wortes bedrängt von Bütte und
Kübel: Kretschmer 1918 Wortgeogr. 186 ff.

Eimer m. From Greek *ἀμ(φι)φορεύς* 'vessel that has something
to carry it by (a handle) on both sides', borrowed into Latin as a
learned loan, *amphora*. Parallel with it (with the Old Latin pronunciation of Greek φ which was preserved in Vulgar Latin [1]),
Latin *ampora*, of which the diminutive, *ampulla*, survives. The
popular word, which the Germanic peoples got to know with the
thing itself, was borrowed in a Romance form with *b* and change to
the masculine gender, and gives OHG *ambar* OE *amber, ambor*.
This form (which continues in Austrian dialect as *amper*) is con-
firmed by the derivatives OHG *amprî* n., OE *embren* (of the same
meaning), as also by OBg *ǫborъ* 'vessel' ORussian *uborъk* Polish
węborek 'do.' (also by OPR *wumbaris* 'emer' [2], borrowed from
Slavonic). The later forms OHG *eimbar, einbar* OS *êmbar* are due
to folk-etymology with *ein* 'one' and OHG *bëran* 'to carry', a
folk-etymology which came into being after the two-eared stone
jar had changed into a pail with a handle.[3] Further, *mb* became
assimilated to *mm* (MHG *emmer* MDutch *emmer*) and, by reason
of the preceding diphthong, simplified to *m*. MnDanish *ember*
MnSw *ämbar* were borrowed from Middle Low German before this
assimilation took place. Like Latin *amphora*, *Eimer* was, from
the beginning, a liquid measure; in the Alps, this last meaning is
to-day the most important. In colloquial German the geographical
area of this word is being threatened by **Bütte** and **Kübel**.[4]

---

[1] See **Elefant**.   [2] i.e. MnHG *eimer*.   [3] See **Zuber**.
[4] See P. Kretschmer, *Wortgeographie der deutschen umgangssprache*, p. 186 ff.

9. W. v. Wartburg, *Französisches etymologisches wörterbuch* [1] :—

nostos (gr.) rückkehr.

1. Nfr. *nostalgie* f. ,, souffrance causée par le regret du pays natal " (seit Lieutaud 1759 ; RPh 1933, 30), ,, regret d'un milieu auquel on a appartenu, d'un genre de vie qu'on a cessé de mener " (seit Ac 1935). — Ablt. Nfr. *nostalgique* adj. ,, qui se rapporte à la nostalgie ; qui éprouve la nostalgie " (seit 1800, Brunot 10), (s. m.f.) ,, personne qui éprouve de la nostalgie " (Besch 1845 — Lar 1874) ; *nostalgiquement* adv. ,, de façon nostalgique " (seit 1921, Proust Guermantes 3, 51).

2. Nfr. *nostomanie* f. ,, nostalgie " (Lavoisier 1793 — LittréG 1907). Die sich bis zur krankheit steigernde sehnsucht nach der heimat, die man verlassen hat, ist besonders bei Schweizern in der fremde beobachtet worden, besonders bei den schweizerischen soldtruppen. Das hat dem schweizerischen wort *heimweh* eingang in die deutsche sprache verschafft. Da sich auch die medizin mit dieser erscheinung befasste, wurde auch zu dem worte eine gelehrte entsprechung geschaffen. 1678 erschien die schrift des Basler arztes J. J. Harder : *Dissertatio medica de* Νοσταλγία *oder Heimwehe oder Heimsucht.* Aus der medizinersprache fand dieses aus νόστος ,, rückkehr ", ἄλγος ,, schmerz " und dem suffix -*ie* gebildete wort eingang ins französische (oben 1). Etwas später wurde eine andere wiedergabe von *heimweh* versucht (2), die sich aber nicht gehalten hat. Eine weitere bildung s. NOSTER II 2.

Nostos (Greek) ' return '.

1. MnFrench *nostalgie* (1) ' souffrance causée par le regret du pays natal ' [2] ; (2) ' regret d'un milieu auquel on a appartenu, d'un genre de vie qu'on a cessé de mener ' [3]. Derivatives :—MnFrench *nostalgique* adj. ' qui se rapporte à la nostalgie ; qui éprouve la nostalgie ' [4] ; noun (m. and f.) ' personne qui éprouve de la nostalgie ' [5] ; *nostalgiquement* adv. ' de façon nostalgique ' [6].

---

[1] vii, 196.

[2] First used by Lieutaud in 1759 (see A. Weil, *Revue de philologie française* 1933, p. 30).

[3] First recorded *Dictionnaire de l'Académie Française* 1935, s.v.

[4] First recorded in 1800 (see F. Brunot, *Histoire de la langue française des origines à 1900*, x, 892).

[5] First recorded in 1845 (" Bescherelle aîné ", *Dictionnaire national* s.v.) see also P. Larousse, *Grand dictionnaire universel du XIX*e *siècle* s.v. (1874).

[6] First recorded in 1921 (Proust, *Le côté de Guermantes* iii, 51).

2. MnFrench *nostomanie* f. ' nostalgie ' [1].

That longing for the native land left behind, which amounts to an illness, was noticed particularly among the Swiss abroad, particularly among the Swiss mercenaries. This gained the Swiss word *heimweh* an entry into German. Since Medicine took account of this phenomenon, a learned correspondant to this word was created. In 1678 there appeared *Dissertatio medica de Νοσταλγία oder Heimwehe oder Heimsucht,* the work of J. J. Harder, a Basle doctor. This word, made up of νόστος ' return ', ἄλγος ' pain ' and the French suffix *-ie,* came into French (No. 1, above) from medical language. A little later, another translation of *heimweh* was put forward (No. 2, above) but this did not survive [2].

10. E. Gamillscheg, *Etymologisches wörterbuch der französischen sprache* [3] :—

grappe 1.   „ Haken "

14 Jhdt., heute champ., pik. *crape,* ist Rückbildung von afrz. *grapon, crapon* „ Haken ", aus fränkisch **kråppo* zu ahdt. *kråpfo* dass. REW 4760.

Germanisch **krappa* bzw. gotisch **krappa,* Bruckner, Char. 12, ist nicht möglich, da nach Kluge s. *Krapfen* 2 altes *-ê-* zugrundeliegt.

2. „ Traube "

12 Jhdt., ist postverb. Subst. von afrz. *graper,* auch *craper* „ die Trauben abnehmen " ; dieses ist spezialisiert aus einem nicht mehr belegten *graper* „ zu sich ziehen " , das vielleicht in nprov. *grapà* „ mit einem Haken die Pflanzen aus einem Graben ziehen " erhalten ist ; (doch kann dieses von der prov. Entsprechung des frz. *grappe* 1 neugebildet sein) ; *graper, craper* aus einem gallorom. **crappare,* das zu fränkisch **kråppo* „ Haken " gehört, also wohl einem fränkischen **kråppôn* entspricht.

Nicht zu irisch *crapaim* „ ich ziehe zusammen " u.ä., da dieses Lehnwort aus anord. *crappr* [sic !] ist, und der gallische PN *Crappao* wegen *-pp-* nicht keltisch sein kann (Pokorny) ; vgl. Dottin 248 ; Jud, AR 6,207.

---

[1] First used by Lavoisier in 1793 (see E. Littré and A. Gilbert, *Dictionnaire de médecine* (1905–8), s.v.).

[2] For a further formation, see **noster** II.2.

[3] p. 483.

3. „ Färberröte "

18 Jhdt., aus ndl. **krap**.

4. „ dem Eisenerz beigemengter Sand oder Steinchen "
19 Jhdt., vgl. nprov. *crapo* „ Müll ", „ der Rückstand des durch-gesiebten Gipses ", „ Abfall ", „ Bodensatz " u.ä., dazu prov. *crapier* „ Siebmist " ; ist in Anlehnung an *grappe* 1–3 umgebildetes *crape*, s.d.

Grappe   1. ' hook '.

First occurrence : XIV c. ; exists to-day in the dialects of Champagne and Picardy (*crape*). Back-formation from OFrench *grapon, crapon* ' hook ', lwf. Franconian **krâppo* (= OHG *krâpfo*).[1] A PrGmc **krappa*, or a Gothic **krappa* [2] is not a possible etymon for, according to F. Kluge. *Etymologisches wörterbuch der deutschen sprache* (10th ed.) s.v. *Krapfen* 2, the OHG word attests a PrGmc *ē*.

2. ' bunch of grapes '.

First occurrence : XII c. Deverbative noun from OFrench *graper* (also *craper*) ' to pluck bunches of grapes ' ; this is semantically specialised from an unrecorded **graper* ' to pull towards one ' which is possibly preserved in MnProv *grapà* ' to pull plants out of a trench by means of a hook ' [3]. OFrench *graper, craper* lwf. a Gallo-Latin **crappare*, lwf. Franconian **krâppo* ' hook ' (above) i.e. **crappare* lwf. Franconian **krâppôn* [4].

3. ' crap-madder '.

First occurrence : XVIII c., lwf. MnDutch *krap*.

4. ' sand or the small stones found mixed with iron-ore '.

First occurrence : XIX c. ; cf. MnProv *crapo* ' dust, rubbish ', ' residue from sieved gypsum ', ' refuse ', ' sediment ', etc., further MnProv *crapier* ' filtered manure ' ; this is **crape** (q.v.), remodelled on **grappe** Senses 1–3, above.

---

[1] W. Meyer-Lübke, *Romanisches etymologisches wörterbuch*, No. 4760.

[2] So W. Bruckner, *Charakteristik der germanischen elemente im Italienischen* (*Wissenschaftliche beilage zum Bericht über das Gymnasium in Basel* 1898 f.), p. 12.

[3] But the word could be modelled on the Provençal correspondant of MnFrench *grappe* in Sense 1, above.

[4] The word cannot be cognate with Irish *crapaim* ' to pull together, etc. ', for this is a borrowing of ON *krappr* (note that the Gaulish personal name *Crappao* cannot be Celtic because of its *pp* (*teste* Professor Pokorny)). Cf. G. Dottin, *La langue gauloise*, p. 248 ; Jud, *Archivum romanicum* vi, 207.

11. R. L. Turner, *A comparative and etymological dictionary of the Nepali language* [1] :—

nāgo, or *năgo*, adj. Barbarous ; —s. A ne'er-do-weel, a rolling stone without wife or family or other responsibilities, (esp.) a soldier freed from the restraint of conjugal life who is free and easy in his behaviour to women. [Sk. *nagnáḥ* naked, *nágnakaḥ* naked, wanton : Pa. *nagga*-, Pk. *ṇagga*- ; Rom. arm. *nəgal*- to unclothe ; B. *nāgā* naked ascetic ; O. *nāgā* naked ; H. *nāgā* m. beggar ; G. *nāgŭ* naked, M. *nāgā* ; Sgh. *naga* younger sister.—In the original sense of ' naked ' (a word liable to replacement : cf. ousting of Eng. *naked* by *nude*) *nagga*- was partially replaced by *naṅga*- as in D.pash. *nənaín* (cf. Kaf. kati *nənə́nə́*), Sh. *nanu̯*, K. *non*ᵘ (< *naṅ*- by assimilation ?—or -*n* < -*gn*- ? There is no other certain example of the group -*gn*- in these languages available) ; Rom. eur. *naṅgo* naked, Ku. *nāṅṛo*, A. *nāṅṭhā* ; B. *nāṅ* paramour ; P. *naṅgā* naked (whence as a lw. in K. *nanga*, Ku. *naṅgo*, H. *naṅgā*, S. *naṅgo*, and prob. N. *nāṅgo*), L. *naṅgā*.]

Commentary.

   s. = noun ; *esp.* = especially ; *Sk.* = Skt ; *Pa.* = Pāli ; *Pk.* = Prākrit ; *Rom.arm.* = Armenian Gypsy ; *B.* = Bengali ; *O.* = Oṛiyā ; *H.* = Hindustānī ; *G.* = Gujarātī ; *M.* = Marāṭhī ; *Sgh.* = Singhalese ; *D.* = the Dardic languages, viz. *pash.* = Pashai, *Sh.* = Shina, *K.* = Kashmiri ; *Kaf.* = Kafiri ; *Rom. eur.* = European Gypsy ; *Ku.* = Kumaonī ; *A.* = Assamese ; *P.* = Panjābī ; *lw.* = loan-word ; *S.* = Sindhī ; *N.* = Nepalī ; *prob.* = probably ; *L.* = Lahndā.

12. Franck's *Etymologisch Woordenboek der nederlandsche taal* (2e Druk door N. van Wijk, 1912 and 1949) [2] :—

   Schril bnw., nog niet bij Kil. Evenals nd. *schrell* „ scherp van toon en smaak, heesch, schril ", nhd. (oorspr. ndd.) *schrill* „ schril ", eng. *shrill* „ id. ", *to shrill* „ gillen, een schril geluid maken "; noorw. *skrella* (sterk) „ klinken " ablautend met ags. *scrallettan* „ luid schreeuwen, een hard geluid voortbrengen ", ijsl. *skrölta* „ schreeuwen ", noorw. *skrella* (zwak) „ id., luid lachen ". Zie ook **schrollen**. De combinatie met **grol** verklaart den oorsprong van **schril** enz. niet ; wel bestaat er jonger associatief verband tusschen beide woordgroepen. *Skrell-* kan uit *skreðl-* ontstaan zijn : dan is mier. *scret* ,, schreeuw ", nier. *sgreadaim* ,, ik schreeuw " verwant. De bet. ,, beschroomd, schuw " in nnl. een schrille blik e. dgl. is blijkbaar secundair.

Schril adj. [1]—and further LG *schrell* MnHG *schrill* (lwf. LG) MnE *shrill* adj. and verb MnNorw *skrella* (strong verb)—is in ablaut to OE *scrallettan* MnIc *skrölta* MnNorw *skrella* (weak verb) ; see also **schrollen.** Putting **schril,** etc. cognate with **grol** does not explain the origin of the former Set, but there was probably associative connection between the two groups of words later. **skrell-* can represent an earlier **skreðl-* ; if it does, MIrish *scret* ' shout ', MnIrish *sgreadaim* ' to shout ' would be cognate.[2]

13. W. Meyer-Lübke, *Romanisches etymologisches wörterbuch* (3rd ed.) [3] :—

1789. **cavea** 1. ,, Höhlung ", 2. ,, Vogelkäfig ", ,, Korb ".

1. Avicent. *gaibo,* venez. *gebo* ,, Flußbett ", ,, Rinnsal " Nigra, Zs. 28,644. — Ablt. : engad. *ǵaviöl* ,, Einschnitt ", ,, Kerbe ", ,, Ohreneinschnitt als Hauszeichen der Schafe ". Auch frz. *chai* ,, Keller " ?

2. It. *gabbia* ,, Hühnerkorb ", ,, Mastkorb " (> pg. *gavea* ,, Mastkorb "), gen. *gaǵa* (> it. *gaggia*) ,, Mastkorb ", neap. (> it.) *gaia* ,, der Platz im Ballastraum, zwischen dem Schiffsbord und den Pumpen ", prov. *gabia* (> frz. *gabie*) ,, Mastkorb ", abruzz. *kayyę* ,, Tragkorb " ; venez. *keba,* engad. *kabǵa,* friaul. *sḱaipie,* frz. *cage,* prov. *gabia,* kat., sp. *gavia* ,, Gefängnis ", afrz. *chage,* wallon. *čef* Thomas R. 41,453, d. *Käfig.* — Ablt. : it. *gabbiuola* ,, kleiner Käfig ", scipr. *gabia* ,, Öffnung, durch die das Wasser aus dem Hauptkana in die Weinberge geleitet wird ". — Diez 150 ; Salvioni, RDR. 5,187. (Frz. *chai* kann nicht aus Bordeaux stammen Dict. Gén., da in Bordeaux *k-* vor *-a-* bleibt, kann aber südwestfrz. sein.).

1789 [4]. **Cavea** 1. ' cavity ', 2. ' bird-cage ', ' basket '.

1. EIt (Vicenza) *gaibo* ' river-bed ', ' water-course ' (Venetian) *gebo*

---

[1] Later than *Etymologicum teutonicae linguae Kiliani.*

[2] The meaning ' timorous, shy ' in MnDutch *een schrille blik* ' a shy glance ', etc., is obviously secondary.

[3] p. 172.

[4] This dictionary has been through several editions and these check-numbers are entered for convenience of reference.

' do.'.[1]—Derivatives : Rhaeto-Romance *ğaviöl* ' incision, nick, earmark as mark of ownership of sheep '. Also French *chai* ?
2. It *gabbia* (ba. Port *gavea*), d. (Genoa) *gağa* (ba. standard It *gaggia*), d. (Naples) *gaia* (ba. standard It *gaia*), Prov *gabia* ' basket for beech-nuts, etc. ' (ba. MnFrench *gabie*) It d. (Abruzzi) *kayyẹ* ' basket for carrying things in ', It d. (Venetian) *keba*, Rhaeto-Romance *kabğa*, It d. (Friuli) *skaipie*, MnFrench *cage*, Prov *gabia*, Catalan *gavia* Sp *gavia*, OFrench *chage* MnFrench d. (Walloon) *čef*[2]. Derivatives : It *gabbiuola*, It d. (San Cipriano in Sanabria) *gabia* ' opening through which the water is led into the vineyard from the main channel '.[3]

14. S. Feist, *Vergleichendes wörterbuch der gotischen sprache* (1939), pp. 25–6 :—

aírþa (nur Dat. Sing. *aírþai* L 19, 44) f. γῆ Erde ; *aírþa-kunds* Adj. von irdischer Abkunft (s.d.) ; *aírþeins* Adj. ἐπίγαιος, χοϊκός irdisch, ὀστράκινος irden 2 K 4, 7 (Suffix *-eins* s.u. *ahmeins*).

Aisl. *jǫrđ*, ae. *eorđ(e)*, afries. *irthe*, as. *erđa*, ahd. *erda* f. Erde ; ahd. *irđīn* irden.

Mir. *-ert* Land, Grund (?) nach Wh. Stokes, BB 25, 255 in *es-ert* (Mann) ohne Grundbesitz, *co-a(i)rt* Besitzer von Land aus idg. St. **u̯ert-* bleibt fern (R.Th.).

Germ. *erþō* ist Weiterbild. von St. *erō* im ἅπ.λεγ. (O. Bremer, Z f d A 31, 205 f.) ahd. *ero* (Wessobr. Gebet) Erde ; gr. St. ἔρᾱ in hom. ἔρα-ζε zur Erde, Gen. ἔρας·γῆς (Hes.), auch πολύηρος· πολυάρουρος. πλούσιος (Hes.) ? *u̯o-*Erw. in aisl. *jǫrfe* m. Sandfeld, Sand[4]): cymr. corn. *erw* f. Landstreifen, Morgen (Feldes), abret. *ero* Furche (Wh. Stokes 41).

---

[1] See Nigra, *Zeitschrift für romanische Philologie* xxviii, 644.
[2] Thomas, *Romania* xli, 451 (and on MnHG *käfig*).
[3] See F. Diez, *Etymologisches wörterbuch der romanischen sprachen*, p. 150 ; Salvioni, *Revue de dialectologie romane* v, 187. (The latter says that MnFrench *chai* cannot come from Bordeaux dialect as A. Hatzfeld et al., *Dictionnaire général de la langue française*, s.v., suggest—for, in Bordeaux dialect, *k* remains before *a* ; *chai* could however originate from the dialects of the South-West.)
[4] Aisl. *jǫru-vǫllr* (nur Gen. Plur. *jǫru-valla* Vǫluspǫ 14), von K. Müllenhoff, D.A.V, 93 als ,, Sandfeld '' gedeutet, bleibt besser ausser Betracht. Es könnte die Wiedergabe eines aus Ägypten stammenden uralten Wanderwortes sein : *Earu*-feld (Binsenfeld), einer der Aufenthaltsorte der Verstorbenen. Dass ägyptische Vorstellungen über das Leben nach dem Tode schon zur Bronzezeit bis zum Norden vorgedrungen waren, zeigt G. Ekholm, Ymer 1916, 275 ff., spez. 292 ff.

Fraglich ai. *urvárā* Fruchtfeld, Erde ; arm. *erkir* Land (H. Pedersen KZ 38, 197).

O. Hoffmann, Festschrift A. Bezzenberger 82 ff. weist in gr. ἐρεσιμήτρη·γεωμετρίαν (Hes.) idg. St. *ereti-* Erde neben *erā-* in gr. ἔραζε, *ertā* in got. *airþa*, *eruo-* in cymr. *erw* Acker, aisl. *jǫru-vollr* [sic] Sandfeld, *jǫrve* Sandhaufen nach. Idg. St. *er-* zu Wzl. *ere-* trennen (P. Persson, Idg. Wortf. 637 ff.) ? Vgl. gr. χῶρος Raum, Land, χώρα Land, eig. Zwischenraum : χωρίς getrennt, abgesondert u ähnl. Beispiele.

Hett. **irras* Erde (?) in *katter(r)as* (aus **katta-irras*) unterirdisch, irdisch hierher nach E.F.

Airþa (only recorded as ds. *airþai* L 19, 44) f. γῇ ' earth ' ; *airþa-kunds* adj. ' of earthly origin ' (see s.v.) ; *airþeins* adj. ἐπίγαιος, χοϊκός ' earthly ' ὀστράκινος ' earthen ' II Cor 4, 7 (suffix *-eins*, see s.v. **ahmeins**) = Ic *jǫrð* OE *eorþe* OFr *erthe* OS *erða* OHG *ërda* f. ; cf. OHG *irdin* [1]. PrGmc **erþō-* is an extension of PrGmc **erō-* in the ἅπ.λεγ. OHG *ero* [2] [3] = Greek ἔρᾱ—in Homeric Greek ἔρα-ζε, gs. ἔρας·γῆς (Hesychius)—cf. also πολύηρος·πολυάρουρος. πλούσιος (Hesychius) ; there is a *uo*-extension in Ic *jǫrfi* [4] Welsh *erw* f. ' strip of land, measure of acreage ' Cornish *erw* f. ' do.' OBreton *ero* ' furrow ' [5] [6] [7]. *Teste* Professor E. Forrer, Hittite

---

[1] MIrish *-ert* ' land, ground ' (which, according to W. Stokes BB xxv, 255, is present in MIrish *es-ert* ' [person] without property ', MIrish *co-a(i)rt* ' owner of land ' to IndE **uert-* is (*teste* Professor R. Thurneysen) not connected.

[2] See O. Bremer, Zeitschrift für deutsches altertum xxxi, 205 f.

[3] In the Wessobrunner Gebet.

[4] OIc *iǫru-uǫllr* (only recorded as gp. *iǫru-ualla*, Vǫluspá stanza 14, interpreted at K. Müllenhoff, Deutsche altertumskunde v, 93 as ' sandy field ') is better omitted from the discussion. It could be the representation of a very early wanderwort deriving from Egypt—the field of *Earu* [' rushes '], one of the resting-places of the Dead (G. Ekholm, *Ymer* 1916, p. 275 ff. (especially p. 292 ff.) shows that Egyptian concepts of the Life after Death had already reached the North as early as the Bronze Age). [But *iʾrw*, later *iʾnrw*, has clear *nr*, that is *l* (usual rendering *Ealu*), A.S.C.R.]

[5] W. Stokes, Urkeltischer sprachschatz, p. 41.

[6] It is doubtful whether Skt. *urvárā* ' field of fruit, earth ' and Arm. *erkir* ' land ' (see H. Pedersen, KZ xxxviii, 197) belong here.

[7] O. Hoffmann, Festschrift Adalbert Bezzenberger zum 14. April 1921 dargebracht, p. 82 ff., suggests IndE **ereti-* ' earth ' for Greek ἐρεσιμήτρη·γεωμετρίαν, beside IndE **erā-* in Greek ἔρα-ζε, **ertā-* for Gothic *airþa*, **eruo-* for Welsh *erw* ' field ' OIc *iǫru-uǫllr* Ic *jǫrfi*. Persson, p. 637 ff., assigns IndE **er-* to the root IndE **ere-* ' to separate ' but this is doubtful ; he compares Greek χῶρος ' space, land ' χώρα ' land ' [essentially ' intervening space '] to Greek χωρίς ' separated, split off ' and similar examples.

*irras ' earth ' in katter(r)as (< *katta-irras) ' underground, earthly '
also belongs here.

15. J. Pokorny, *Indogermanisches etymologisches wörterbuch* [1]
[Pokorny] :—

3. ĝher- und ĝherə-, ĝhrē- , strahlen, glänzen, schimmern '.
Aisl. *grár* (*ĝhrē-u̯o-s*), ags. *grǣg* (*ĝhrē-u̯i̯o-s*), engl. *gray*, afries.
grē, as. *grā, grē*, ahd. *grāo* (Gen. *grāwes*) , grau ' ;
lit. *žeriù, žcrĕti*, , im Glanze strahlen ', *žĕruóti* , glühen, funkeln ',
ablaut. *žarijà* f. , glühende Kohle ', apr. *sari* f. , Glut ' ;
aksl. *zьrjǫ, zьrĕti* , sehen, blicken ', russ. *zrĕtь*, sloven. *zréti*, čech.
zŕíti, poln. *źrzeć* ds., aksl. *zorja* , Schein, Glanz ', *zarja* , Strahl ',
klruss. *zórja* , Stern, Gestirn, Morgenröte ', russ. *zaŕá* , Röte am
Himmel ', skr. *zòra* , Morgenrot ', čech. *zoře* , Morgenröte ', *záře*
, Schein, Glanz, Strahl ', poln. *zorza* , Morgenröte ' ; aksl. *pozorь*
, θεωρία ', russ. *pozór* , Anblick, Schande ', *nadzór* , Aufsicht ',
čech. *pozor* , Aufmerksamkeit, Acht ', *názor* , Anschauung, Ansicht ' ;
hierher auch aksl. *zrakъ* , Anblick, Form, Art ', russ. dial. *zórok*
, Blick, Angesicht ', skr. *zrâk* , Licht ', čech. *zrak* , Sehen, Gesicht,
Sehkraft ', poln. *wzrok* , Sehkraft, Gesicht ' ; ablaut. aksl. *zrъcalo*
n., skr. dial. *zŕcalo*, čech. *zrcadlo* , Spiegel ' ;
über lat. *grāvastellus* s. WH I 620.
Wurzelerweiterung **ĝhrēi-** :
Air. *grían* f. , Sonne ' (*ghrĕinā*) ;
afries. as. ahd. mhd. *grīs* , grau ', nhd. *greis* , grau, alt ', wozu
wohl auch aisl. *grīss* , Ferkel ', aschwed. *grīs* ds., schwed. dän.
gris , Ferkel, Schwein '.
Wurzelerweiterung (***gherĕu-**): **ĝhrū-**.
In aisl. *grȳiandi* f. , Morgenröte ', aschwed. *gry* ,(vom Tage)
grauen ', dän. *gry* ds., *gry* n. , das Grauen ' ; hierher auch aisl.
grey n. , Hündin, Feigling ', *greyhundr* , Windhund ', ags. *grīeghund*
, Windhund ' ?
WP. I 602 f., Persson Beitr. 300 ff., Trautmann 366.

3 [2] ĝher- and ĝherə-, ĝhrē- ' to radiate, shine, glimmer '.
Ic *grár* (< IndE *ĝhrē-u̯o/ā-) OE *grǣg* (< IndE *ĝhrē-u̯i̯o/ā-)
(> MnE *gray*) OFr *grê* OS *grâ grê* OHG *grâo* (gsmn. *grâwes*)
(> MnHG *grau*) ;

---

[1] pp. 441-2.   [2] i.e. this is the third root of this form.

Lith *žeriù žerĕti* ' to shine radiantly ', *žĕruóti* ' to glow, sparkle ' and—in ablaut—Lith *žarijà* ' glowing coals ', OPR *sari* ' glut ' ; OBg *zьrjǫ zьrĕti* ' to see, look ' Russian *zret'* Slovene *zrĕti* ' do.' Czech *zříti* ' do.' Polish *źrzeć* ' do.', OBg *zorja* ' shining, brilliance ', *zarja* ' ray ' Ukr *zórja* ' star, stars, dawn ' Russian *zar'a* S-Cr *zòra* ' dawn ' Czech *zoře* ' do.', *záře* ' light, brilliance, ray ' Polish *zorza* ' dawn ' ; OBg *po-zorь* ' θεωρία ' Russian *po-zor*, *nad-zor* Czech *po-zor* ' attention, care ', *ná-zor* ' opinion, view ' ; here also OBg *zrakь* ' view, form, kind ' Russian d. *zorok* ' glance, countenance ' S-Cr *zrȃk* ' light ' Czech *zrak* ' seeing, sight, power of sight ' Polish *wzrok* ' power of sight, seeing ' ; and—in ablaut—OBg *zrьcalo* ' mirror ' S-Cr d. *zȑcalo* ' do. ' Czech *zrcadlo* ' do.'.[1]

Extended Root **ĝhrēi-** :—

OIrish *grian* ' sun ' (< IndE **ĝhrēinā-*, **ĝhreinā-*) ; OS *grîs* OFr *grîs* OHG *grîs* (> MHG *grîs* MnHG *greis*)—here also, probably, Ic *gríss* OSw *grīs* (> MnSw *gris*) MnDanish *gris*.

Extended Root [**ĝherēu-*] **ĝhrū-* :—

OIc *grýiande* OSw *gry* MnDanish *gry* ; here also Ic *grey, greyhundr* OE *grīeg-hund* ?[2]

16. A. Walde and J. Pokorny, *Vergleichendes wörterbuch der indogermanischen sprachen* [WP][3] :—

meug- ,, heimlich und tückisch lauern ".

Lat. *muger* ,, der Falschspieler beim Würfelspiel " (Zupitza Gutt. 216 ; Vf. LEWb². s.v.) ;

air. *formūigthe, formūchthae* ,, absconditus ", *formūichdetu* ,, occultatio' ; ahd. *mūhhari, mūhho, mūhheo* ,, Wegelagerer, Straßenräuber ", *muhhēn, -ōn* ,, heimlich lauernd anfallen ", mhd. *vermūchen* ,, heimlich auf die Seite schaffen ", spätahd. *mūhhilāri*, nhd. *Meuchler*, mhd. *miuchel* ,, heimlich " (weiteres aus dem. Dt., z.B. ahd. *mūhheimo* ,, Grille ", bei Birlinger KZ 20, 316 ff.), mhd. *mocken* ,, versteckt liegen ", mengl. *micher* ,, Dieb ", engl. mdartl. *to mitch* ,, versteckt sein ". Die Verb. der germ. und kelt. Worte nach Zimmer KZ 24, 210 f. ; Stokes KZ 40, 248 f. will nicht existierendes ir. *mugh* ,, schlimm " (nur O'Davorens Glossar) anreihen, dies ist aber *mugh* ,, Sklave "!

---

[1] For Latin *grāuastellus*, see Walde-Hofmann i, 620.
[2] See WP i, 602 f. ; Persson, pp. 300 ff. ; Trautmann, p. 366.
[3] ii, 255.

meug- ' to lurk secretly and spitefully '.

Latin *muger* [1]; OIrish *for-mūigthe for-mūchthae* ' absconditus ', *for-mūichdetu* ' occultatio ' ; OHG *mûhhâri mûhho mûhheo, muhhên muhhôn* MHG *ver-mûchen,* late OHG *mûhhilâri* MnHG *meuchler,* MHG *miuchel* [2], *mocken* ME *micher* MnE d. *mitch* [3].

17. É. Boisacq, *Dictionnaire étymologique de la langue grecque* (4th ed.) [4] :—

βροτός ' mortel ' < *μβροτός, cf. ἄ-μβροτος ' immortel ' τερψί-μβροτος ' qui réjouit les mortels ' Ἀκεσί-μβροτος etc. (Fick-Bechtel Personenn. 198) μορτός ἄνθρωπος, θνητός Hésych. Arm. *mard* ' homme ' et βροτός < i.-e. *mórto-* ' mortel ' + *mr̥tó-* ' défunt ' (Hübschmann Arm. Gr. I 473), cf. skr. *mr̥táḥ* zd *mərəta-* ' défunt ' skr. *mártaḥ* ' mortel, homme ' *mártyaḥ* ' mortel ' v. pers. *martiya-* zd *mašya-* ' homme ' zd *marəta- marətan-* ' mortel, homme ' skr. *măraḥ* m. ' mort, peste ' *mriyátē máratē* zd *mirye'te* (< *mə'rye'te*) ' mourir ' skr. *amŕtaḥ* ' immortel ' etc., arm. *meṙanim* ' mourir ' *anmer* ' immortel ' (Hübschmann l. cit.), lat. *morior* ' mourir ' (< *mr̥io-*) *mortuus* ' défunt ' *mors* gén. *mortis* f. ' mort ' (= skr. *mr̥tíḥ* lit. *mirtìs* v. slav. *sŭ-mrŭti*) *morbus* ' maladie ' (?), v. irl. *marb* gall. *marw* ' défunt ' (< celt. *maryo-s* Fick II[4] 203. Henry Bret. 196), got. *maúrþr* v.h.a. *mord* ' meurtre ', lit. *miřti* ' mourir ' *māras* ' peste ' *merdę́ti* ' être à la mort ' lett. *mēris* ' peste ' v. slav. *mrěti* ' mourir ' *morŭ* ' peste ' *mrŭtvŭ* ' défunt ' (cf. lat. *mortuus*). Curtius [5] 331. Fick I[4] 107.284.514. Etc. I.-e. *mer-* ' mourir ' ; voy. s.v. μαραίνω.

βροτός < *μβροτός, cf. ἄ-μβροτος, τερψί-μβροτος, Ἀκεσί-μβροτος, etc. [5] ; μορτός · ἄνθρωπος, θνητός (Hesychius). βροτός (and Arm *mard* ' man ' also [6]) < IndE *mórto-* ' mortal '

---

[1] Zupitza, *Die germanische gutturale,* p. 216 ; A. Walde, *Lateinisches etymologisches wörterbuch* (2nd ed.) s.v.

[2] Further High German material—for instance OHG *mûh-heimo*—is given by Birlinger *KZ* xx, 316 ff.

[3] The connection of the Germanic and Celtic words is due to Zimmer, *KZ* xxiv, 210 f. ; at *KZ* xl, 248 ff., W. Stokes wishes to add in a non-existent Irish *mugh* ' bad ' (only in O'Davoren's *Glossary* [see Pedersen i, 9])—but this is actually *mugh* ' slave '.

[4] p. 134.

[5] F. Bechtel and A. Fick, *Die griechischen personennamen,* p. 198.

[6] Hübschmann, *Armenische grammatik* i, 473.

+ *mṛtó- ' dead ' ; Skt mṛtá- ' dead ' Av mərəta- ' dead ' Skt márta-
' mortal, man ', mártya- ' mortal ' OPersian martiya- ' do.' Av
mašya- ' man ' Av marəta- marətan- ' mortal, man ' ; Skt māra-
nara- ' death, pestilence ' Skt mriyáte márate ' to die ' Av miryeite
(< *meiryeite) ' do.' ; Skt amṛta- ' immortal ', etc. ; Arm meṙanim
' to die ', Arm anmer ' immortal ' [1] ; Latin morior (< *mṛi̯o-),
mortuus, mors (gs. mort-is) (= Skt mṛti- ' death ' Lith mirtìs ' do. '
OBg sъ-mrъtь ' death '), morbus (?), OIrish marb ' dead ' Welsh
marw ' do.' (< PrCeltic *maru̯o- [2]) ; Gothic maúrþr OHG mord ;
Lith miŕti ' to die ', māras ' pestilence ', merdĕti ' to be at the point
of death ' ; Lettish mêris ' pestilence ', OBg mrĕti ' to die ', morъ
' pestilence ', mrъtvъ ' dead ' (cf. Latin mortuus).[3] IndE root *mer-
' to die ', see also μαραίνω, below.

18. Z. Gombocz and J. Melich, Magyar etymologiai szótár [4] :—

boroszlán [első adat Márt. 1807] 1. , Daphne mezereum, seidel-
bast, kellerhals ' Márt., CzF. ; 2. , Syringa vulgaris, flieder '
PP. m. 1801, Kassai, I, 358, Királyföldy 1846, CzF.

Eredete nincs tisztázva. Pontosan megfelelne szláv *brъstan-
(vö. szerb-horv. br̀stan , hedera, epheu ' HASz.) vagy *breštan-nak
(vö. ó-cseh brziestan Gebauer, Slov. brečtan alatt | lengy.
brzestan, brzostan , epheu ' Linde). Az szl ∞ st megfelelésre vö m.
zászló < szláv zastava ; poroszló < pristav ; Noszlop (hn., régi
Noztup), vö cseh Neostup, l. Melich SzlJöv. I, 2 : 120. Alaki
nehézségek miatt alig gondolhatunk a köv. szláv szócso-
portra : brъšljàn : bolg. brъršljàn bròšlen , Hedera helix, epheu '
Ger. ; bъ̀ršlan Revue Slav. IV, 115 ; bъ̀šl'an Mil. OB. 56 ; bъršlen,
brъšlen Duv. ; brùšlĕ̀n Cank. | szerb-horv. bršljan ua. Vuk [3] ;
bršljàn gen. bršljàna Nem. I, 396 ; beršljan, beršljen Jambr.,
Belloszt. | szlov. bršljàn bršlẹ̀n bršlîn Plet.—Asbóth Trt 27,
aki a m. boroszlán ∞ szláv brъšljan egybevetést egyébként elfo-
gadja, a szl. šl ∞ m. szl megfelelést feltünőnek mondja. Nem

---

[1] Hübschmann, loc. cit.
[2] A. Fick, Vergleichendes wörterbuch der indogermanischen sprachen, vol. II
(4th ed.), p. 203 ; Henry, Lexique élémentaire des termes les plus usuels du breton
moderne, p. 196.
[3] For βροτός see also Curtius, Grundzüge der griechischen etymologie (5th ed.),
p. 331 ; Fick, op. cit. vol. I (4th ed.), pp. 107, 284, 514.
[4] i, 489-90.

fejtik meg a m. szót a szl. -sl-es alakok sem : szlov.   bŕslej,
bŕslek ua. Plet. | kaj-horv. berszlyan Jambr. (sajtóhiba ?).
Hibásan : Leschka, El. ; Mikl. Slav. el., Nyr. XI, 117.—A
magyarból : oláh boroşlén [Tiktin ; boroşlean Cihac, II, 484]
, epheu ', vö. Alexics, Nyr. XVI, 401.

Boroszlán[1] 1. ' Daphne mezereum '[2] 2. ' Syringa vulgaris '[3].
The origin of the word cannot at all be elucidated ; a PrSlav
*brьstan- (cf. S-Cr bŕstan ' ivy ' [4]) or *breštan- (cf. OCzech brziestan
' do.' [5] Slovak brečtan ' do.' Polish brzestan brzostan ' ivy ' [6])
would correspond exactly.   For the correspondence Hungarian
szl ∽ Slavonic st, cf. Hungarian zászló ' flag ' lwf. Slavonic zastava,
Hungarian poroszló ' sheriff ' lwf. Slavonic pristav, Hungarian
Noszlop (male personal name, early form Noztup): Czech Neostup[7].
Because of the morphological difficulties we can hardly make
reference in this connection to the following family of Slavonic
words : PrSlav *brъšljàn : MnBg brъršljàn bròšlen[8] ' ivy ', bъršlan[9]
bъšl'an[10] bъršlen brъšlen[11] brùšlên[12] ' do.' ; S-Cr bršljan[13] bršljàn
(gs. bršljàna)[14] beršljan beršljen[15] ' do.' ; Slovene bršljân bršlęn
bršlîn ' do.' [16]. Ásboth[17] who, in fact, does maintain that Hungarian
boroszlán and Slavonic *brъšljan are connected, finds the correspondence Slavonic šl : Hungarian szl surprising (and Slavonic

---

[1] First occurrence : J. Márton, Német-magyar és magyar-német lexicon [1807] s.v.
[2] Márton, loc. cit. ; G. Czuczor and J. Fogarasi, A magyar nyelv szótára s.v.
[3] P. Páriz, Dictionarium latino-hungaricum et hungarico-latinum, vol. II s.v. ;
J. Kassai, Magyar diák szó-könyv s.v. ; E. Királyföldy, Ujdon-új magyar szavak
tára s.v.
[4] Yugo-Slav Academy : Rječnik hrvatskoga ili srpskoga jezika s.v.
[5] J. Gebauer, Slovník staro-český s.v.
[6] S. B. Linde, Słownik języka polskiego s.v.
[7] J. Melich, Szláv jövevényszavaink I.ii.120.
[8] N. Gerov, Rechnik na bъlgarskii yazyk s.v.
[9] N. Gerov, Rocznik slawystyczny iv, 115.
[10] Lj. Miletič, Das ostbъlgarische, p. 56.
[11] A. Duvernois, Slovar' bolgarskago yazyka s.v.
[12] A. and D. Kyriak Cankof, Grammatik der bulgarischen sprache.
[13] S. K. Vuk, Lexicon serbico-germanico-latinum (3rd ed.), s.v.
[14] Nemanió, Čakavisch-kroatische studien i, 396.
[15] A. Jambressich, Lexicon latinum interpretatione illyrica s.v. ; J. Belosztenecz,
Gazophylacium, seu latino-illyricorum onomatum aerarium s.v.
[16] M. Pleteršnik, Slovensko-nemški slovar s.v.
[17] O. Ashbot, Refleks slov vida trъt—trьt i tlъt—tlьt v mad'yarskikh zaimstvo-
vaniyakh iz slavyanskago yazyka, p. 27.

forms with -sl-, such as Slovene *bŕslej bŕslek* ' ivy ' [1] [2] do not at all explain the Hungarian word.[3] [4]

19. E. Berneker, *Slavisches etymologisches wörterbuch* [5] :—
medvĕdь—ksl. *medvĕdь* m. ' Bär '. **r.** *medvĕdь* ds. ; *medvĕditsa* ' Bärin '. **klr.** *médvid'*, durch Metathese *védmid'* ; *medvédycha*, *medvédýća* ; *vedmízyna* ' Brombeere, Himbeere '. **bg.** *medvĕd* (beachte auch *medún*, von *medъ* abgeleitet). **skr.** *mèdvjed* ; Koseform *médo* ; *mèdvjedica*. **sl.** *médvĕd*, G. *-ĕda* ; *medvĕdica*, *medvĕdka*. **č.** *medvĕd*, *nedvĕd* ; *medvĕdice*, *nedvĕdice* (*n* durch Fernassimilation an *d* und Anlehnung an die mit *ne-* komponierten Wörter). **p.** dial. *miedźwiedź*, gew. *niedźwiedź* ; *niedźwiedzica* (*n* wie im Č.). **os.** *mjedwjédź*, *mjedźwjédź*, **ns.** *mjadwjéź* ; *mjëdwjéź*, älter *mjeźwjeź*.

Auf neuer Komposition von **medъ* u. **ĕsti* beruhen :
r. *medo-édka* ' Honigdachs '. **klr.** *medo-jída* ' Honigesser '. **sl.** *medo-jĕd* ds. **č.** *medo-jed*, *-jedka* ds. ; ' Hummel '. **p.** *miodo-jad* ' Honigdachs '.

Eine Kurzform zu *medvĕdь* ist *mešьka* (vgl. Brückner A. 21, 14) : **r.** alt (Sreznevskij Mat. II 132) *meshьka*. **p.** alt *Mieszka*, Königsnamen. Aus dem Slav. entlehnt lit. *meszkà* ' Bär ' ; *mẽszkinas* ' männlicher Bär ' ; le. *meschka*. Dazu das Denominativum *mešьkati* : **r.** *méshkatь* ' zaudern, zögern, lange verweilen ' (*ь* graphisch für *e*). **klr.** [*méškańe* ' Wohnen ' aus dem P.]. **č.** *meškati* ' sich aufhalten, versäumen, zaudern ' ; auch tr. ' jemd. aufhalten '. **p.** *mieszkać* alt ' zögern, zaudern ', heute ' wohnen ' („ an einem Orte verweilen " ; über die Nebenform *mięszkać* s. Brückner aaO.). Die Grundanschauung war „ täppisch wie ein Bär gehen, nicht von der Stelle kommen " : vgl. lit. *meszkiúti* ' wie ein Bär gehen '.

|| Altes Kompositum, idg. **medhu̯-ēdi-s* (s. *medъ* u. *ĕmь*, *ĕsti* ; vgl. lit. *mès-ēdis* ' Fleischfresser '), entsprechend ai. ved. *madh(u)v-ád-* ' Honigesser '. Vgl. nhd. *honig-bär* ; mkymr. *melfochyn* ' Bär '

---

[1] Pleteršnik, *op. cit.* s.v.
[2] *berszlyan* in Jambressich, *op. cit.*, is probably a misprint.
[3] Failed etymologies : S. Leschka, *Elenchus vocabulorum Europaeorum cumprimis Slavicorum Magyarici usus*, s.v. ; F. Miklosich, *Die slavischen elemente im magyarischen*, s.v. ; the same, *Magyar Nyelvŏr* xi, 117.
[4] Borrowed from Hungarian : Roumanian *boroşlên* ' ivy ' (H. Tiktin, *Rumänischdeutsches wörterbuch*, s.v.—A. de Cihac, *Dictionnaire d'étymologie dacoromane*, ii, 484, has *boroşlean*) ; cf. Alexics, *Magyar nyelvŏr* xvi, 401.
[5] [ii], 30–1.

(,, Honigschwein "). Daβ die Herkunft des Wortes vielfach nicht mehr gespürt wurde, ersieht man aus den Umgestaltungen.— *medvědь ist ein Euphemismus. Vgl. über die Benennung des Bären in den idg. Sprachen Meillet Quelques hypothèses sur des interdictions de vocabulaire dans les langues indo-européennes 7 ff. ; Śmieszek Mat&Pr. 4,406 f.—Aus dem Slav. magy. medve ' Bär '.

PrSlav *medvědь :—OBg medvědь ' bear ' Russian medved', medveditsa ; Ukr médvid' (védmid' by metathesis) ' do.' ; medvédycha medvédýća ' she-bear ' ; vedmízyna ' blackberries, raspberries'; MnBg medvěd 'bear' (note also MnBg medún ' bear', derived from PrSlav medъ) ; S-Cr mèdvjed ' do.' (hypochoristic form médo ' do.'), mèdvjedica ' she-bear '. Slovene médvěd ' do.' (gs. -ěda), medvědica medvědka ' she-bear '. Czech medvěd nedvěd ' bear ', medvědice nedvědice ' she-bear ' (n by distant assimilation to the d and by folk-etymology with the compounds beginning with ne-). Polish d. miedźwiedź, standard Polish niedźwiedź ' bear ', niedźwiedzica ' she-bear ' (n as in Czech). osorb mjedwjédź mjedźwjédź ' bear ' nsorb mjadwjéź mjĕdwjéź (earlier mjeźwjeź) ' do. '.

The following are due to recent compounding of *medъ ' honey ' and *ěsti ' to eat ' :—Russian medo-edka Ukr medo-jída ' honey-eater ' Slovene medo-jěd ' do.' Czech medo-jed, medo-jedka ' bumble bee ' ; Polish miodo-jad ' honey-badger '.

PrSlav *mešьka is a shortened form of *medvědь [1]—in ORussian meshьka [2] OPolish Mieszka name of a king. Lith meškà ' bear ', měškinas ' male bear ' ; Lettish meška ' bear '. Here also the denominative verb PrSlav *mešьkati in Russian meshkat' [3][4] Czech meškati ' to rest, stop, hesitate ', also tr. ' to halt [someone] ' Polish mieszkać, earlier ' to linger, hesitate ', present-day ' to live ' [i.e. ' to pause in a place '].[5] The basic idea was ' to walk clumsily like a bear, not to come away from a spot ' (cf. Lith meškiuóti ' to walk like a bear ').

The word is an old compound, IndE *medhu-ēdi- (see medъ and ěmь, ěsti) ; cf. Lith més-ēdis ' carnivore ' [i.e. meat-eater '] ;

---

[1] Brückner, Archiv für slavische philologie xxi, 14.
[2] Sreznevskii, Materialy dlya slovar'a drevne-russkago yazyka s.v.
[3] In мюшкamь, ю is an orthography for e.
[4] Ukr méškaňe ' dwelling ' is a borrowing of the Polish word.
[5] On the parallel form mięszkać, see Brückner, loc. cit.

it corresponds to Skt (Vedic) *madhu(v)-ád-* 'honey-eater'; cf. MnHG *honig-bär* 'brown bear' [i.e. 'honey-bear'] MWelsh *melfochyn* 'bear' [i.e. 'honey-pig']. The deformations of this word show that, in large part, its origin has been forgotten. *Medvĕdь* is, of course, a euphemism [1].[2]

20. M. Mayrhofer, *Kurzgefasstes etymologisches wörterbuch des altindischen* [3]:—

ásuraḥ mächtig, m. Herr, später : böser Geist, Dämon/powerful, m. lord, later on : evil spirit, demon, = aw. *ahurō* Herr, *Ahurō Mazdå*, ap. *Aura Mazdā* „ Ormazd ", wohl zu *ásuh,* das aus *ṇsu-* (: *ániti*) kommt und ursprünglich soviel wie „ gesteigerte Lebenskraft, *Orenda* " bedeutete (Güntert, Ar. Wk. 101 ff. ; Dandekar 24 ff.), mit der die *Ásurāḥ* ausgestattet waren. Die Überwindung der *ásu*-Vorstellung durch den geistigeren *mánas*-Begriff hat wohl (vgl. Dandekar 40 ff.) zum Abstieg der *Ásurāḥ* zu Dämonen geführt. Hierher got.-lat. *ansēs,* an. *ōss* „ Ase " (vgl. WH I 50, P. 48)? Ist in dem urind. Namensglied -(*a*)*ššura* (von Götze jedoch = *śúrah* gesetzt) *ásuraḥ* zu sehen (Brandenstein 142 ff.)? Vgl. noch *Ásurih.*

Nicht besser E. Polomé, Études Germaniques 8, 36 ff. ; Lg. 28, 453, nach dem arisch **asura-s* und german. **ansu-* zu heth. *hassu-* „ König " („ **xònsus* ") gehören sollen, das weiter als „ maître des liens " zu gr. *ἡνία* „ Zügel ", lat. *ānsa* usw. gestellt wird. — Venet. *ahsu-* bleibt wohl fern, vgl. Whatmough, Lg. 25, 287.

Eine Beeinflussung durch das akkad. *Assur* nehmen K. R. V. Rājā, Comparative Studies, 1, 38 ff. ; F. W. Thomas, JRAS 1916, 364 ; Kretschmer, WZKM 33, 14 ff. an. Vgl. auch Sköld, JRAS 1924, 265 ff.— Nicht überzeugend ist die Etymologie, welche *ásuraḥ* von *ásra-* = aw. *anra- (ma¹nyu-),* Attribut des bösen Geistes, herleitet (Wack. II 38).— Sicher nicht zu lat. *erus* Herr (siehe WH 419).—

Der Name des *Ásuro Mayaḥ,* des auch in Astronomie, Magie und Kriegswissenschaft bewanderten Bildners und Architekten der Daityas, war Gegenstand vieler kühner Deutungen : Weber, Ind. Stud. 2, 243 sah in ihm den gr. *Πτολεμαῖος* (ínschr. *Turamaya-*!) ; Spooner, JRAS 1915, 77 ff. leitet ihn aus iran. *Ahura Mazdā* her (doch siehe F. W. Thomas, JRAS 1916, 362 ff.). Der Name ist aber wohl nicht von

---

[1] On the names of the bear in the Indoeuropean languages, see A. Meillet, *Quelques hypothèses sur des interdictions de vocabulaire dans les langues indoeuropéennes*, pp. 7 ff. ; Śmieszek, *Materyały i prace komisyi językowej Akademii Umiejętności w Krakowie* iv, 406 f.

[2] Hungarian *medve* ' bear ' lwf. Slavonic.

[3] pp. 65–6.

asuramāyấ dämonische Zauberkunst, bzw. der häufigen vedischen Formel *ásurasya māyẩ* (Neisser 1, 141) zu trennen ; da aber Volksetymologie vorliegen kann, ist wenigstens Webers Vorschlag nicht sogleich zu verwerfen.

Ásura- ' powerful ; lord ', later ' evil spirit, demon ' = Av *ahurō* ' lord ' *Ahurō Mazdā* OPersian *Aura Mazdā* ' Ormazd '. Probably to *ásu-* < IndE **ṇsu-* (cf. Skt *ániti* ' to breathe '), originally meaning ' enhanced life-force, *Orenda* ',[1] with which the Ásurāḥ were endowed. It was probably the prevailing of the more spiritual *mánas*-concept over the *ásu*-idea [2] which led to the degradation of the Ásurāḥ into demons. Here belong Gothic-Latin *ansēs* pl. Ic *áss*.[3] Is *ásura-* to be seen in the PrIndian name-element *-(a)śśura* ? [4] Cf., also, *Ấsuriḥ*.

The suggestion of E. Polomé [5]—that PrAryan **asura-* and PrGmc **ansu-* belong to Hittite *hassu-* ' king ' (< **xonsu-*), further (assuming the basic meaning ' maître des liens ') to Greek ἡνία Latin *ānsa*, etc.—is no better than the one here given [6]. Several scholars [7] have assumed an influencing by Akkadian *Assur* [8].

The name *Ấsuro Mayaḥ* (the former and architect of the Daityas) which penetrated into Astronomy, Magic and Theory of War also, has been the subject of many astute interpretations.[9] But this name is, in all probability, not to be separated from Skt. *asuramāyấ* ' dæmonic magic ', nor from the common Vedic formula *ásurasya*

---

[1] H. Güntert, *Der arische Weltkönig und Heiland*, p. 101 ff. ; R. N. Dandekar, *Der vedische mensch*, p. 24 ff.

[2] Cf. Dandekar, *op. cit.*, p. 40 ff.

[3] Walde-Hofmann i, 50 ; Pokorny, p. 48.

[4] So W. Brandenstein, *Die alten Inder in Vorderasien und die chronologie des Rigweda*, p. 142 ff. ; but A. Götze, *Oriental Studies in honour of Cursetji Erachji Pavry*, pp. 127–9, equates the word to Skt *śúra-* ' strong, powerful '.

[5] *Études germaniques* viii, 36 ff., and *Language* xxviii, 453.

[6] Venetian *ahsu-* is probably a different word ; see Whatmough, *Language* . xxv, 287.

[7] K. R. V. Rājā, *Comparative studies* i, 38 ff. ; F. W. Thomas, *JRAS* 1916, p. 364 ; Kretschmer, *Wiener zeitschrift für die kunde des Morgenlandes* xxxiii, 14 ff. ; cf. also Sköld, *JRAS* 1924, p. 265 ff.

[8] The etymology which derives *ásura-* from **ásra-* = Av *aṅra(ma'nyu-)*, attribute of the Evil Spirit (J. Wackernagel, *Altindische grammatik* ii, 38), is not convincing ; again, *ásura-* is certainly not cognate with Latin *erus* (see Walde-Hofmann, p. 419).

[9] Weber, *Indische studien* ii, 243, saw Greek Πτολεμαῖος in it (but it is *Turamaya-* in an inscription) ; Spooner, *JRAS* 1915, pp. 77 ff., derives it from Iranian *Ahura Mazdā* (but see F. W. Thomas, *JRAS* 1916, pp. 362 ff.).

māyá [1] ; however, since there can well be question of folk-etymology, at least Weber's suggestion cannot be rejected out of hand.

21. A. Walde and J. B. Hofmann, *Lateinisches etymologisches wörterbuch* [Walde-Hofmann] [2] :—

brevis, *-e* ,, kurz, klein, gering, schmal, flach, seicht " (seit Plaut., rom. ; *-is* [sc. *libellus*] seit Diocl. und *-e* n. [seit 6.Jh., rom.] ,, kurzes Schreiben, Urkunde ", daraus ahd. *brief* ,, Brief, Urkunde ", engl. *brief* ,, Aktenstück ") : aus **mreĝh-u̯-i-* **bre(χ)u̯i-* (zum Lautlichen s. Sommer Hdb². 225, Persson Beitr. 929, Reichelt KZ 46, 324, Leumann-Stolz⁵ 149 f. ; zum *i*-St. vgl. *gravis, levis* usw.) zu idg. **mr̥ĝhús* in av. *mərəzu-ǰiti-, mərəzu-ǰva-* ,, βραχύβιος ", sogd. *murzak* ,, kurz " (Wackernagel GGA. 1910, 15 f., Gl. 10, 22 f.), gr. βραχύς ,, kurz ", βράχεα ,, seichte Stellen " (vgl. lat. *brevia* seit Verg., wohl Bed.-Lw. ; dazu βραχίων ,, Oberarm ", Kompar. neben βράσσων, Bechtel Lexil. 83 ; aber βράγος· ἕλος Hes. kaum als maked. nach Fick BB 29, 199 f. hierher, sondern zu ahd. *bruoch* ,, Sumpf ", s. Walde-P. II 235) ; got. *gamaúrgjan* ,, verkürzen " (von **maúrgus* ,, kurz "), ahd. *murg(i)* ,, kurz ", *murg-fāri* ,, hinfällig ", ags. *myrge* ,, kurzweilig " (de Saussure MSL. 5,449 [Rec. 406 f.] usw. ; nicht mit Solmsen KZ. 34, 30 nach J. Schmidt u.a. zu lat. *murcus*, dessen Bed. ,, verstümmelt " nicht aus ,, verkürzt " zu gewinnen ist ; unannehmbar auch Pedersen I 105 : air. *meirc* ,, Rost "). Fern bleibt abg. *br̆zo* Adv. ,, Schnell " (s. Berneker 109 f. und unter *festīnō*).—Verfehlt Bezzenberger BB. 2, 271 (*brevis* : lit. *gražùs* ,, schön ") ; Fick GGA. 1894, 232 (: got. *anapraggan* ,, bedrängen " usw., s. Walde-P. II 135).—S. noch *brūma.*—Walde-P. II 314.

Breuis (mf. : *breue* n.),[3] *breuis* [sc. *libellus*] [4] and *breue* n. noun [5][6] < IndE **mreĝh-u̯-i-* (> **bre(χ)u̯i-*) [7] to IndE **mr̥ĝhu-* in Av *mərəzu-*

---

[1] W. Neisser, *Zum wörterbuch des Rigveda* i, 141.

[2] i, 115.

[3] Plautus onwards ; exists in the Romance languages.

[4] Diocletian onwards.

[5] From VI. c. A.D. onwards : exists in the Romance languages.

[6] ba. OHG *briaf* (> MnHG *brief*) MnE [*lawyer's*] *brief*.

[7] For the phonology see F. Sommer, *Handbuch der lateinischen laut- und formenlehre* (2nd ed.), p. 225 ; Persson, p. 929 ; Reichelt, *KZ* xlvi, 324 ; M. Leumann, *Laut- und formenlehre* [in Stolz and Schmalz, *Lateinische grammatik* (5th ed.)], pp. 149 ff. For the *i*-declension of the word cf. *grauis, leuis*, etc.

fīti, mərəzu-jva ' βραχύβιος ' Sogdian *murzak* ' short '[1] Greek βραχύς, βράχεα,[2] further βραχίων, comp., beside βράσσων [3][4]; Gothic *ga-maúrgjan* (from a **maúrgus*) OHG *murg murgi, murg-fári* OE *myrge* [5].[6] (OBg *brъzo* adv. ' quickly ' must be kept separate [7]) [8] [9]. See also **brūma**.

22. E. Fraenkel, *Litauisches etymologisches wörterbuch* [10] :—

(j)ēknos, (j)ā́knos, jekanas (Bretkun 3. Mos. 3, 10, nach Bezzenberger Btr. 291) ' Leber ', lett. *akna, -e,* gew. Pl. *aknas* (in Dondangen *jęknas*) etc. (Būga KS 149) ; cf. ai. *yákr̥t* (Gen. *yaknā́ḥ*), av. *yakārə*, griech. ἧπαρ (Gen. ἥπατος), lat. *iecur* (Gen. *iecinoris*) ' Leber ' (s. Benveniste Orig. 8 ff. 26. 181 ff., Specht Dekl. 297). Für av. *huyā́γna-* (Yašt 10, 116) liest Krause KZ 56, 304 ff. *hayākana-* ' von gemeinsamer Leber ', d.h.s.v.a. ' Geschwister '. Er äußert sich über die Leber als besonders wichtiges Lebensorgan und erinnert an aisl. *lifri* ' der zur selben Leber (*lifr*) Gehörige ' als Umschreibung für ' Bruder '. Schwierigkeit macht der Anlaut von aisl. *lifr*, ahd. *lёbara*, arm. *leard* ' Leber ' (unwahrscheinlich darüber J. Schmidt Plurbldg. 198 ff.). Nach Neckel bei Krause KZ 56, 308 soll germ. *Leber* vielmehr mit *leben* verwandt sein. Die balt. Formen ohne Anlauts-*j* sind aus denen mit diesem Kons. im Satzsandhi entstanden (vgl. über ähnliche Fälle s.v. (*j*)*ёgёrė*.) Über evtl. Zushg. von *ikras* 2. ' Fischrogen ' mit lit. (*j*)*ēknos* s.s.v. *ikras* 2.

---

[1] Wackernagel, *Göttingische gelehrte anzeigen* 1910, p. 15 and *Glotta* x, 22 f.

[2] Cf. Latin *breuia* (Virgil onwards) probably calqued on the Greek.

[3] F. Bechtel, *Lexilogus zu Homer*, p. 83.

[4] But Hesychius' βράγος· ἕλος can hardly (with Fick *BB* xxix, 199 f.) be taken as Macedonian and as belonging here—it is, rather, to OHG *bruoch* (so WP ii, 235).

[5] F. de Saussure, *MSL* v, 449 (and *Notice* of this *MSL* v, 406 f.), *et al.*

[6] The Germanic words are not to be taken (with F. Solmsen, *KZ* xxxiv, 30—he is following J. Schmidt and others) as cognate with Latin *murcus* (whose meaning ' mutilated ' cannot be derived from ' to shorten '). Pedersen i, 105, puts OIrish *meirc* ' rust, wrinkle ' as a cognate but this view, too, is not tenable.

[7] See **festīnō** and E. Berneker, *Slavisches etymologisches wörterbuch* [i], 109 f.

[8] Failed etymologies :—A. Bezzenberger, *BB* ii, 271 (*breuis*: Lith *gražùs* ' beautiful ') ; Fick, *Göttingische gelehrte anzeigen* 1894, p. 232 (to Gothic *ana-praggan*—see WP ii, 135).

[9] On *breuis* see also WP ii, 314.

[10] pp. 192–3.

(J)ēknos (*j*)*āknos jekanas* [1] 'liver' Lettish *akna akne* 'do.' [2]
= Skt *yákr̥t* (gs. *yaknáḥ*) 'do.' Av *yakārə* 'do.' Greek ἧπαρ (gs.
ἧπατος) Latin *iecur* (gs. *iecinoris*). [3] Krause, *KZ* lvi, 304 ff.,
takes Avesta *huyāγna-* [4] as *hayākana-* 'from a common liver', that is, as
much as to say, 'brothers and/or sisters'. He expresses views as to
the liver being a particularly important part of the body and calls
attention to OIc *lifre* 'he who belongs to the same liver (Ic *lifr*)'
as a circumlocution for 'brother'. The initial of Ic *lifr* OHG *lĕbara*
Arm *leard* 'liver' is difficult [5] and, according to Professor Neckel, [6]
" liver " is much better brought into connection with " to live ".
The Baltic forms without initial *j* are derived, in sandhi, from those
with it [7] [8].

23. Y. H. Toivonen, *Suomen kielen etymologinen sanakirja* [9] :—
airo, murt. myös (esim. Verml.) *aira*, (Lemi) *airu*, karj.-aun. *airo*,
lyyd. *air*, *airo*, veps. *air*, vatj. *airo*, *air*, (Kukk.) *hairo*, vir. *aer*
(g. *-ru*), murt. myös *air*, *âr*, *ajur*, *ajor* jne. ' airo ', *aeruda*, *aerutada*
' soutaa ', liiv. *àiraz*, *airᴈz*, (Sal.) *air* ' airo ', *airᴈ* ' soutaa ' (lpL *ai'ru*,
N *ai'ro*, I *ǎi̯r̄ᵘ*, Nrt. *ajr*, Kld. *ārj*, T *ārja* ' airo ') < germ., ksk.
*airō- : ags., mn. *ár*, mr. *ār*, nr. *ǎr*, *ǎra* jne. ' airo ' (lappiin nähtävästi
ksm. välityksellä ; liiv. > lät. *airis*, *aire* ' airo ', *airēt* ' soutaa ').

Airo ' oar ' (d. also *aira* [10] *airu* [11]): Karelian and Aunus *airo*
' do.' Lüd *air airo* ' do.' Veps *air* ' do.' Vatya *airo air hairo* [12]
' do.' Estonian *aer* (gs. *aeru*) ' do.' (d. also *air âr ajur ajor*, etc.)

---

[1] J. Bretkun, *Biblija* [1591] Leviticus 3,10 (according to A. Bezzenberger,
Beiträge zur geschichte der litauischen sprache, p. 291).
[2] In Lettish, the normal plural is *aknas*, but *jęknas* in Dondangen (see K. Buga,
Kalba ir senovė, p. 149).
[3] See E. Benveniste, *Origines de la formation des noms en indo-européen* pp. 8 ff.,
26, 181 ; F. Specht, *Der ursprung der indogermanischen deklination*, p. 297.
[4] Yašt 10, 116.
[5] For an improbable suggestion on this point, see J. Schmidt, *Die pluralbildungen*
der indogermanischen neutra, p. 198 ff.
[6] See Krause *KZ* lvi, 308.
[7] On similar forms see s.v. **(j)ęgėrė**.
[8] On a possible connection between Lith (*j*)*ēknos* ' liver ' and Lith *ìkras* ' roe ',
see **ikras 2**.
[9] i, 10.
[10] For instance, in Värmland.
[11] At Lemi.
[12] At Kukkosi.

aeruda aerutada ' to row ' Livonian *àiraz airŝz air* [1] ' oar ', *airŝ* ' to
row ' ; (cf. further, Luleå-Lappish *aiᵉru* ' oar ' Norwegian Lappish
ai⁺ro ' do.' Enare Lappish *äȳⁱʳᵘ* ' do.' Lappish of Lake Nuorti *ajr*
' do.' Kildin Lappish *ārj* ' do.' Kola Lappish *ārja* ' do.') ; lwf.
ON. *airō- (> Ic *ár*, OSw *ār* (> MnSw *àr åra*)) = OE *ār* [> MnE
oar] ; the Lappish forms are apparently borrowings from Primitive
Finnish.[2]

The scientific " Etymology " that I have described above is, of
course, the only subject to which this name can properly be applied.
As will now be appreciated, it is not, in any sense, a subject for the
amateur, and it is, on the whole, a subject singularly little-known
to the General Public. There is however another subject to which
the General Public applies the name *etymology*, a subject which
philologists often call *Popular Etymology*.[3] This subject is one quite
without value but, since it is one of the great breeders of popular
fallacies, it may be as well to devote a little space to its discussion.
In order to do this, it will, however, be necessary to submit to
examination something that I may best epitomise by saying that
what falls here for examination is, in fact, the views of the General
Public considered under the illumination of our basic Axioms I
and II.

It may be as well to begin by drawing a fairly obvious Corollary
from what has gone before. Above, I defined Comparative Philology
as all consequences arising from a consideration of the Axioms. It
therefore follows that, in the context of Comparative Philology,
anything that is not a consequence of the Axioms is non-existent,
i.e. is nonsense. This means that we may conveniently use the
Axioms as touch-stones for assessing whether or not a popular
belief is nonsense ; if it is deducible from the Axioms, it is not
nonsense, but, if it is not so deducible, it is nonsense.

A large group of popular fallacies is directly to be ascribed to
the use of the words *like* and *similar* in linguistic contexts by the
General Public. In the context of the second Axiom it is quite clear

---

[1] At Salats.

[2] Lettish *airis aire* ' oar ', *airēt* ' to row ', lwf. Livonian.

[3] *Popular etymology* is again distinct from *Volksetymologie* (often translated
as *folk-etymology*) which is a phenomenon (not a subject) whose nature will have
become clear from the examples in the dictionary-citations just given.

what the General Public means by these words—and it is upon this
use of them that all Popular Etymology rests. There is, for instance,
a Danish word *hoppe* meaning ' mare ' ; the General Public's view
of this word might well be " it is ' like ' Greek ἵππος, meaning
' horse ' " and this, to the General Public, constitutes an etymological
statement about Danish *hoppe*. But nothing as to the necessity of
congruent or cognate words being similar is deducible from Axiom II
and the attaching of any importance to such a similarity is therefore
nonsense. As indeed we have already seen (cf. *cow* = *beef*, p. 42).
In fact, Danish *hoppe* has not the faintest connection with Greek
ἵππος—and, I may add, one of the best-known congruents of
Greek ἵππος is a most " dissimilar " one viz. Latin *equus*.

In the context of the First Axiom, the General Public's use of the
words *like* and *similar* is far from clearcut. The use I have in
mind occurs in remarks such as " Spanish is ' like ' Italian " or
" Serbian is ' similar to ' Russian " ; what are the actual cases
here, of course, is that Spanish is related to Italian and Serbian
is related to Russian in the sense of Axiom I. If asked to explain
what he means by *like* or *similar* in such a context, the questionee
sometimes indicates that he means similarity in sound, sometimes
that he means similarity in grammar, but, usually, he has little
precise idea as to what he does mean. It may be noted that, to
English ears, Finnish and Italian (unrelated languages) are similar
in sound ; further, that English and Welsh (related languages)
are very dissimilar in grammar. Lay speakers of a language (A)
apparently often consider two other languages (B and C) to be
similar in grammar solely because B and C possess in common a
grammatical feature unknown in A. On this view it would be reasonable to consider the unrelated languages English and Hungarian
as related because Hungarian and Somerset dialect have a remarkable feature in common, the so-called objective conjugation [1] !

It will thus be seen that it is not at all a question of a popular
etymology being wrong or providing matter for discussion—it can
only be by pure chance that a popular etymology is right, and an
etymology cannot ever be matter for discussion between a philologist
and a non-philologist.

---

[1] See A. S. C. Ross, *Notes and Queries for Somerset and Dorset* xx, 259–60.

CHAPTER TWO

AN APPARATUS FOR ENGLISH ETYMOLOGY

IN THE first chapter of this book, I have endeavoured to give some indication of the nature of Etymology. In Chapter II, I discuss the apparatus necessary for dealing with the etymologies of English words. Ideally, such an Apparatus must be excessively large. It falls naturally into two parts, the first being essentially connected with Axiom I, the second with Axiom II. In Part I we are thus concerned with the relationships of the English Language and, to a much lesser extent, with the relationships of those languages from which English, or any of its direct parents (Anglo-Saxon, Primitive Germanic, Indo-european) have taken loan-words. Part I is thus, ideally, little less than a classification of the languages of the world by families. In Part II, we are thus concerned with the history of the phonemes of English (and a little with its morphology) and with any necessary controls or aids to understanding that we may encounter in the relevant discussions. The furthest attainable parent of English is Indoeuropean ; ideally, then, we should first enumerate the pho-nemes of Indoeuropean (adding an account of Ablaut) and describe its morphology, and then set out the historical phonology and morphology of every Indoeuropean language. Thus, ideally, our Part II comprises nothing less than most of the whole corpus of Indoeuropean Philology.

Practice, in a book on Etymology, must naturally and of necessity fall hugely short of this ideal. Nevertheless it is convenient and desirable to keep the Ideal in mind when establishing the Apparatus.

In practice, I have made my Apparatus as follows (it being prefaced that each Section is to be as short as possible) :—

(i) An account of the Indoeuropean family of languages.

(ii) An enumeration of the phonemes of Indoeuropean.

(iii) Some remarks upon Ablaut.

(iv) The fate of the Indoeuropean phonemes in certain selected non-Germanic Indoeuropean languages (mostly ancient ones).

(v) The fate of the Indoeuropean phonemes in Primitive Germanic.

(vi) An enumeration of the phonemes of Primitive Germanic.

(vii) The fate of the Primitive Germanic phonemes in certain selected non-English Germanic languages (mostly ancient ones).

(viii) The fate of the Primitive Germanic phonemes in English.[1]

(ix) Some remarks upon the Morphology.

The justification of most of this Apparatus is self-evident ; only (iv), (vii) and (ix) perhaps require some comment. In order to justify (iv), it is only necessary to consider an example such as MnE *bear* = Latin *fero* : from (v) and (viii) we shall know that IndE *bh* > *b* in MnE *bear*, but the equation will not be intelligible unless we know also that IndE *bh* > *f* in Latin *fero*, and this is a part of (iv). The example MnE *eat* = MnHG *essen* justifies (vii) in a similar manner—we require to know that PrGmc *t* > [s] in MnHG *essen*. Lack of space must, naturally, keep (ix) to a minimum and this will, in the event, be no very great disadvantage at least as far as later English is concerned for, as a general rule, the morphology plays much less part in the etymology of later English than it does in that of Anglo-Saxon.

(i) The Indoeuropean Family of Languages

The Indoeuropean Family falls into ten sub-families :—

I. HITTITE, of which the most important member is the language from which the group takes its name. *Hittite* is the language of the Hittite Empire, which had its centre at the present-day Boghaz-Köy in Asia Minor. Mostly written in cuneiform, the language is chiefly known from the archives of this site, which extend from XIX–XIV c. B.C.

II. INDO-IRANIAN, which falls into two sub-groups, INDO-ARYAN and IRANIAN.

INDO-ARYAN. The most ancient member of the group is *Sanskrit*, which exists in two forms : *Vedic*, the language of a number of religious texts, which cannot be dated accurately, but of which some certainly originate in the Second Millennium B.C., and *Classical*, the form of Sanskrit which became fixed owing to the labours of certain grammarians (notably Pāṇini, of IV c. B.C.). It is in the Classical form that the huge mass of Sanskrit literature is written—and

---

[1] Cf. my remarks p. 137.

continues to be written to this day (in somewhat the same way as
that in which Latin continued as a written language for many
centuries after its death as a spoken language). Side-by-side with
standard Sanskrit there grew up a series of regional languages,
known collectively as the *Prākrits* ; the earliest dated Prākrit
texts are the Inscriptions of Aśoka (III c. B.C.). The Prākrits may
appropriately be called *Middle Indian* ; there is also at least one
important Middle Indian religious language, *Pali*. The modern
Indo-Aryan languages are very numerous and are spoken by a
vast number of people. Some of the most important are *Kashmiri*,
Western Punjabi, *Sindhi*, *Gujarati*, *Marathi* (Bombay area) the
Rajasthani dialects, *Punjabi* proper, *Nepalese*, *Western Hindi*
(roughly between the Punjab and Cawnpore), *Eastern Hindi* (from
Cawnpore nearly as far as Benares), *Bengali*, *Bihari*, *Oriya*, *Assamese*,
Singhalese (in Ceylon)—finally I may mention the various *Gypsy*
languages, which achieved their present widespread distribution as
a consequence of the many migrations of these people, who left
the North-West of India about V c. A.D. (The most important
dialect of Western Hindi was christened *Hindustani* by the English
and this became a common language over a very large part of India ;
it has two literary forms, *Urdu* and *Hindi*, both very widely-used).

IRANIAN. In the most ancient period, Iranian is known in two
forms, *Old Persian* (for which the inscriptions of Darius (521–486
B.C.) and Xerxes (485–465 B.C.) are the main sources) and *Avestic*,
the language of the Avesta, the sacred book of the Zoroastrians
(probably to be assigned to VIII c. B.C.). There are several *Middle
Iranian* languages and, of these, the western ones are, collectively,
called *Pahlavi*. Of the modern languages, *Persian* (texts from
VIII c. A.D.) is the most important ; *Baluchi*, *Pushtu* (the language
of the Afghans) and *Ossete* (spoken in the Caucasus) also deserve
mention here.

III. " TOCHARIAN ". This language, existing in two dialects
(A and B), is the most recent discovery in the Indoeuropean Family ;
its texts were found in Chinese Turkestan at the beginning of the
present century (at least one is as early as VII c. A.D.). When the
texts were first investigated they were assigned to the people called
Τόχαροι in the Greek sources ; this attribution is now known to
be false but the nomenclature has persisted (hence the customary
inverted commas).

IV. ARMENIAN, with texts from IX c. A.D.; the classical form of the language seems to have been fixed in V c. A.D.

V. THRACO-PHRYGIAN, comprising *Thracian* (with an inscription of V. c. B.C.), *Phrygian* (with two sets of inscriptions, VII–VI c. B.C. and III–IV c. A.D.) and, possibly, *Old Macedonian* (glosses and proper names).

VI. GREEK ; until recently it was thought that Homeric Greek (IX–VIII c. B.C.) was the earliest form of Greek known to us but M. Ventris and J. Chadwick's recent decipherment of the hieroglyphs known as " Minoan Linear *B* " [1] means that Homer is antedated by many centuries.

VII. ALBANIAN (first text, 1462 A.D.).

VIII. ITALO-CELTIC, which falls into two sub-groups, ITALIC and CELTIC.

ITALIC comprises *Umbrian* (known from the Tables of Iguvium, 200–70 B.C.), *Oscan* (the language of the Samnites—inscriptions of III c. B.C.—I c. A.D.) and *Latin*. The earliest Latin inscription is c. 600 B.C., the literary monuments start in III c. B.C. Latin has given rise to the ROMANCE Family of Languages whose members are the following :—

1. *Italian* (first text, c. 960 A.D.).
2. *Sardinian*.
3. *Provençal* (the literature begins c. 1000 A.D.).
4. *French* (first text, 842 A.D.).
5. *Spanish* (first texts, X c. A.D.), also spoken in all of Latin America save Brazil and Haiti.
6. *Catalan* (first text, 1171 A.D.).
7. *Portuguese* (first text, 1192 A.D.) ; also spoken in Brazil.
8. *Rhaeto-Romance*, the " fourth language " of Switzerland.
9. *Dalmatian*, recently died out on the Adriatic Coast.
10. *Roumanian* (first texts, later XVI c. A.D.).

CELTIC comprises *Gaulish* (the language of the inscriptions of Gaul, III c. B.C.—I c. A.D.), *Q-Celtic* and *P-Celtic*. *Q*-Celtic (or *Goidelic*) consists of *Gaelic*, which is of three kinds : *Irish* (the first texts are the Ogam inscriptions of V c. A.D.), *Manx* and *Scots Gaelic* (first texts, XVI c. A.D.). *P*-Celtic (or *Brythonic* or *British*)

---

[1] Evidence for Greek dialect in the Mycenaean archives, *Journal of Hellenic Studies* lxxiii [1953], 84–103.

comprises *Welsh* (first texts, VIII c. A.D.), *Cornish* (IX c. A.D. until its dying-out, c. 1800) and *Breton*.

IX. GERMANIC. This falls into three groups, the first containing only *Gothic* (texts of IV and VI c. A.D., also fragments of *Crimean Gothic* recorded 1560 A.D.), the other two being NORTH and WEST GERMANIC.

NORTH GERMANIC (NORSE or SCANDINAVIAN) falls into two sub-groups, *East* and *West Norse*. *Old Norse* is attested in a number of runic inscriptions II–VIII c. A.D. East Norse comprises *Swedish* and *Danish* (texts from XIII c. A.D., both languages), West Norse *Old Norwegian* and the forms this latter language has taken in the colonies populated directly or indirectly from Norway viz. *Icelandic* (first texts, X c. A.D.), *Færoese* and *Shetlandic* (of which fragments of texts survive, but which is best-known in the form of *Shetland Norn* (only recently entirely superseded by the Lowland Scots dialect now used in the Islands)). The dialects of Norway are, of course, predominantly the descendants of Old Norwegian ; the normal language of the country (*Riksmål*) is, however, a form of Danish. During XIX c. A.D. there was created a somewhat artificial mixture of the dialects known as *Landsmål*, which is now a rival to Riksmål.

WEST GERMANIC consists of *High German*, customarily called *German* (first texts, VIII c. A.D.), *Low German* (i.e., in chronological order of descent, first, *Old Saxon* (main text, c. 830 A.D.), then, *Middle Low German* and, to-day, the *Plattdeutsch* dialects), *Dutch* and *Flemish* (also *Afrikaans*), *Frisian* (first texts, XIII c. A.D.) and *English* (the first *Anglo-Saxon*, or *Old English* texts are of VIII c. A.D.).

X. BALTO-SLAVONIC falls into two sub-groups, BALTIC and SLAVONIC.

BALTIC consists of *Old Prussian* (texts of XV and XVI c. A.D., extinct in XVII c.), *Lithuanian* (first text, 1547 A.D.) and *Lettish* (first text, 1585 A.D.).

SLAVONIC falls into three groups, *South Slavonic*, *West Slavonic* and *Russian*. There are old South Slavonic texts of IX c. A.D. ; their language, which continued, is usually called *Old Bulgarian* or (*Old*) *Church Slavonic* and, with Orthodox Christianity, it spread to other parts of the Slavonic world (so that we may, for instance, distinguish a *Russian Church Slavonic*). The individual languages of the Southern Group are *Slovene* (first text, X c. A.D.), *Serbo-Croatian* (texts from XV c. A.D.) and *Bulgarian*. West Slavonic comprises *Czech* (first texts, XIII c. A.D.), *Polish* (first texts, XIV c. A.D.), *Slovak* and some other languages. The Russian Group consists of *Russian* proper, *White Russian* and *Ukrainian*.

(ii) The Phonemes of Indoeuropean

The Phonemes of Indoeuropean may be classified as *Vocalic, Consonantal, Semi-Vocalic* and *Diphthongal.*

Vocalic. There are both long and short vowels :—*a e o ə ъ ā ē ō.*

Consonantal. The Consonants fall into two groups, *Stops* and *Spirants.* The Stops are classified according as they are (1) unvoiced and unaspirated, (2) unvoiced and aspirated, (3) voiced and un-aspirated, (4) voiced and aspirated ; in respect of this classification, it is customary to make use of the Latin terminology of the early nineteenth century ; a stop is thus (1) a *tenuis,* (2) a *tenuis aspirata,* (3) a *media,* (4) a *media aspirata.* Stops are further classified according as they are *Labial, Dental* or *Guttural* and there are three kinds of Guttural viz. *Palatal, Velar* and *Labio-Velar.* There are thus twenty stops viz. :—

	Tenuis	Tenuis aspirata	Media	Media aspirata
Labial	p	ph	b	bh
Dental	t	th	d	dh
Palatal	$\hat{k}$	$\hat{k}h$	$\hat{g}$	$\hat{g}h$
Velar	k	kh	g	gh
Labio-Velar	k^u	k^uh	g^u	g^uh

The Spirants are voiced and unvoiced, aspirated and unaspirated :—
s sh z zh þ þh ð ðh.

Semi-Vocalic. As their name implies, the semi-vowels can function either as vowel or consonant ; in the former function they are either long or short ; the notation differs according to the function. We thus have :—

Short Vowel :	i	u	l	m	n	r
Long Vowel :	$\bar{i}$	$\bar{u}$	$\bar{l}$	$\bar{m}$	$\bar{n}$	$\bar{r}$
Consonant :	i	u	l	m	n	$r.$

Diphthongal. A diphthong is a combination of a vowel and a semi-vowel. The number of diphthongal combinations which are theoretically possible is thus very large but some of these do not actually eventuate (e.g. vowel + long semi-vowel, as *oī*), while others are more conveniently treated in their two parts, as vowel + consonant (e.g. *el*), or consonant + vowel (e.g. *le*). The list of diphthongs thus reduces to the following :—*ai āi ei ēi oi ōi əi au āu eu ēu ou ōu əu.*

(iii) Ablaut
Vocalic

For the reasons given in the Preface it will be desirable to keep this Section to a minimum and it will probably be sufficient to say that the majority of vocalic ablauts encountered are of two kinds, the first being much the more common.

In the First Case the alternation is :—

$$e \infty o \infty \bar{e} \infty \bar{o} \infty \mathtt{b} \infty \text{-}$$

($\mathtt{b}$ being virtually confined to the position before *l, m, n, r*). Examples :—

1) **ped-* : Latin as. *pedem* Greek as. $\pi\delta\delta a$ Latin *pēs* ($<$ **pēd-s*) Gothic *fotus* Skt. *upa-bd-á-* ' trampling '.

2) **bheidh-* : Greek $\pi\epsilon i\theta\omega$, 1st sg. 2nd perf. $\pi\epsilon\pi oi\theta a$ Gothic ppart. *bidans.*

3) **ƙleu-* : Greek 1st pl. future middle $\kappa\lambda\epsilon\nu\sigma\delta\mu\epsilon\theta a$ OIrish *cluas* ' ear ' ($<$ **ƙloustā-*) Skt. 1st sg.aor. *a-śrāušam* ' to hear ', ppart. *śruta-* ' famous '.

4) **bher-* : Greek $\phi\epsilon\rho\omega$, $\phi\delta\rho a$ Gothic 1st pl.pret. *berum* Greek $\phi\omega\rho$ Gothic ppart. *baúrans* Greek $\delta i\text{-}\phi\rho os$.

5) **bhendh-* : Gothic *bindan* ($<$ **bhendhono-*), sg.pret. *band* ($<$ **bhondha*), ppart. *bundans* ($<$ **bhṇdhono/ā-*).

6) **gʷem-* : Gothic *qiman* ($<$ **gʷemono-*), sg.pret. *qam*, 1st pl.pret. *qemum*, ppart. *qumans* Greek $\beta a i\nu\omega$ ($<$ **βaνι̯ω*).

In the Second Case the alternation is :—

$$\bar{e} \infty \bar{o} \infty \theta$$

Examples :—

1) **sē-* : Latin *sēmen* Russian *sad* Latin ppart. *satus.*

2) **dhēi-* : Lettish *dêju* ' to suck ' Greek $\theta oi\nu\eta$ ($<$ **θωινη*) Gothic *daddjan* ($<$ **đajjan-* $<$ *đai̯an-* *$<$ **dhəi̯ono-*).

Consonantal

The only common consonantal ablaut in Indoeuropean is the alternation between forms with initial *s* + consonant and those without the *s*. Examples :—Greek στέγος ∾ τέγος ; Lith *skaidrùs* ' bright, clear ' ∾ MnHG *heiter* ; OE *nearu* ∾ MnHG *schnurren*.

(iv) The Fates of the Indoeuropean Phonemes
VOWELS

Under this head I deal with the vocalic phonemes and with the semi-vocalic phonemes in vocalic function. It is convenient to treat *ḹ m̥̄ n̥̄ r̥̄* separately and to take with them also *ъ* (which virtually occurs only before *l m n r*).

PRELIMINARY NOTES

1. *a, ā* and the long semi-vowels (*ī ū ḹ m̥̄ n̥̄ r̥̄*) are of moderately rare occurrence.

2. *ə > i* in Indo-Iranian but is everywhere else treated exactly as is *a* :—Skt *pitár-* ' father ' Greek πατήρ Latin *pater* OIrish *athir* ' do.' ; Skt ppart. *sthitá-* ' standing ' Greek στατός Latin ppart. *status* Lith *stataũ* ' to place ' OBg *stojǫ* ' to stand '.

TABLE

	Sanskrit	Greek	Latin	Old Irish	Lithuanian	Old Bulgarian
a	a	α	a	a	a	o
ā	ā	η	ā	á	ō	a
e	a	ε	e	e	e	e
ē	ā	η	ē	í	e	ě
o	a	o	o	o	a	o
ō	ā	ω	ō	á	uo	a
i	i	ι	i	i	i	ъ
ī	ī	ῑ	ī	í	y	i
u	u	υ	u	u	u	ъ
ū	ū	ῡ	ū	ú	ū	y

EXAMPLES

a. Skt *ati* ' more than, very ' Greek ἀτάρ Latin *at* OIrish *ad-*

aith-, prefix ' again ', etc. Lith *at- ati-* ' back, off ' OBg *ot otъ* ' out,
away '.

ā. Skt *mātár-* ' mother ' Greek μήτηρ Latin *māter* OIrish *máthir*
' do.' Lith *motě* (gs. *moteřs*) ' woman, wife ' OBg *mati* (gs. *matere*)
' mother '.

e. Skt *šát* ' six ' Greek ἕξ Latin *sex* OIrish *sé* ' do.', *seser* ' group
of six men ' Lith *šeši* ' six ' OBg *šestь* ' do.'.

ě. Skt *mās-* ' month ' Greek μήν Latin *mensis* OIrish *mí* ' do.'
Lith *měnů* ' moon ' OBg *měsęcь* ' month, moon '.

o. Skt *aštáu* ' eight ' Greek ὀκτώ Latin *octo* OIrish *ocht* ' do.'
Lith *aštuoni* ' do.' OBg *osmь* ' do.'

ō. Skt *dāna-* ' gift ' Greek δῶρον Latin *dōnum* OIrish *dán* ' do.'
Lith *duonis* ' do.' OBg *danь* ' uectigal '.

i. Skt *vidhávā* ' widow ' Greek ἠΓίθεος Latin *uiduus* OIrish
fedb ' do.' Lith *vidùs* ' middle, inside ' [1] OBg *vьdova* ' widow '.

ī. Skt (Vedic) nan. *trī* ' three ' Latin *trī-ginta* OIrish namn.
trí ' do.' Lith *trý-lika* ' thirteen ' OBg nanf. *tri* ' three '; Greek
κλίνη Latin *in-clīno* Lith *pa-šlýti* ' to become crooked '.

u. Skt *yugá-* ' yoke, pair ' Greek ζυγόν Latin *iugum* Gaulish
Uer-iugo-dumnus (OIrish *cuing* ' yoke ' < IndE **kom-įung-* ?) Lith
jùngas ' do.' OBg *igo* ' do.' (< *jьgo < *jьzgo).

ū. Skt *dhūmá-* ' smoke, steam ' Greek θῦμός Latin *fūmus* MIrish
dúil ' desire ' [2] (= Skt *dhūli-* ' dust ') Lith pl. *dúmai* ' smoke ' [3]
OBg *dymъ* ' do.'.

Į m̥ n̥ ŋ̥

In the different languages the development of the nasals (n̥ ŋ̥)
and that of the liquids (r̥ l̥ [4]) is somewhat similar and may be
summarized as follows.

---

[1] The semantics are noteworthy : the root **ṵeidh-* has ' to separate ' as its
basic meaning (hence the meaning ' widow ') ; Lith *vidùs* probably had ' the
division between two parts ' as its earlier meaning, applied, for instance, to a belt
of forest separating two plots of ground in the middle—hence, finally, the application to trees and wood—for MnE *wood* = Lith *vidùs*.

[2] For the semantics, cf. the meaning of the Greek cognate.

[3] Cf. Latin np. *fūmi* ' smoke '.

[4] In Sanskrit *l̥* behaves as if it had been *r̥*.

(A) SHORT.

1. The vocalic quality is retained only in the case of the liquids in Indo-Iranian and Slavonic.

2. Normally, a vowel is developed before the nasal or liquid viz. a in Indo-Iranian and Greek, i in Lithuanian, $ь$ in Old Bulgarian, o^u in Germanic, in Latin e in the case of nasals, o in that of liquids.

3. The nasal is lost before a following t in Indo-Iranian, Greek and Old Bulgarian (in this last language IndE $n̥t > et$).

4. Occasionally, metathesis takes place e.g. IndE $r̥t >$ OIrish rit.

(B) LONG.

1. In Germanic the four long semi-vowels are not distinct from the corresponding short ones, nor are they in Old Bulgarian (though they are in Serbo-Croatian) ; in Lithuanian, they are distinct only in respect of the intonation.

2. In Greek and Italo-Celtic a vowel is developed after the relevant consonant ; this vowel is $ā$ in Italo-Celtic, $ā$ for the Greek nasals, $ω$ for the Greek liquids, whereas in Indo-Iranian $ā$ is developed before a nasal (the latter being lost if a t follows), $ī$ before a liquid.

(C).

$ьn$, $ьm$, $ьl$, $ьr$ are treated exactly as $n̥$, $m̥$, $l̥$, $r̥$.

SOME EXAMPLES

$m̥$. IndE *$k̑m̥tó$- ' hundred ' :—Skt $śatám$ ' do.' Greek $ἑ$-$κατόν$ Latin $centum$ Welsh $cant$ ' do.' [1] Lith $šim̃tas$ ' do.' OBg $sъto$ ' do.'.

IndE *$g^x m̥$- :—Skt $gámati$ ' to walk ' Greek $βαίνω$ ($<$ *$βανι̯ω$) Latin $uenio$.

$ьm$. IndE *$sьmo/ā$- :—Skt $samá$- ' similar, the same ' Greek $ἁμό$-$θεν$.

$n̥$. IndE *$m̥nto$- :—Skt ppart. $matá$- ' thought ' Greek $αὐτό$-$ματος$ Latin ppart. com-$mentus$ OIrish der-met ' oblivion ' Lith ppart. $miñtas$ ' thought of ' ; cf. OBg pa-$mętь$ ' memory '.

$ьn$. IndE *$g^x ьnā$- :—Skt $ganā$ ' lady of the Gods ' Greek (Boeotian) $βανᾱ́$ OIrish ban-$chú$ ' bitch '.

$n̥̄$. IndE *$ĝn̥̄to/ā$- :—Skt ppart. $jātá$- ' born ' Latin ppart. $gnātus$ $nātus$ Gaulish $Cintu$-$gnatus$.

---

[1] The Irish phonology is not entirely clear : OIrish $cét$ ' hundred '.

ʀ. Skt ppart. *mr̥tá-* 'dead' Latin *mortuus* Lith *mirtìs* 'death' OBg *sъ-mrъtь* 'do.'. Skt *puraḥ* 'in front', etc. Greek πάρος.

ʙʀ. Skt *giráti* 'to swallow' OBg *žь̄reti* 'do.' Greek βάραθρον.

ʀ. Skt *pūrvyá-* 'first' Greek πρῶτος (< *πρωϜατος) Latin *prandium* (< *prām-[e]dịo-) Lith *pìrmas* 'do.'

ʟ. IndE *u̯l̥kᵘo-* 'wolf':—Skt *vŕ̥ka-* 'do.' Lith *vil̃kas* 'do.' OBg *vlьkъ* 'do.' S-Cr *vûk* 'do.'.

ʙʟ. Skt *tulấ* 'weighing-scales' Greek τάλᾱς OLatin *tulo.*

ʟ. IndE *pl̥no/ā-* 'full':—Skt *pūrṇá-* 'do.' OIrish *lán* 'do.' Lith *pìlnas* 'do.' OBg *plьnъ* 'do.' S-Cr *pȕn* 'do.'.

DIPHTHONGS

These are called *short* or *long* according as the first element is so (the latter class is rare).

SHORT

Preliminary Note. əi, əu are not distinct from *ai, au,* even in Indo-Iranian [1]: Skt *dhenú-* 'in milk' Lith *diena* 'pregnant [of animals]' (cf. Skt *dháyati* 'to suck'); Greek σταυρός Latin *rē-stauro* Ic *staurr.*

TABLE

	Sanskrit	Greek	Latin	Old Irish	Lithuanian	Old Bulgarian
ei	e	ει	ī	ē ia	ei ë	i
oi	e	οι	ū	oi oe	ai ë	ě
ai	e	αι	ae	ai ae	ai ë	ě
eu	o	ευ	ū	ó ua	au	u
ou	o	ου	ū	ó ua	au	u
au	o	αυ	au	ó ua	au	u

EXAMPLES

ei. Skt *éti* 'to go' Greek 3rd sg. pres. εἶσι Latin 3rd sg. pres. *it* Lith *eĩti* 'do.' OBg *iti* 'do.'; Greek στείχω OIrish *tiag-* 'to go'.

[1] Cf. p. 77.

oi. IndE npm. def. art. **toi* :—Skt *té* ' do.' Greek *τοί* Lith *tiẽ* ' do.' OBg *ti* ' do.' ; Greek *οὔνη* Latin *ūnus* OIrish *óen* ' one '.

ai. Skt *édha-* ' fire-wood ' Greek *αἴθω* Latin *aedēs* OIrish *áed* ' fire ' ; Skt *setu-* ' band, fetter, dam, boundary-mark ' Latin *saeta* Lith *pá-saitis* ' connecting strap ' OBg *sětь* ' string '.

eu. Skt *bódhati* ' to awake (intr.), perceive ' Greek *πεύθομαι* Lith *baudžù* ' to correct, punish ' OBg *bljudǫ* ' to take care of ' ; Greek voc. *Ζεῦ* Latin *Iuppiter* (< **Iū-piter*) ; OIrish *túath* ' race ' Lith *tautá* ' country, people '.

ou. Latin *rūfus* OIrish *rúad* ' red ' Lith *raũdas* ' do.' OBg *ruda* ' ore '.

au. Skt *o-gaṇá-* ' isolated, pitiable ' Greek *αὐ-χάττειν* Latin *au-fero* OIrish *ó úa* ' from, by means of ' Lith *au-linkai* ' henceforward, later ' OBg *u-myti* ' to wash off '.

LONG

The long diphthongs hardly survive save in Indo-Iranian and, to a limited extent, in Greek ; in general, they are treated in the same way as the corresponding short ones. Two examples :—1) **ēi** : Skt 1st pl. perf. *áima* ' to go ' = Greek 1st pl. imperf. *ῆμεν* ; 2) **ōu** : Skt *gāuḥ* ' head of cattle ' = Greek *βοῦς* = OIrish *bó* ' cow '.

CONSONANTS

Under this head I include the consonantal phonemes (viz. the stops and the spirants) and the semi-vocalic phonemes in consonantal use.

STOPS

PRELIMINARY NOTES

1. The tenues aspiratae (*ph th ḱh kh kʷh*) and the media *ḅ* are rare ; the following examples will serve to show the development of the former (which are thus not entered in the Table) :—Skt *phála-* ' fruit ' Greek *ὄ-φελος* Latin *pollex* MIrish *oll* ' large ' OBg *palьсь* ' thumb ' ; Skt *granthi-* ' knob, joint, swelling ' Greek *γρόνθος* OHG *kranz* ; Greek *φάλλη* Latin *squalus* OPR *kalis* ' welz '.[1]

2. The three sets of gutturals are not kept distinct in the Indo-

---

[1] i.e. MnHG *wels*.

D

european languages [1]; languages which conflate the palatals and velars but keep this dual group distinct from the labio-velars are called " *centum* "-languages ; those which conflate the velars with the labio-velars but keep this dual group distinct from the palatals are called " *satəm* "-languages.[2]

3. " Grassmann's Law " states that there is a strong tendency to avoid consecutive aspiratae ; they are eliminated by dissimilation ; thus IndE **dhughəter-* ' daughter ' > Skt *duhitár-* ' do.' (first aspiration lost), Greek θυγάτηρ (second aspiration lost).

4. Under certain conditions the conflate velars were palatalised in Indo-Iranian and Slavonic ; before IndE *e-* and *i-*vowels in the former, in a more complicated manner in the latter. (In the Table, the palatalised variant is given in square brackets [ ].)

TABLE

	Sanskrit	Greek	Latin	Old Irish	Lithuanian	Old Bulgarian
p	p	π	p	—	p	p
b	b	β	b	b	b	b
bh	bh	φ	f, b	b	b	b
t	t	τ	t	t	t	t
d	d	δ	d	d	d	d
dh	dh	θ	f, b, d	d	d	d
k̂	ś	κ	c	c	š	s
ĝ	j	γ	g	g	ž	z
ĝh	h	χ	h, g	g	ž	z
k	k [c]	κ	c	c	k	k [č, c]
g	g [j]	γ	g	g	g	g [ž, z]
gh	gh [h]	χ	h, g	g	g	g [ž, z]
kʷ	k [c]	π, τ, κ	qu, c	c	k	k [č, c]
gʷ	g [j]	β, δ, γ	gu, u, g	b	g	g [ž, z]
gʷh	gh [h]	φ, θ, χ	f, gu, u, g	g	g	g [ž, z]

---

[1] It should be noted here that, in this respect, the Albanian and Thracian positions are not entirely clear.

[2] The nomenclature is based upon the initial consonant of the word for ' hundred ', IndE *k̂m̥to-* (thus, a palatal) : Skt *śatám* Av *satəm* Greek ἑ-κατόν Latin *centum* OIrish *cét* Welsh *cant* Gothic *hund* Lith *šimtas* OBg *sъto*—from which it may be seen that Indo-Iranian and Balto-Slavonic are *satəm-*, while Greek, Italo-Celtic and Germanic are *centum-*.

EXAMPLES

p. Skt *pitár-* 'father' Greek πατήρ Latin *pater* OIrish *athir* 'do.';
Skt *svápiti* ' to sleep ' Greek ὕπνος Latin *sopor* Lith *săpnas* ' dream '
OBg *sъpati* ' to sleep '.

b. Skt *bála-* ' strength, power ' Latin *dē-bilis* OBg comp. *bolijь*
' larger ' (? also Greek βέλτερος).

bh. Skt *bhrátar-* ' brother ' Greek φράτηρ Latin *fräter* OIrish
bráthir ' do.' Lith *broter-ělis* ' little brother ' OBg *bratrъ* ' brother '.

t. Skt nm. *tráyaḥ* ' three ' Greek namf. τρεῖς Latin n. *trēs* OIrish
nam. *tri trí* ' do.' Lith n. *trỹs* ' do.' OBg nm. *trьje* ' do.'.

d. Skt nam. *dváu* ' two ' Greek na. δύω Latin nam. *duo* OIrish
dáu dó ' do.' Lith nam. *dù* ' do.' OBg nam. *dъva* ' do.'

dh. Skt *dháyati* ' to suck ' Greek θῆσθαι Latin *fēmina* OIrish
dith ' suxit ' Lith *dělě* ' leech ' OBg *dojǫ* ' to give suck '.

k. Skt *śatám* ' hundred ', etc. [p. 82].

ĝ. Skt *jānámi* ' to know ' Greek γνωτός Latin *ignōtus* OIrish
gnáth ' known, accustomed ' Lith *žinóti* ' to know ' OBg *znajǫ*
' to know '.

ĝh. Skt *háryati* ' to find pleasure in, desire ' Greek χαίρω Latin
horior OIrish *gor* ' pious '; Skt *viji-hite* ' to gape apart ' Greek
χάσμα Latin *hio* Lith *žióti* ' to yawn ' OBg *zějǫ* ' hio '.

k. Skt *krṇátti* ' to twist the thread, spin ', *cṛtáti* ' to bind, join
together ' Greek κάρταλλος Latin *crātis* MIrish *ceirtle* ' hank, skein '
Lith *krōtai*, pl. ' trellis-work ' OBg *krǫstǫ* ' torqueri ', *črьstvъ*
' solidus '.

g. Skt *gola-* ' ball ' Greek γῦρός Latin *guttur* MnIrish *guaire*
' hair ' Lith *gauraî*, pl. ' body-hair ' OBg *gyža vinьnaja* ' vine '.

gh. Greek χναύω Lith *gniũsai* pl. ' vermin ' OBg *gnusьnъ* ' dis-
gusting '; Greek χανδάνω Latin *pre-hendo* MIrish *gataim* ' to steal '
OBg *gadati* ' to think '; Skt *gardha-* ' desire ' OBg *gladъ* ' hunger '
Serbian Church Slavonic *žlъždǫ* ' desiderare ' (= Skt *gṛdhyati* ' to
be greedy, desire ').

kᵘ. Skt nsm. *káḥ*, nsf. *ká* ' who ? ' Greek τοῦ ? πη ? Latin *qui
quae quod* (Latin *quid* = Skt *cit*, generalising particle) OIrish nsmf.
cia ' do.' Lith nsm. *kàs*, nsf. *kà* ' do.' OBg nsmn. *kъ-to* (gsmn.
če-so) ' do.'.

gᵘ. Skt *ganā* ' lady of the Gods ', *jani-* ' woman ' Greek (Boeotian)
βανά OIrish *ben* ' lady ' OBg *žena* ' woman '; Skt *giráti* ' to swallow ',
intensive *ni-gal-galīti ni-jal-galīti* ' to swallow violently ' Greek

βορά Latin *uoro* Lith *gérti* 'to drink' OBg *grъlo* 'throat', *žrěti* 'to swallow'.

gʷh. Skt *hánti* 'to strike' (3rd pl. pres. *ghnánti*) Greek θείνα· Latin *dē-fendo* OIrish *gonim* 'to wound, kill' Lith *giñti* 'to hunt, drive' OBg *gъnati* 'do.' (1st sg. pres. *ženǫ*).

SPIRANTS

The only spirant of common occurrence is *s*, which alternates with *z* before voiced phonemes. *s* remains in all the languages of the Tables save Greek where it often becomes "rough breathing" (mostly before vowels) :—IndE **septm̥* 'seven' : Skt *saptá* Greek ἑπτά Latin *septem* OIrish *secht* Lith *septynì* OBg *sedmь*. The developments of *z* are more diverse ; cf., for instance, IndE **ni-sd-o-* (to root **sed-* 'to sit', **ni-* 'down') > **nizdo-* : Skt *nīdá-* 'resting-place' Latin *nīdus* MIrish *net* 'nest' Lith *lìzdas* 'do.' OBg *gnězdo* 'do.' (the initials of the last two have been altered by folk-etymology) ; IndE **zdhi* : Av 2nd sg. imp. *zdī* 'to be' Greek 2nd sg. imp. ἴσθι. *sh, zh* are very rare ; cf., for instance, **menth-s-* > **mensht-* in OBg sg. aor. *męsъ* to *mętǫ* 'turbare' and Skt *psāti* 'to chew' Greek ψώω < **bzhō* to Skt **babhasti* (3rd pl. pres. *bapsati*) 'to devour'. *þ* ∽ *đ, þh* ∽ *đh*, only occur after the gutturals and are not distinct from the *s*-sounds save in Greek (and, possibly, Celtic), where they appear as dentals ; cf., for instance, **r̥kþo-* : Skt *r̥kṣa-* 'bear' Greek ἄρκτος MIrish *art* 'do.' Latin *ursus* ; **ĝhđem-* (and ablauts) : Skt *kṣáḥ* 'earth, ground' Greek χθών Latin *humus*? OIrish *dú*, gs. *don* 'place' Lith *žěmė* 'earth, land' OBg *zemlja* 'do.'.

SEMIVOCALIC PHONEMES

For the most part these remain unchanged in the languages of the Tables ; note, however, that *l* and *r* are to some extent confused in Sanskrit, that *u̯* is digamma (ϝ) in Greek, which is lost in classical Greek, while *i̯* > ζ (in several cases *u̯* suffers slight phonetic change to *v* or *f*).

EXAMPLES

i̯. Skt *yugá-* 'yoke, pair' [see p. 78].

u̯. Skt *vamiti* 'to vomit' Greek ἐμέω Latin *uomo* Lith *vémti* 'do.' ; Skt *api-vr̥ṇóti* 'to shut', *apa-vr̥ṇóti* 'to open' Latin *aperio*

(< *ap-ṷeriō) OIrish *fern* 'shield' Lith *vérti* 'to open *or* shut' OBg *vrěti* 'do.'.

m. Skt *mádati* 'to be drunk, intoxicated with something, to enjoy oneself' Greek μαδάω Latin *madeo* OIrish *maidim* 'to break (intr.)'; Latin *mare* OIrish *muir* 'sea' Lith *mãrės* 'Haff, bes. das kurische' OBg *mor'e* 'sea'.

n. Skt *nãsã* 'nose' Latin *nãres*, pl. Lith *nósis* 'do.' OBg *nosъ* 'do.'; Skt agd. dual encl. *nãu* 'us two' Greek na. dual νώ Latin nap. *nōs* OIr *ni*, 1st pl. pronoun, augens OBg acc. dual *na* 'us two'.

r. Skt *rikháti likháti* 'to tear' Greek ἐρείκω Latin *rixa* OIrish *róen* 'road' Lith *rievà* 'gorge, rock' OBg *rěšiti* 'soluere'.

l. Skt *lubhyati* 'to desire strongly' Greek λυπτά · ἑτάιρα, πόρνη Latin *libet lubet* MIrish *co-lba* 'love' Lith *liaupsẽ* 'glorification' OBg *ljuby* 'love'.

(v) The fates of the Indoeuropean Phonemes in Primitive Germanic

Very many of the Indoeuropean Phonemes remain virtually unchanged by their passage into Primitive Germanic (e.g. *s* of Latin *sedeo* : MnE *sit*) and, to save space, these phonemes are not hereinafter referred to.

VOWELS [1]

Only three sound-changes require notice :—

1. IndE *o* > PrGmc *a* : Latin *octo*, etc. [p. 78] Gothic *ahtau*.
2. IndE *ā* > PrGmc *ō* : Latin *frāter*, etc. [p. 83] Gothic *broþar*.
3. As stated above (p. 79), the long liquids and nasals are indistinguishable from the short ones in Germanic ; the latter develop *o*ᵘ before them and, similarly, *ḷ* changes to PrGmc *o*ᵘ before them. Thus IndE *ḱm̥tó-* (> Skt *śatám* 'hundred', etc. [p. 82]) > Gothic *hund* ; IndE *ṷḷkʷo-* (> Skt *vŕka-* 'wolf', etc. [p. 37]) > Gothic *wulfs* ; IndE *pḷno/ā-* (> Skt *pūrṇá-* 'full' S-Cr *pŭn* 'do.', etc. [p. 80]) > Gothic *fulls* [2] ; Latin *uenio* (< IndE *gʷm̥i̯ō*) = OE *cuman*. [3]

---

[1] For some remarks on those of the unaccented syllables, see p. 139.
[2] Assimilation *ln* > *ll*.
[3] IndE *o*, *a* (unchanged) and *ə* (falls with IndE *a* everywhere save in Indo-Iranian—p. 77) are thus indistinguishable—as *a*—in Primitive Germanic.

DIPHTHONGS

The development of the Indoeuropean diphthongs in Primitive Germanic is self-evident, for each part of the diphthong is " treated separately ". Thus IndE *oi* > PrGmc *ai* (npm. def. art. Greek τοί = Gothic *þai*) for, by the immediately foregoing, IndE *o* > PrGmc *a* and IndE *i* remains unchanged [1] [2].

EXCURSUS I : THE REDISTRIBUTION OF E, I, O, U IN EARLY
PRIMITIVE GERMANIC

I have dealt with this matter in a suitable manner in my *Tables* (Table A).

On examination it will be seen that, essentially, this Table is of self-evident form. It is divided into five main columns ; the first shows when the bipartite phoneme o^u (< IndE ь, or developed from IndE *ḷ m̥ n̥ r̥*) appears as *o* and when as *u* ; the second shows the conditions under which (*a*) IndE *e* appears as *e* or *i* and (*b*) IndE *i* appears as *i* or *e*; the two remaining columns deal with the treatment of the diphthongs IndE *ăi, ŏi, ǝi, ău, ŏu, ǝu* and IndE *ĕu*, respectively.

For convenience of reference some forms from Germanic languages other than English are here cited :—

o (*A2a* [3]) IndE **ĝhḷtīno/ā-* : Gothic *gulþeins* OHG *guldîn* OS *guldin* OFr *gelden* (with *i*-umlaut *u* > *y* > *e*) ;

(*A4a*) IndE **dhurā-* : Gothic *daúrons*, pl. Ic *dyrr*, pl. OHG *turi* OS *duru* OFr *dure* ;

(*Bi*) IndE **ĝhḷto-* : Gothic *gulþ* OIc *gull goll* OHG *golt* OS *gold* OFr *gold* ;

e ≷ i (*A1*) IndE **bhendhono-* : Gothic *bindan* Ic *binda* OHG *bintan* OS *bindan* OFr *binda* ;

(*A2a*) IndE **sedi̯ono-* : Ic *sitja* OHG *sizzen* OS *sittian* OFr *sitta* ;

(*A2b*) IndE **steighono-* : Gothic *steigan* Ic *stíga* OHG *stîgan* OS *stigan* OFr *stîga* ;

(*A3*) IndE **nemono-* : Gothic *niman* Ic *nema* OHG *nĕman* OS *niman neman* OFr *nima nema* ;

---

[1] For the later developments of IndE *ei, eu* see immediately below.

[2] As stated above (p. 81), the long diphthongs fall with the corresponding short ones in Germanic.

[3] These references are to my Table A.

(*A4a*) IndE ns. **melʊĝ-s* : Gothic *miluks* Ic *mjǫlk* OHG *miluh* OS *miluk* OFr *melok* ;

(*Biii*) IndE **lipǝro-* : Ic *lifr* OHG *lëbara libara* MLG *lever* OFr *livere* [1].

ae[1]. (*A2a*) IndE **kǝideti* : 3rd sg. pres. Gothic *haitiþ* Ic *heitr* OHG *heizit* OS *hêtid* ;

(*Biii*) IndE **kǝidono-* : Gothic *haitan* Ic *heita* OHG *heizan* OS *hêtan* OFr *hêta*.

ao[n]. (*A2a*) IndE **kloubeti* : 3rd sg. pres. Gothic *-hlaupiþ* Ic *hleypr* OHG *hloufit* OS *-hlôpid* ;

(*Biii*) IndE **kloubono-* : Gothic *hlaupan* Ic *hlaupa* OHG *hloufan* OS *-hlôpan* OFr *hlâpa*.

[1]eo[n]. (*A1a*) IndE **bhcudheti* : 3rd sg. pres. Gothic *-biudiþ* Ic *býðr* OHG *biutit* OS *biudid* ;

(*A4a*) IndE **bheudhō* : 1st sg. pres. Gothic *-biuda* OHG *biutu* OS *biudu* OFr *biâde* ;

(*Biii*) IndE **bheudhono-* : Gothic *-biudan* Ic *bjóða* OHG *biotan* OS *biodan beodan* OFr *biâdda*.[2]

EXCURSUS II

In Primitive Germanic, *a i u* before nasal $+ h > ą į ų + h$, later *ā ī ū + h*. Later, in certain parts of West Germanic (including the "parent area" of Anglo-Saxon, Frisian and part of Old Saxon) the same change took place before nasal $+ s f þ$. I deal with this matter in my *Tables* (Table B).

CONSONANTS

It is only the Stops of Indoeuropean that require much notice here,

---

[1] It is Old High German that has the largest number of "ideal" instances here : *spĕc, lĕckôn, hĕrot, zwĕhôn, quĕc*, etc. ; Anglo-Saxon has only *nest, wer* and *spec* (beside *spic*). Some scholars would limit the regular operation of the change to High German.

[2] The effects of the redistribution of *e* and *i* can be seen in the Germanic conjugational system. There are two infinitival types of Class III strong verbs :— Ic *hjalpa* (with *a*-breaking) OHG *hĕlfan* OS *helpan* OFr *helpa* OE *helpan* ᴄᴏ Ic *binda* OHG *bintan* OS *bindan* OFr *binda* OE *bindan*. Similarly, the division of the bipartite phoneme *o*ᵘ explains the relationship between the *-o*-participles of Class III strong verbs (as OHG *giholfan* OE *holpen*) and those having *-u-* (as OHG *gibuntan* OE *bunden*) ; and also the apparently "irregular" *i*-umlaut-relationship *o* ᴄᴏ *y* (p. 86) in OE *gold* (< **ʒulpa-*) beside OE *gylden* (< **ʒulpina/ō-*), Ic *hollr* ᴄᴏ *hylli*.

for the semi-vocalic consonants and the common spirant s [1] remain unchanged in Germanic.[2] It is, however, the changes affecting the Stops that are one of the most marked characteristics of Germanic. Nearly all these changes are grouped under a Main Change—called " Grimm's Law "—and an exception to this Main Change known as " Verner's Law ". By Grimm's Law, the Indoeuropean tenues (and tenues aspiratae) change into the corresponding unvoiced spirants in Primitive Germanic, the mediae aspiratae into the corresponding voiced spirants, while the mediae become unvoiced. Germanic is a " centum "-language, so the palatals and velars fall together ; in the case of the labio-velars, each " part " is treated separately, the first part according as it is tenuis (or tenuis aspirata), media aspirata, or media, the second part, $\unicode{x1D5CF}$, by what has gone before, merely remaining [3][4]. Verner's Law may be stated as " A non-initial stop which, by Grimm's Law would have given a Primitive Germanic unvoiced spirant, gives, instead, the corresponding voiced spirant, if the Indoeuropean accent does *not* precede it ". Thus we have the following correspondences :—

INDOEUROPEAN	PRIMITIVE GERMANIC
'p [5] 'ph	f
't 'th	þ
'ḱ 'ḱh 'k 'ḱh k (*of* 'kᵘ) k.h (*of* 'kᵘh)	x
bh p' ph'	ƀ
dh t' th'	đ
ĝh gh g.h (*of* gᵘh) k' kh' ḱ' kh' k	ʒ
(*of* kᵘ') k.h (*of* kᵘh')	
b	p
d	t.
ĝ g g (*of* gᵘ)	k

[1] IndE z + media became s + tenuis as OE *nest* = Latin *nĭdus* (< IndE **nizdo-*, p. 84) ; in the combination z + media aspirata the z remains and the second element is treated normally (Gothic *mizdo* Greek μισθός OBg *mьzda* ' reward ').

[2] Save that IndE s > PrGmc z (> WG r, p. 102) under Verner's Law conditions (below) : OE *snoru* = Skt *snuṣā́* ' daughter-in-law '.

[3] Thus, at first sight, Latin *equus* = Gothic *aiƕa(-tundi)* might suggest an IndE **eḱᵘo-* (cf. Latin *sequor* = Gothic *saiƕan* to root **sekᵘ-* in Greek ἕπομαι Skt *sacate* *siṣakti* ' to accompany, follow ') but Skt *aśva-* ' horse ' (not **aka-*) shows that the form is really **eḱu̯o-*.

[4] It is usually written w (just as IndE i " becomes " PrGmc j).

[5] A preceding accent denotes that the stop is either initial or is preceded by the accent, a following accent that it is not preceded by the accent.

Note. It seems that the combination $\mathfrak{z}w$ was early eliminated in Primitive Germanic by the suppression of one of the components, but the conditions of the respective suppressions are not entirely clear——*w* was certainly suppressed before a following *j* ; thus to *sekʷ-* (of Latin *sequor*) we have 3rd pl. pret. *sēkʷn̥t* > PrGmc *sēȝwun* > (i) *sēwun* > WGmc *sāwun* > OE *sǣwun* > WS *sāwon*, (ii) *sēȝun* > WGmc *sāȝun* > OA *sēgun* ; IndE *sokʷi̯o-* (> Latin *socius*) > PrGmc *saȝwja-* > *saȝja-* > OE *secg*.

f

< 'p.   Latin *pater*, etc. [p. 83] Gothic *fadar*.

þ

< 't.   Latin n. *trēs*, etc. [p. 83] OE nam. *þrī*.

x

< 'k.   Skt *śatám* ' hundred ', etc. [p. 82] Gothic *hund*.

< 'k.   Skt *kraviṣ-* ' raw meat ' Ic *hrár*.

< 'kʷ   Latin *sequor*, etc. [p. 88] Gothic *saíƕan*.

ƀ

< bh.   Skt *bhrátar-* ' brother ', etc. [p. 83] Gothic *broþar* ; Skt *lubhyati* ' to desire strongly ' OE *lufu*.

< p'.   Skt *saptá* ' seven ', etc. [p. 84] OHG *sibun* (< PrGmc *sibun*).

đ

< dh.   Skt *duhitár-* ' daughter ' Greek θυγάτηρ Gothic *daúhtar* ; Skt *vidhávā* ' widow ' Gothic *widuwo*.

< t'.   OE pl. pret. *wurdon* (: Skt 1st pl. perf. *va-vr̥timá*)—to OE *weorþan* (cf. Skt *vartate* ' to turn (intr.), exist, live ').

ȝ

< ĝh.   Skt *haṁsá-* ' goose, swan ' Greek χήν Lith *žąsìs* ' goose ' OHG *gans*.

< gh.   Greek χανδάνω OBg *gadati* ' to think ' Gothic *bi-gitan*.

< gʷh.   Skt *hánti* (3rd pl. pres. *ghnánti*) ' to strike ' OBg *gъnati*, *ženǫ* ' to drive, hunt ', etc. [p. 84] OHG *gund-fano* OE *gūþ*.

< **k̑**. OE pl. pret. *tigon* < IndE *dik̑n̥t* (cf. Skt *diśáti* ' to show '
Latin *dīco*).

< **k̑**. **kenk-* in OE *hungor* ; cf. Skt *kákate* ' to thirst ' Gothic
hūhrus (< IndE **kn̥kru-*).

< **kʷ**. OE pl. pret. *sēgun* : Latin *sequor* [p. 89].

p

< **b**. OBg *slabъ* ' weak ' Gothic *slepan*.

t

< **d**. Skt *dváú* ' two ' Gothic *twai* nm.

k

< **ĝ**. Skt *jānámi* ' to know ' Greek γνωτός OE *cnāwan*.

< **g**. Skt *gola-* ' ball ' Ic *kjóll*.

< **gʷ**. Skt *ganā* ' lady of the Gods ', *jani-* ' woman ' OIr *ben*
' lady ' OE *cwene* (> MnE *quean*), *cwēn* (> MnE *queen*).

EXCEPTIONS

1. After *s* an Indoeuropean tenuis [1] remains unchanged e.g. Latin
piscis Gothic *fisks*.

2. In Germanic, an Indoeuropean labial followed by *t* appears as
ft, a guttural $+$ *t* as *xt*, a dental $+$ *t* as *ss* (*s*).[2] Examples :—Latin
rego, supine *rectum* Gothic *raíhts* ; further the " alternations "
Gothic *-skapjan* ∞ *ga-skafts*, *giban* ∞ *fra-gifts* ; OE 1st, 3rd sg. pres.
mæg ∞ sg. pret. *meahte* ; Gothic *witan* ∞ sg. pret. *wissa*.

A few other sound-changes affected the consonants. Save for the
introduction of *t* in the group *sr* (OE *strēam* : Skt *srávati* ' to flow '),
these may all be classed under the head of Assimilation and are as
follows :—

1. Those things which, by the foregoing, should have given
PrGmc *ðn ðn ʒn* or PrGmc *pn tn kn*, give instead PrGmc *pp tt kk*
if the Indoeuropean accent followed immediately ; after a long
vowel these long consonants are shortened ; thus Ic *kroppr* < IndE

---

[1] The tenuis aspirata is treated as if it had been the tenuis : Greek ἀσκηθής
Gothic *skapjan*.

[2] This " rule " is really composite : first, it states that *t* is unchanged in such
positions, second, that various assimilations occur.

*gʷrebhn-' (Greek βρέφος); Gothic *h̨eits* : Skt *śvitna- śvitnyá-* 'white'.

2. IndE -*nu̯-* > PrGmc *nn* : Skt *rínvati* 'to let flow, run away, let go' = Gothic *rinnan*.

3. IndE *ln* > PrGmc *ll* : Skt *pūrṇá-* 'full' [p. 80] = Gothic *fulls*.

(vi) The Phonemes of Primitive Germanic

Vowels and Diphthongs

a	e	i	oᵘ	
	ē₁ ē₂ ¹	ī	ō	ū
aiᵉ	aoᵘ	ⁱeoᵘ		

Consonants

p t k b d g f þ s x b̵ đ z ʒ j w l m n r

(vii) The fates of the Primitive Germanic Phonemes

VOWELS

EAST GERMANIC (GOTHIC) MODIFICATIONS

1. PrGmc *e* > Gothic *i* : Gothic *itan* OHG *ëzzan* OE *etan*.

2. PrGmc *o* > Gothic *u* : Gothic *guþ* OS *god* OE *god*.

Note. Gothic *i u* before *h* (*h̨*) *r* > [ɛ] [ɔ] (written *aí aú*) : Gothic *baíran* = Latin *fero*, beside Gothic *itan* = Latin *edo* ; Gothic *taíhun* = Latin *decem*, beside Gothic *sibun* = Latin *septem* ².

3. PrGmc *ē₁* remains as Gothic *ē*, which sometimes > *ī*. Gothic -*redan* (OHG *rátan* OE *rǣdan*) represents the norm ; but Wulfila has a fair number of *ei*-spellings ³ e.g. 3rd sg. pres. *greitiþ* J 16, 20 ; *qeins* L 1, 5 ; L 2, 5 (= OS *quán*) beside *gretiþ*, *qens* ; cf., also, Crimean Gothic *schlipen*, *mine*, etc. (= Gothic *slepan*, *mena*)

4. PrGmc *ō* remains as Gothic *ō* ⁴ which sometimes > *ū*. Gothic *fotus* (OHG *fuoz* OE *fōt*) represents the norm ; but cf. Wulfila's

---

¹ *ē₂* is a rare phoneme and of obscure origin ; sometimes it is certainly derived from an IndE *ei* as in OE *hēr* OHG *hiar* < IndE *k̂ei-r* (cf. Latin *cis*).

² This change is sometimes called *breaking* (cf. p. 93).

³ *ei* was written in imitation of Greek ει which was pronounced [i:] in IV c. A.D.

⁴ *e o* must be long in Gothic (the corresponding short vowels being *aí aú*) so it is not necessary to mark them so as *ē ō*.

3rd pl. pret. *uhtedun* Mk 11, 32, and sg. pret. *supuda* Mk 9, 50, beside *ohtedun, supoda* (the only instances), further Crimean Gothic *bruder* (= Gothic *broþar*).

5. In all stressed positions, the PrGmc diphthongal phonemes *ae^i, ao^u, ^{i}eo^u* materialise as *ai, au, iu* respectively in Gothic; thus, corresponding to the forms given in Table A (p. 86) we have in Gothic *haitan*, 3rd sg. pres. *haitiþ*; *-hlaupan*, 3rd sg. pres. *-hlaupiþ*; *-biudan*, 3rd sg. pres. *-biudiþ*.

NORTH AND WEST GERMANIC MODIFICATIONS

PrGmc $\bar{e}_1 > \bar{a}$: Latin 1st pl. perf. *ēdimus* Gothic 1st pl. pret. *etum*: OIc 1st pl. pret. *ǫtom* (< *$\bar{a}$tum) OHG 1st pl. pret. $\bar{a}$zum OE pl. pret. $\bar{æ}$ton.[1]

DEVELOPMENTS WITHIN GERMANIC LANGUAGES

1. Except for developments in Anglo-Frisian (p. 104), changes mentioned in (2) below and various combinative changes set out in (3) below, the West Germanic vowels [2] of accented syllables remain unaltered in the earliest period of each of the Germanic languages :—

a. Skt *pitár-* 'father' Gothic *fadar* Ic *faðir* OHG *fater* OS *fadar*.

e. Latin *edo* Gothic *itan* Ic *eta* OHG *ëzzan* OS *etan*.

i. Latin *piscis* Gothic *fisks* Ic *fiskr* OHG *fisc* OS *fisk*.

ā (< PrGmc $\bar{e}_1$). Latin *sē-men* Gothic *mana-seþs* Ic *sáð* OHG *sât* OS *sâd*.

ī. Latin *suīnus* Gothic *swein* Ic *svín* OHG *swîn* OS *swîn*.

ū. Lith *súras* 'salty' Ic *súrr* OHG *sûr*.

2. Old High German dialects have the diphthongal phonemes *ie ia* (as well as *ē*) corresponding to PrGmc $\bar{e}_2$, and diphthongal *uo* corresponding to WG *ō* :—OHG *hiar hêr* : Gothic *her* OS *hêr* OFr *hîr* OE *hēr*; OHG *miata mieta mêta* : OE *mēd*; OHG *fluot* : Ic *flóð* OE *flôd*; OHG *muoter* : Ic *móðir* OE *môdor*. But, in Middle High German, these diphthongal forms were again monophthongised so that Modern High German has *hier, miete, flut, mutter* (all monophthongal).

3. Extensive diphthongisation occurred in the North and West

---

[1] I may note here that PrGmc $\bar{e}_2$ appears in the preterite stems of originally reduplicating verbs in North and West Germanic : sg. pret. Gothic *haíhait* Ic *hét* OHG *hiaz* OE *hēt*.

[2] For some remarks on the diphthongs see p. 95.

Germanic languages as a result of various *umlauts* and *breakings*. The following brief survey indicates the general trend.

I-UMLAUT

(i) *Old Norse* [1]. The main effects are :—

a > e. Ic *ketill*, cf. Gothic gp. *katile* ; with later *w*-umlaut (p. 95), Ic *sløkkva* (< PrGmc **slakwjan-*).

ā > ǣ. Runic *mariʀ* (Thorsberg, c. 250 A.D.) > Ic *mærr*, cf. Gothic *waila-mereis*.

ŏ > ø̆. Runic np. *ðohtriʀ* (Tune, V c. A.D.) > **dœhtr* > Ic *dœtr* ; Ic *sœkja* = Gothic *sokjan*.

ŭ > ў̆. Ic *fylla* = Gothic *fulljan* ; Ic nap. *mýss* (< np. **mūsiʀ*) to sg. *mús*.

au > Ic ey. Ic *eyrir* (< **auriaʀ*, lwf. Latin *aureus*) ; Ic. *leysa* beside Ic *lauss*.

iu > ў̄. Runic 3rd sg. pres. *ƀariutiþ* (Stentoften, first half VII c.) > Runic *ƀarutʀ* (Björketorp, VIII c.) Ic *brýtr* ; Ic *sýki* beside *sjúkr*.

(ii) In *Old High German* and *Old Saxon*, *i*-umlaut (which began c. 800 A.D.) affected only *a*, giving *e*, and this not when certain consonant-groups (especially *h*, *l*, *r* + consonant) followed. Examples :—with umlaut : OHG *brennen* (Gothic *-brannjan* OE *bærnan*) ; OS *sendian* (Gothic *sandjan* OE *sendan*) ; OHG 3rd sg. pres. *ferit*, to *faran* ; OS 3rd sg. pres. *ferid*, to *faran* ; without umlaut : OHG 3rd sg. pres. *wahsit*, *haltit* (Bavarian) ; OS *mahtig*. In Old Saxon there are a few instances in which vowels other than *a* are affected (e.g. *mêri* beside *mâri*) ; these, together with fairly frequent examples of umlauted vowels in Middle Low German, probably indicate that *i*-umlaut was more widespread than the surviving texts show.

(iii) *Old Frisian* (beginning VI c. A.D.). All back vowels are affected, as in Old Norse and Old English, and *ŭ* > *ў̆* > *ĕ* as in the Kentish dialect of Anglo-Saxon. Examples :—OFr *here* (Gothic *harjis* OE *here*) ; OFr *bêta* (Gothic *botjan* OE *bētan*) ; OFr *kere* (OHG *kuri* OS *(self-)kuri* OK *cere*) ; OFr *rêma* (OHG *rûmen* OK *rēman*) ; OFr *dêpa* (Gothic *daupjan* OS *dôpian*).

(iv) *Old English* (beginning VI c. A.D.)—see p. 109.

---

[1] On the evidence of runic inscriptions, the change seems to have begun c. 600 A.D.

BREAKING

There are terminological difficulties here, for, in different languages, unlike processes have been called *breaking* (lwf. MnHG *brechung* in such a sense). Here the term is applied to the processes by which a simple vowel in a stressed syllable is diphthongised through the influence of a following velar sound, which can be either vocalic or consonantal. In this sense, Breaking is confined to Old Norse, Old Frisian and Old English.

(i) *Old Norse* breaking occurs before a syllable. containing *a*, *u* or *w*. By *a*-breaking, *e* > *i̯a*:—Ic *hjarta* (Gothic *haírto* OHG *hërza*), Ic *hjalpa* (Gothic *hilpan* OE *helpan*). By *u* and *w*-breaking, *e* > *i̯ǫ* [1] : Ic *jǫrð* (< **erþu* < PrGmc **erþō*) beside Gothic *aírþa* OHG *ërda* ; Ic *fjǫr*, ds. *fjǫrvi*, beside Gothic *faírhvus* OE *feorh*. In both these Norse breakings the intermediate stages are obscure and disputed, and it is not clear whether the vowel first velarised the intervening consonant or alone sufficed to effect the change, though the former view seems more probable [2].

(ii) *Old Frisian* shows a trace of breaking similar to that of Old English. Thus *īxt* > *iuht* (OFr *liuchte* OE *lēoht* : OHG *lihti*) ; OFr *riucht* = OE *riht*. It also shares with Old East Norse traces of *w*-breaking :— *i* > *iu* before *ggw*, *ngw*, *nkw* as OFr *siunga* OSw *siunga* ODanish *siunga* (Gothic *siggwan* OIc *syngua*) ; OFr *diunk(er)* *dionker* (< **dinkwaz-*) Ic *døkkr* OS *dunkar* ; OSw *siunka* (Gothic *sigqan* Ic *søkkva*).

(iii) *Old English*—p. 107.

OTHER UMLAUTS

These are confined to Old English (p. 111) and Old Norse and are especially common in the latter. Old Norse has palatal umlaut (OIc ppart. *tekenn* < **takanʀ*, beside ppart. OIc *farenn*), labial umlauts (below), and combined labial umlaut (Ic *spónn* < **spǫnn*

---

[1] The earliest written forms of the ON breaking-diphthongs were *ea* and *eo* but the main literary texts of XIII c. already have *ia* (= *ja*) and *io* (= *jǫ*).

[2] This sound-change closely resembles Old English back-mutation (p. 111). It has less in common with Old English " breaking " except that it does have the general principle of a back glide to a following velar sound. Recent discussions of these changes include articles by G. Flom at *Language* xiii, 123–36, and by I. Hoff at *Norsk tidsskrift for sprogvidenskap* xiv, 315–40 and *Arkiv för nordisk filologi* lxiv, 177–210.

< *spānuʀ). The more important labial umlauts are *u*-umlaut (occurring before a syllable containing *u* (of any origin)) and *w*-umlaut. Examples :—

U-UMLAUT[1] ǎ > ǒ. Ic nap. *lǫnd* (< *landu* < PrGmc *landō*) beside *land* ; OIc nap. *ǫr* (< *jāru*) beside *ár* (Gothic *jer* OE *gēar*).

W-UMLAUT. a > ǫ. Ic *dǫgg* (< *daggwu* cf. OE *dēaw*).

æ > ø. Ic *øx* (< *ækwisiʀ*, cf. Gothic *aqizi*).

e > ø. Ic *søkkva* (< *sekkwa*, cf. Gothic *sigqan*).

ī > ȳ. Ic *tryggr* (Gothic *triggws*); Ic *Týr*, cf. OE *Tīw* (= Latin *dīuus*).

ei > øy > Ic ey. OIc *ey* (Gothic *aiw*).

DIPHTHONGS

On the whole, the development of the diphthongal phonemes of Primitive Germanic presents considerable difficulties ; indeed, the intermediate stages of some of the developments must be regarded as unknown. There has been much discussion, for instance, of the problems afforded by the western West Germanic developments of *ae*[2]. I have already discussed the simple Gothic development of the diphthongs at p. 92, above. In Norse, *ae* gives, first, *æi*, save before *h* and *r*, where it gives *á* ; in general, this *æi* remains in Old Norwegian, gives *ei* in Icelandic and *ē* in East Norse (save in Old Gutnish, which has *ai*): Ic *steinn* ONorw *stæin* OGutnish *stain* OSw *stēn* ODanish *stēn*, but Ic *sár* OSw *sār* ODanish *sār* (ba. Finnish *sairas* ' ill '). In East Norse (save for Old Gutnish), PrGmc *aoᵘ* > *ē* ; PrGmc *ao* > ON *ǫu* > ONorw *ou* Ic *au* OGutnish *au* ; and PrGmc *au* when *i*-mutated > ONorw *øy* Ic *ey* OGutnish *oy* : ONorw *hloupa* Ic *hlaupa* OSw *hlōpa* OGutnish *hlaupa* ODanish *hlōpa* ∞ 3rd sg. pres. ONorw *hløypr* Ic *hleypr* OSw *hlōper* OGutnish *hloyper* ODanish *hlōper*. The developments of PrGmc *ᵗeoᵘ* in Norse are complicated[3] ; if *i* or *u* follows in the next syllable, or ʀ immediately, *ᵗeoᵘ* > *iu* (*ȳ* everywhere by *i*-mutation), otherwise it gives *iǫu* (cf. Finnish loan-word *joulu* ' Christmas ' : Gothic *jiuleis* pl.).

---

[1] Cf. Old English " back-mutation " (p. 111)—but the results are different : PrGmc *aluþ* (cf. Finnish *olut*—p. 141) > Ic *ǫl* but OE *ealu*.

[2] I have set forth my own views on this subject, *English Studies* xxxii, 49–56. See further A. Campbell, *TPS* 1939, p. 90 ff. (where further literature).

[3] The earliest evidence for it is *eu* of Finnish *keula* ' stem [of a ship] ' which is a Norse loan-word (: Ic *kjóll*—cf. p. 90).

In West Norse the rare *iu* remains (Runic nsf. *liuƀu* (Opedal) :
Ic. *ljúf*), while *iǫu* gives *iú* before *ƀ f ʒ k p*, otherwise *ió*—hence
the variation in the infinitive of the second class of strong verbs in
Icelandic (*fljúga, krjúpa* but *bjóða*). In East Norse, *iǫu > iū*
generally but *iau* in Old Gutnish : Ic *djúpr* = OSw *diuper* OGutnish
diaupr ODanish *diupær*, Ic *jól* = OSw *iūl* OGutnish *iaul*. The
High German developments are also difficult. PrGmc *ae^i >* OHG
ê before *h r w*, otherwise *ai*, which soon becomes *ei* : OHG *sêr*
(: Finnish loan-word *sairas* 'ill' Gothic *sair*, noun), OHG *heizan*
= Gothic *haitan*. PrGmc *ao >* OHG *ô* before *h* and the dentals,
otherwise *au*, which soon becomes *ou* : hence the variation in the
second stem of the second class of strong verbs : sg. pret. OHG
zôh, kôs, bôt but *loug, kloub* (cf. Gothic sg. pret. *-bauþ*). *i*-umlaut
of the descendants of PrGmc *au* does not take place until the Middle
High German period : Gothic *hausjan* OHG *hôren* MHG *hœren*,
3rd sg. pres. Gothic *-hlaupiþ* OHG *hloufit* MnHG *läuft*. In general,
PrGmc *eo >* OHG *io*, PrGmc *'eu > iu*, but in oberdeutsch the
first change only takes place before *h* and the dentals, *iu* being
otherwise the norm there : OHG *biotan*, 1st sg. pres. *biutu*, 3rd sg.
pres. *biutit* [1], Franconian *liogan* (oberdeutsch *liugan*), 1st sg. pres.
liugu, 3rd sg. pres. *liugit*. The position in Low German and Frisian
is again difficult. PrGmc *ae^i >* OS *ê ei* OFr *â ê* : OS *hêtan* OFr
hêta (Gothic *haitan*) ; PrGmc *ao^u* is *â ô* in Old Saxon (*-hlôpan*
= Gothic *-hlaupan*), *â* (*i*-umlauted, *ê*) in Old Frisian (*hlâpa* = Gothic
-hlaupan, hêra : Gothic *hausjan*) ; PrGmc *eo* is OS *eo io* OFr *iâ*
(OS *biodan* OFr *biâda*) ; PrGmc *'eu* is OS *iu* OFr *iu* (3rd sg. pres.
OS *biudid*).

CONSONANTS

GENERAL

Some of the consonants—*l, m, n, r, s*—undergo no "significant"
change in themselves [2] (though they often have important influence
on neighbouring sounds) and are scarcely hereinafter referred to.

The Primitive Germanic consonantal system remained largely
unaltered in Gothic and Old Saxon but was greatly modified in
High German by the second sound-shift (p. 98 ff.), in Anglo-Saxon

---

[1] Cf. Table A of my *Tables*.

[2] Except of course where they disappear, as *l, r* of *talk, bark* in many varieties
of Modern English.

and Old Frisian by the palatalisation of the stops *k*, *g* and in Old Norse (especially) [1] by numerous assimilations (e.g. Ic sg. pret. *batt* < **bant* < **band* = Gothic *band* ; Ic *hodd* < **hoʀd* = Gothic *huzd*). The West Germanic languages acquired lengthened consonant-groups by "West Germanic doubling" (p. 98). Gothic and Old Norse had a special development of the semi-vowels *j*, *w* ("Holtzmann's Law ", p. 102) differing from that in West Germanic.

In the following account particular attention is paid to the consonantal relationships of English and Modern High German words. I have done this because more people speak these two languages than any other pair of Germanic languages [2]. A comparison of English and Dutch, or of any other pair of Germanic languages would, of course, have been equally possible and equally remarkable resemblances and differences would have been shown [3].

EAST GERMANIC (GOTHIC) MODIFICATIONS

1. PrGmc *ƀ đ z* became unvoiced to *f þ s* when final after vowels and also when before voiceless consonants :—Gothic sg. pret. *gaf* (< PrGmc **ʒaƀ*) ; sg. pret. *baiþ* (OE *bād*) ; *dius* (< PrGmc **đeuza-*) ; 2nd sg. pret. *gaft* ; *naups* (OS *nôd*).

2. In other positions, PrGmc *z* remains in Gothic (Gothic *mizdo* : OE *meord*), giving *s* in Crimean Gothic (*schnos* [4] : OE *snoru*).

3. PrGmc *-jj- -ww-* > Gothic *-ddj-* (Norse *-ggj-*), *-ggw-* :—Gothic g. *twaddje* (: PrGmc **twajjǭ* > Ic g. *tveggja*) ; Gothic *triggws* (< PrGmc **trewwa/ō-* > Ic *tryggr*).

4. PrGmc *-ēj-* appears written *ai* in Gothic : *saian* OS *sâian* Lith *sė́ju* ' to sow '.

NORTH AND WEST GERMANIC MODIFICATIONS [5]

(a) Common to both.

1. PrGmc *þl þr* > *fl fr* :—Gothic *þliuhan* Ic *flȳja* OE *flēon* OHG *fliohan* ; Gothic *þrafstjan* : OE *frōfor* OHG *fluobara* (< **fruobra*).

---

[1] For some examples of assimilation in the other Germanic languages, see p. 103.

[2] It is perhaps of interest to recall that W. W. Skeat, when writing his *Principles of English Etymology* (published in 1887), found it necessary to condemn the prevalent belief that English " was derived from " German (i, 73 ff.).

[3] For example, the Danish tendency to voice final consonants is shown by the equations MnE *book, foot, deep, deaf* = MnDanish *bog, fod, dyb, døv* but the initial consonants are the same in the two languages.

[4] Text : *schuos*.

[5] See also immediately above, § 3.

2. PrGmc *xw* > *x* intervocalically : Gothic *saíhvan* = Ic *sjá* OE *sēon* (< *sexan) OS *sehan* OHG *sëhan*.

3. PrGmc *z* > *r*—See p. 102.

(b) Specifically West Germanic.

1. *West Germanic Consonant-lengthening (doubling).*

(i) All single consonants except *r* were lengthened when following a short vowel if an original *j* followed :—Gothic *bidjan* Ic *biðja* : OHG *bitten* OS *biddian* OE *biddan* ; Gothic *sibja* : OHG *sippia* OS *sibbia* OFr *sibbe* OE *sibb* ; Gothic *nasjan* beside PrGmc **nazjono-* > OHG *nerien* OE *nerian*.

(ii) PrGmc *p t k* were usually lengthened before *r l* and a vowel inserted before *r l* subsequent to the lengthening :—OBg *jablъko* ' apple ' Ic *epli* : OHG *apful* (> MnHG *apfel*) OS *appul(-grê)* OFr *appel* OE *æppel* ; Gothic *baitrs* Ic *bitr* : OHG *bittar* OS *bittar* OE *bit(t)er* ; Latin *ager* Gothic *akrs* Ic *akr* : OHG *ahhar acchar* OS *akkar* OFr *ekker* (but OE *æcer*, without lengthening).

(iii) There are a few cases of gemination before *w*, e.g. OHG *ackus* OS *accus* = Gothic *aqizi*.

2. PrGmc *đ* > WG *d* (> OHG *t*) in all positions (in Gothic and Norse, only in certain positions).

STOPS
p t k

For the most part, PrGmc *p t k* remain unchanged in all positions, save that :—

(i) In Anglo-Frisian, initial and medial *k* before a front vowel > [ts] [tš] :—OS *kiosan* OFr *sziâsa* OE *cēosan* ; Gothic *lekeis* OFr *lêtza* OE *lǣce*.[1]

(ii) In Old High German [2], the Second Sound-Shift operates here in that PrGmc *p t k* (*a*) when initial, geminated or post-consonantal > OHG [pf] [ts], oberd [kx]—written *pf ph*, *z zz*, *ch kh cch* [3] and (*β*) when post- or inter-vocalic, > OHG *ff zz hh* (often written *f z h* after long vowels and when final) [4]. Examples :—

p. Gothic *puggs* Ic *pungr* OE *pung* : OHG *pfung* ; Gothic

---

[1] A similar fate befell *g* (p. 102).

[2] There are numerous dialectal variations within Old High German here ; they cannot be discussed adequately in the present context.

[3] This is the ultimate explanation of MnE *p*ound *t*ongue = MnHG *pf*und *z*unge.

[4] This is the ultimate explanation of MnE o*p*en ea*t* ma*k*e = MnHG o*ff*en e*ss*en ma*ch*en.

greipan Ic *grîpa* OS *grîpan* OFr *grîpa* OE *grīpan* : OHG *grîfan* (> MnHG *greifen*).

t. Gothic *tuggo* Ic *tunga* OS *tunga* OFr *tunge* OE *tunge* : OHG *zunga* ; Gothic *itan* Ic *eta* OS *etan* OFr *îta* OE *etan* : OHG *ëzzan*.

k. Gothic *kaúrn* Ic *korn* OFr *korn* OE *corn* : OHG (oberd) *chorn* ; OS *makon* OFr *makia* OE *macian* : OHG *machôn*.

b d g

In Primitive Germanic, these were developed from the corresponding voiced spirants *ƀ đ ʒ* in the following circumstances [1] :—

(i) *ƀ* [2] *đ* initially and *ƀ đ ʒ* after nasals and when geminated gave *b d g*. Examples :—Gothic *baíran* (< IndE **bherono-*) ; Gothic *daúrons*, pl. (: IndE **dhurā-*) ; Gothic *lamb* Ic *lamb* OE *lamb* ; Ic *land* OE *land* ; Gothic *laggs* OS *lang* OE *lang* ; OE *crabba* ; Gothic g. *twaddje* ; Gothic *triggws*.

(ii) *lđ zđ* > *ld zd* :—Skt *pṛthiví* ' earth ' Ic *fold* OS *folda* OE *folde* ; Gothic *huzd* MnHG *hort* OE *hord*. In other positions *ƀ đ ʒ* remained spirantal in Primitive Germanic (for the developments, see p. 100).

The newly-developed voiced stops remained everywhere save in Old High German dialects where, as part of the Second Sound-Shift, they often became unvoiced to *p t k* : oberd *pintan* = Gothic *bindan* ; oberd *tac* = Gothic *dags* ; oberd *ouca* = Gothic *augo*. This *t* (and a few *p*-forms such as MnHG *pappeln* = MnE *babble*) generally remains in Modern High German so that the normal relationship between English and German is here MnE *b d g* = MnHG *b* [3] *t g* :—MnHG **b**ier, **t**aube, **g**ott = MnE **b**eer, **d**ove, **g**od.

SPIRANTS
f þ x

f, þ remained in all positions in Gothic (*fadar*, np. *wulfos*, *þank* (L 17, 9), *qiþan*, sg. pret. *warþ*). In Norse and English they remained initially (Ic *þing* OE *þing*) but became voiced in voiced surroundings

---

[1] Recently discussed by W. G. Moulton, " The stops and spirants of Early Germanic ", *Language* xxx, 1–42 (cf. also A. S. C. Ross, *LSE* iii, 2–6).

[2] The oft-cited Scandinavian runic forms 3rd sg. pres. *ƀarutʀ* (Björketorp) = Ic *brýtr* and np. *đohtriʀ* (Tune) = Ic *dœtr* are not evidence for the spirantal quality of the initial letters, for the runic alphabet had only one symbol each for any *b*- or *d*-sound.

[3] On the medial relationship MnE *v* = MnHG *b* (*even* = *eben*). see p. 101.

(Ic np. *ulfar, kveða*; OE nap. *wulfas, cweþan*)[1]. The position in Old Saxon is much the same : *folk, wulf* but ap. *uulbos, queðan*[2].

From the earliest times there was a High German tendency to voice *þ* to *đ* and then to *d* in all positions, though the process was not completed in all areas until the Middle High German period :—MnHG *dünn, dorn* < MHG *dünne, dorn* < OHG *dunni, dorn*, earlier *thunni, thorn* (= MnE *thin, thorn*).

In Middle English (perhaps earlier) and the Scandinavian languages there was a tendency to voice *þ*- in pronominal and un-stressed forms. In Modern English, [ð] has remained in *that, there, thou*, etc., as against [θ] in *thing, thank, three*, etc. The same contrast is seen in Norse (save for Icelandic) in respect of the corresponding stops (MnDanish *det, der, du*, etc., as against *ting, tak, tre*, etc.).[3]

x is preserved as *h* initially before vowels in all the Germanic languages : Gothic *haúrn* Ic *horn* OE *horn*, etc. In other positions it is frequently lost : Ic *þó* < **þauh*; MnHG *sehen* [ze:ən] ; OE *miht* > LME [mi:t] > MnE *might*. Where it is preserved it is, according to the nature of the surrounding sounds, a velar or a palatal spirant (cf. MnHG *nacht, nicht*).

Initially before *l r n w*, *x* disappeared during the course of the Old High German and Old English periods (except that *hw* is still preserved in many varieties of English—as of *white, which*) ; the same loss took place in East Norse—the position in West Norse is more complicated (cf. [kv] of MnIc *hvítur*). Thus Latin *nux* < **dnuks* < **knud-s* : MnIc *hnot* OHG *hnuz* OE *hnutu* : OSw *nut* MnDanish *nød* MnHG *nuss* MLG *note* MnDutch *noot* ME *nóte* (> MnE *nut*).

ƀ đ ʒ

In various circumstances, some of the details of which are imperfectly known, these voiced spirants developed into the corresponding

---

[1] Cf. MnE *wife* ∞ *wives, wolf* ∞ *wolves*, etc. On the use of the symbols *f þ* (*ð*) for [ƀ] [đ], see p. 120. The English voicing occurred in the course of VIII c. A.D.

[2] A minor development, affecting a few words, is PrGmc -*þl*- > OHG and OS -*hl*- : Gothic *maþl* (< PrGmc **maþla*-) OE *mæþel* but OHG *mahál* OS *mahal* (OHG *Madal*- in place-names) ; Ic *bilda* (< **bīðla*) but OHG *bíhal*.

[3] Thus to-day, of all the Germanic languages, it is only English and Icelandic that preserve *þ* : as [θ] in MnE *thin, thank* = MnIc *þunnur, þakka*, and as [ð] in MnE *clothes, bathe* : MnIc *klæði, baða*. (With MnE *thou* : *thistle*, cf. MnHG *du* : *distel*, MnSw *du* : *tistel*, MnDanish *du* : *tidsel*, MDutch *du* : MnDutch *distel*).

voiced stops, *b d g*, where they had not already done so in Primitive Germanic, or had other developments. The more important of these are :— [1]

ƀ đ. (i) In Gothic, PrGmc *ƀ* > *b* after *l r* (*silba, -swairban*) and PrGmc *đ* > *d* after *r* (*waúrd*). It is possible that stops developed here after other consonants too.

(ii) PrGmc intervocalic and final *ƀ* remained spirantal (generally voiceless when final or before voiceless sounds) in Gothic (written *b*), Norse, Old Saxon, Old Frisian and Old English (Gothic *giban* Ic *gefa* OS *geƀan* OFr *jeva* OE *giefan*) but became the stop in all positions in High German (OHG *gëban*) [2].

(iii) PrGmc intervocalic *đ* remains in Gothic (written *d*) and Old West Norse, but becomes *d* in West Germanic (OHG, > *t*) :— Gothic *-biudan* Ic *bjóða* : OHG *biotan* OS *biodan* OFr *biáda* OE *bēodan* [3].

3. The developments of *ʒ* in the Germanic languages are complex and many of the intermediate steps are unknown. Thus the following statements are partly based on unprovable assumptions (though they are the assumptions of the majority of philologists) :—

(i) PrGmc initial *ʒ* > *g* in Gothic (?) [4], Norse and High German (oberd *k*) and before back vowels and consonants in tenth century Old English. Like early Old English, Old Saxon probably also retained *ʒ* initially (if the evidence of the alliterative poetry is to be trusted). Examples :—Gothic *greipan* Ic *grípa* OHG *grîfan* OS *grîpan* OE *grîpan* ; Gothic *guma* Ic *gumi* OHG *gomo* OE *guma* (< IndE *ĝhьmen-* —p. 84).

(ii) PrGmc intervocalic and final *ʒ* generally remained spirantal except in High German where it became *g* (oberd sometimes *k*).

---

[1] In general the alphabets of the separate languages did not have separate symbols for the different materialisations of the phonemes /b/ /d/ /g/. Confusion will result unless it is remembered, for instance, that in Old West Norse and Anglo-Saxon, *þ* and *ð* are used indifferently, denoting the voiceless or the voiced spirant according to position, and that, in these two languages too, the voiced spirant *ƀ* is written *f* (Ic *gefa* OE *giefan* as against OS *geƀan*) but the voiced stop as *b*.

[2] This is the ultimate explanation of the difference in medial consonant between MnE *carve give have love* and MnHG *kerben geben haben lieben*.

[3] This explains the equations MnE *ride wade* = MnHG *reiten waten*.

[4] From the meagre evidence it cannot be certainly ascertained whether Gothic initial *g* was a voiced stop or a voiced spirant. Latin writers consistently use *g* in spelling Gothic names, but the loan-words *Kreks*, dp. *marikreitum* (lwf. Latin *graecus, margarita*), obscure the issue.

The spirant was probably velar after a back vowel (as in MnHG pl. *tage*, in some pronunciations), and a front spirant when following a front vowel (as in MnHG *liegen*, some pronunciations) :—Gothic np. *dagos* Ic np. *dagar* OHG nap. *tagâ* OS nap. *dagos* OE nap. *dagas* ; Gothic as. *wig* Ic as. *veg* OHG *wëg* OS *weg* OFr *wei* OE *weg*.

(iii) In Anglo-Frisian (*a*) PrGmc ʒ before and after a front vowel was palatalised to *j* (written ᵹ by the Anglo-Saxons but often as *ǵ* or *g* in text-books, written *i* or *j* in Old Frisian) : PrGmc **ʒebana-* **reʒna-* > OE *giefan regn* OFr *jeva rein* (contrast OHG *gëban rëgan*) [1]. (*b*) WG -ʒʒj- (p. 98) > *dz dž* : OE *licgan* OFr *lidza* (contrast OS *liggian* OHG *liggen* Ic *liggja*).

z

Medial *z* (< *s* by Verner's Law—p. 88) remained in Gothic but moved to *r* (" Rhotacism ") in North and West Germanic [2]. An intermediate stage is shown in early Norse runic inscriptions which have separate symbols for the product of PrGmc *z* (transcribed ʀ) and PrGmc *r*. In literary Old Norse, ʀ and *r* have fallen together as *r*. Examples :—comp. Gothic *maiza* Ic *meiri* OHG *mêro* OS *mêro* OE *māra* ; Gothic *huzd* Ic *hodd* (< *hoᚾd) MnHG *hort* OS *hord* OE *hord*.

PrGmc final *z* (< IndE *s*) remained in Gothic and Old West Norse but was lost in West Germanic :—ns. Gothic *dags* Ic *dagr* OHG *tag* OS *dag* OE *dæg* (< PrGmc *daʒaz). By contrast, PrGmc *r* (< IndE *r*) remains everywhere :—Latin *pater* Gothic *fadar* Ic *faðir* OHG *fater* OS *fadar* OE *fæder*.

SEMI-VOWELS

j w

In their consonantal function *j w* had an extensive influence on neighbouring sounds but, in themselves, showed little tendency to change, except, from the earliest times, to alternate with vocalic *i u* in medial and final position :—Gothic as. *hari < PrGmc *xarjq, but gs. *harjis* < PrGmc **xarjiz-*.

By " Holtzmann's Law ", intervocalic *j w* were lengthened to *jj ww*. Then, (*a*) in West Germanic, the first element of the lengthened semi-vowel forms a diphthong with a preceding short vowel, while

---

[1] This is the origin of the *y* of MnE *yield*, *yard*, etc.
[2] Cf. the similar change in Latin : as. *flōrem* < *flōsem.

(b) in Gothic and Norse the first element becomes a stop (*jj* > Gothic *ddj* Ic *ggj* ; *ww* > Gothic *ggw* Ic *ggv*). Examples :—PrGmc **ajjǫ* > Crimean Gothic *ada* Ic *egg* OHG *ei* OS *ei* OE *ǣg*, pl. *ǣgru* ; IndE **ĝhlōu̯o/ā-* > **ĝhlou̯o/ā-* (: Greek χλωρός) > Gothic *glaggwo*, adv. Ic *glǫggr* OHG *glauuêr* OS *glau* OE *glēaw*.

In Old West Norse, initial *j*, and *w* + *l*, *r*, or rounded vowels, disappeared :—Gothic *juk* OHG *joh* OS *juk(-rôda)* OE *geoc ioc* = Ic *ok* ; Gothic *wrikan* OS *wrekan* OFr *wreka* OE *wrecan* = Ic *reka* ; OHG *Wuotan* OS *Wôdan* OE *Wōden* = Ic *Óðinn*.

In Old High German, and in the course of Middle and Early Modern English, initial *w* was lost before *l r* : OHG *rëchan* (cf. immediately above), MnE *write*.

In all the Germanic languages save English, *w* had become a spirant by the Middle Ages. In present-day Dutch, High German, Low German and Norse it is either a bilabial or labio-dental spirant.

DEPENDENT CHANGES

The Germanic languages have many examples of the common linguistic phenomena, such as assimilation, dissimilation, metathesis, glide sounds and the simplification of " difficult " consonant-clusters. A few examples will suffice to show how these processes may obscure the etymology of a word :—

Assimilation. WG *ƀn* > OE *mn* (*mm*) : Gothic *stibna* = OE *stefn stemn* ; OE *wīf-mann* > ME *wimman* > MnE *woman*.

Dissimilation. In Anglo-Frisian, *h* > *k* before spirant : OFr *oxa* OE *oxa* [1] = Gothic *aúhsa* MnHG *ochse* ; Shakespeare's *heykfer* ' heifer ' < OA *hēh-fore*.

Metathesis. OE *sc* > *cs* (*x*) : OHG *eiscôn* = OE *ācsian* (beside *āscian*) ; *l*-metathesis : Ic *heimull* (< **heimold*) : Gothic *haimoþli* ; OE *rǣdels*—OS *râdisli* ; *r*-metathesis : Gothic *-brannjan* = OE *bærnan*.

Glide Sounds. Gothic *timrjan* = OHG *zim-b-ren* OE *tim-b-ran* ; OE *buruh* (> MnE *borough*) beside OE *burh*.

Simplification of Consonant-Clusters. OIc *enskr engskr* < *englskr* (beside *engliskr*) ; MnE *worship* < OE *weorþscipe*.

---

[1] *x* is [ks].

(viii) The fates of the Primitive Germanic Phonemes in English

This Section in no way attempts to rival, but rather to supplement and interpret, the standard handbooks of English Historical Phonology—K. Luick, *Historische grammatik der englischen sprache* is certainly the greatest of these—for they contain a wealth of material not possible to give in the limited space here. Some of the sound-changes of Old English are very complex and are best dealt with in Tabular form ; I have printed tables setting out these changes in my *Tables*; for lack of space, and other reasons, these can hardly be reprinted here, so that a reference to the relevant *Table* must suffice.

I follow general custom in using the terms Old English, Middle English and Modern English for the periods A.D. 700–1100, 1100–1500 and 1500–present-day, respectively. The divisions are in practice, of course, not absolute. We have no English texts dateable before c. 700, and this period is called Primitive (Old) English or pre-literary Old English. In the period for which we have texts, literary Old English, as is well known, consists of four main discernible dialects, West Saxon, Kentish, Mercian and Northumbrian. The last two have many features in common and are frequently grouped together and termed *Anglian*. In the Middle English period there are more texts and, as a consequence, more discernible dialects.

PRIMITIVE AND OLD ENGLISH
VOWELS AND DIPHTHONGS

ANGLO-FRISIAN AND PRIMITIVE ENGLISH DEVELOPMENTS

VOWELS [1]

Certain sound-changes which are not found in the dialects of Middle and Upper Germany and the Rhineland are common to Old English and Old Frisian. These changes presumably began, and may have been completed, before the migration to Britain,

---

[1] It is unfortunately not possible in the scope of this book to make any but the most incidental remarks about the fate of vowels in unaccented syllables in Old English, important though they are. The heavy stem-stress greatly reduced their number so that, for instance, in the course of the literary period -*e* -*i* -*æ* become simplified to -*e* ; and in the late OE period most unstressed vowels become weakened to -*ə*, -*i* (p. 117). Readers are referred to Luick's excellent treatment and to a convenient table at p. 98 of J. Wright, *Old English Grammar*, in which the main developments are set out.

while the two peoples were still in contact. Some of the changes
are shared with Old Saxon, but the reasons for this phenomenon
are not precisely known. The changes of the vowels of accented
syllables may be listed as follows [1].

1. PrGmc *a* (except before nasals) is fronted to Anglo-Frisian *æ*,
which is retained in West Saxon and Northumbrian, but is further
fronted (" Second Fronting " or " Zweite Aufhellung ") in Old
Frisian, West Mercian [2] and Old Kentish to *e* : WS *fæt* OFr *fet*
VPs *fet* OK *fet* (Ic *fat* MnHG *fass*).

According to the ordinary view this *æ* (where it is retained)
reverts to *a* (i) when followed by a back vowel in the next syllable :
WG nas. **dag*, gp. **dago* (OHG *tag, tago*) > WS *dæg, daga*—the
corresponding forms in the Vespasian Psalter and the Old Kentish
Charters are *deg, dæga*, and in the Kentish Glosses, *deg, daga* [3] ;
(ii) before *w*, providing *i j* did not originally follow :—OE
gds. *clawe* (< PrGmc **klawōz, *klawai*); (γ) in Anglian, before
l, r + consonant :—*all, cald, darr, arm* (WS *eall, ceald, dearr, earm*).

The retraction of *æ* to *a* should mean that there existed in West
Saxon a bipartite phoneme *æ*ᵃ materialising either as *æ* or as *a*.
But in West Saxon, surprisingly, the difference *æ/a* is in fact a
difference between phonemes, for the two components are kept
apart by at least the pairs :—

　　ds. *stæle* (to *stæl* ' place ')/agds. nap. *stale* (to *stalu* ' theft ') ;
　　ds. *wæle* (to *wæl* ' slaughter ')/agds. nap. *wale* to *walu* (1) ' ridge ',
　　　　(2) ' wale '.

and perhaps by other pairs as well [4]. Clearly we have an instance
of the phenomenon that has been called the " phonematologisation

---

[1] Old Frisian forms are sometimes given less prominence here than are Old
English ones, for our main concern is, after all, with English.

[2] The dialect of the Vespasian Psalter.

[3] Further details of the Second Fronting may be briefly stated here :—(i) in
VPs, PrE *æ* > *e*, retracted *a* > *æ*, but Second Fronting did not take place before
a following *l* :—VPs *deg*, gp. *dæga* ; *ald*, comp. *ældra* (with *i*-umlaut) ; **hwæl*—
nap. *hwalas*. (ii) In IX c. Kentish Charters PrE *æ* > *e* ∽ *æ*, retracted *a* > *æ* :
ðet ∽ *ðæt* ; *reacoluensae* (Sweet *OET*, p. 442), with back-mutation of *æ*. (iii) In
the X c. Kentish Glosses, PrE *æ* > *e* (even before *l*), retracted *a* remains : *siðfet* 20 ;
welhriou 367 ; pl. *siðfata* 27. The " Kentishness " of the Old Kentish Charters
has been doubted (see R. Vleeskruyer, *The life of St Chad*, p. 47 note) and thus
the complete phenomena of Second Fronting (*æ* > *e*, *a* > *æ*) may be confined to
West Mercian.

[4] See my article " Old English *æ* ∽ *a* ", *English Studies* xxxii, 49–56.

of a phonetic difference"[1]. Evidence for the phonematologisation of
æ/a in the non-West Saxon dialects seems to be lacking[2] and it is
possible that the phenomenon is purely West Saxon. It is then
probable that the Frisian state of affairs, at first sight rather similar
(cf. forms such as ns. *fere, seke* = OE *faru, sacu*, as against ns. *klage*
= OHG *klaga*), is not to be directly connected with that in West
Saxon. It may well be due to various analogies ; in any case its
further investigation would be a matter for the Frisian specialist,
for it is clear that the present-day dialects would be deeply involved.

The West Saxon phenomenon, on the other hand, may most
simply be regarded as being due to the occurrence of an " irregular "
a before front vowels in certain paradigms, e.g. as. nap. *sace* to *sacu*
(ā-stem, short root syllable), gsmn. *hwates*, ismn. apf. napm. *hwate*
to *hwæt* (strong adj., o/ā-stem).

2. WG *a* + nasal > AFr *ą* (apparently intermediate in sound
between *a* and *o*) + nasal, which in some OE texts is regularly
written *a* (Epinal Glossary), in others *o* (VPs), in others *a* or *o* (early
Northumbrian Poems) :—OE *cómb* OFr *kómb* (p. 114, for the
lengthening) beside *a*-forms (= Ic *kambr*). In lightly-stressed
words *o* is the norm :—OE *on, hwonne.*

3. WG *ā* (< PrGmc *ē₁*) > WS *ǣ*[3] OFr OA OK *ē* :—Gothic
(*mana-*)*seþs* Ic *sáð* WS *sǣd* OFr *sêd* OA *sēd* OK *sēd*. WS *ǣ* usually
reverts to *ā* when followed by a labial or velar consonant (*w p g k*)
+ back-vowel :—*mǣg*, nap. *māgas* ; pl. pret. *sāwon* (p. 89).

4. WG *ąh* > AFr *ōh* (p. 87) :—sg. pret. Gothic *brāhta* OFr
brochte OE *brōhte.*

5. WG *ą* + *s f þ* > AFr *ō* (p. 87) + *s, f, þ* :—OHG *gans* OFr
gôs OE *gōs* ; adv. OHG *samfto* OE *sōfte* ; Gothic *anþar* OFr *ôther*
OE *ōþer.*

6. WG *ā* + nasal > AFr *ō* + nasal :—Gothic *mena* OS *mâno*
OFr *môna* OE *mōna* ; Gothic 1st pl. pret. *nemum*, pl. pret. OS
nâmun OFr *nômon* OE *nōmon.*

It is convenient to mention here two further phenomena shared
by Frisian and English but which occurred *after* the migration to

---

[1] Cf., my remarks *LSE* v, 99.

[2] Thus Lind has *fær* ' journey ' (implying a ds. **fære*) beside *fære* pres. subj.
of *fara* ' to go '. Contrast WS ds. *fære* (to *fær*), agds. nap. *fare* (to *faru*), 1st sg. pres.
ind. and sg. pres. subj. *fare* (to *faran*).

[3] Called *ǣ₁* in its later developments—see p. 127.

Britain :—(i) Old Frisian and Old English both have widespread effects from *i*-umlaut (pp. 93, 109) ; note that, both in OFr and OK, *ă* > *ȳ̆* > *ĕ* ; (ii) Frisian shares with English the lengthening of short vowels before certain consonant-groups (p. 114) :—OS *wildi, findan* OFr *wīlde, fīnda* OE *wīlde, findan*.

DIPHTHONGS

These have already been dealt with in part in Table A of my *Tables* and dialectal differences in the distribution of diphthongs are hinted at there (WS *hlę̄apan* Ru² *hlę̄opa*) ; these may be somewhat elaborated by reference to the following table (for convenience, I have included the main developments in Norse and the other West Germanic languages—cf. p. 95).

BREAKING [1]

It is assumed that, just before this change took place, the consonants *h l r* had, or acquired, a back pronunciation (*h* as *ch* of MnHG *nacht*, *l* as *l* of Russian *loshad'*, *r* as *r* of MnHG *reiten*, or the like). It is difficult to pronounce a front vowel before such a consonant, but the difficulty can obviously be avoided by either (*a*) changing the front vowel into a back vowel, or (*b*) inserting a back vowel between the front vowel and the back consonant. Hence :—PrE **æld* (< PrGmc **alþa/ō-* > MnHG *alt*) (*a*) > Mercian *ald* ; (*b*) > **æold* > WS *eald* (with *ea* written for *aea*). Whether or not diphthongisation takes place depends upon (1) the nature of the vowel (*æ, e* or *i*) ; (2) its quantity ; (3) the nature of the following consonant(-group). Table B of my *Tables* sets out the matter in a suitable manner.[2]

DIPHTHONGISATION AFTER PALATALS

Two great changes are involved here viz. (i) in Primitive English, PrGmc *k g* were palatalised to [*č*] *j* before front vowels (so that,

---

[1] On traces of breaking in Old Frisian and Old Norse see p. 94.

[2] In the historical period the phenomena are unevenly distributed in the dialects. Thus :—(i) many unbroken *al*-forms are found in early WS texts and in early Kentish Charters (? due to Mercian scribes) ; (ii) PrE *elf* > A, EOK *eolf* in *seolf* (only) ; (iii) breaking before *r*-groups is normal in all dialects, but unbroken *ar* is sometimes found, especially in the early Northumbrian remains ; in parts of Anglian (including VPs) unbroken *ir* is normal :—VPs *afirran*, *hirtan* ; Lind *firr* (hence A.Wisse *fir firrest* (not **fe(o)r*, etc.) ; (iv) in West Saxon and Kentish breaking was earlier than *r*-metathesis (thus *birnan, irnan* = Gothic *brinnan, rinnan*) ; in Anglian *r*-metathesis preceded breaking (thus VPs Ru¹ *beornan, eornan* (see further E. G. Stanley, *EAGS* v, 103 ff.)).

OS	OHG	Ic	OFr	Gothic form (Type-word)	Epinal Corpus	Aelfric	Ru²	Lind	VPs	KGl
ê	ei (ê before r h w)	ei	ê	stains	ā	ā	ā	ā	ā	ā
ô	ou (ô before dental or alveolar).	au	â, ô	-hlaupan	ẹ̄a	ẹ̄a	ẹ̄o	ẹ̄a	ẹ̄a	ẹ̄a
eo (io)	eo io	jó jú	iā	-biudan (iu < IndE eu)	ẹ̄o	ẹ̄o	ẹ̄o	ẹ̄a	ẹ̄o	īo (ẹ̄o īa)
iu	iu	jú	iu	3rd sg. pres. -biudiþ	īo	ȳ[1]	īo	īo	ẹ̄o (īo)	īo (īa)

[1] $g <$ *ie* by *i*-umlaut, which operates on this diphthong in West Saxon only (for the effect of *i*-umlaut on the other diphthongs, see p. 110).

before a PrE front vowel, PrGmc *j* and *g* both appear as *j* (written *g*))[1]. Similarly, PrGmc *sk* > OE [š] before all vowels (but earlier before front vowels than before back); (ii) Vowels preceded by PrE *j*[č][š] were diphthongised. I have set out the rather complex results arising in a suitable manner in Table D of my *Tables*.[2] [3]

I-UMLAUT [4]

At this stage in their development most of the stressed vowels undergo an important and characteristic change in those word-forms where they were followed by a WG *ĭ* or *j*. In recorded Old English the normal weakening of the unstressed syllables has generally removed or disguised the *i/j*; and, conversely, some endings have a non-umlauting *i* as a weakened form of other vowels as e.g. *-ig* in *hunig* < *-æg* < PrGmc *-aʒa-*; *-i(g)an* in the infinitive of Class II weak verbs (*-i(g)an* < *-ejan* < *-œjan* < *-ǣjan* < *-ōjan*). The primitive forms have therefore to be sought in the related languages (most instructively in Gothic and Old Saxon).[5]

The results of *i*-umlaut in Old English may be briefly summarised as follows.

a > æ. OA *ældra* < PrGmc *alpizan-* [6].

a + nasal > æ + nasal > e + nasal. Leiden Riddle 2, sg. pret. *cændæ*; OE nap. *menn* to *mann* [7].

---

[1] This is thus an Anglo-Frisian consonantal change.

[2] Forms such as OE *ceorl* (not *cierl*) show that palatal diphthongisation was later than breaking.

[3] The diphthongisation is virtually confined to West Saxon and Northumbrian. Mercian and Kentish forms such as VPs *gēamrung* and KGl 183 *gionne* (= asm. *giongne*) are extremely rare and are confined to *g* < WG *j*. MK forms such as Ayen *yemere, beyende* seem to represent OK *giōmor*, *beggondan* with later shift of stress.

[4] On the effects of *i*-umlaut in other Germanic languages, see p. 93 ff.

[5] Certain sounds are not affected :—(i) *i* and *ī* could not be; (ii) a short *e* no longer existed before *i/j* (p. 86); (iii) *ē* and *ǣ* are apparently not affected.

[6] In parts of the Anglian area a following *l* + consonant later produced " secondary umlaut " of *æ* (as did *n*, see next paragraph) to *e*, leaving an *ældra*-area and an *eldra*- area. Thus VPs apm. *ældran* but Ru[1] *eldra*. In Middle English, the *ældra*-area is represented, for example, by the Gawain MS. (sg. pret. *malt* to OA *mæltan*; cf. WS *mieltan* Gothic *ga-malteins*) and the Royal MS. of the Ancrene Wisse. The *eldra*-area is represented, for example, by Orm (*elldre, melltenn*), and by some MSS. of the Ancrene Wisse.

[7] A small area in Essex (no OE texts extant) must have retained the intermediate stage *æ* (nap. *mæn*, *sændan*), for *a*-forms (< OE *æ*) occur, for instance, in Vices and Virtues (nap. *man, sanden*), an Essex text of c. 1200.

æ > e (before a single consonant or a WG geminate) :—OE *ege* (Gothic *agis*) ; OE *settan* (Gothic *satjan*).

ǣ (< WG *ai*) > ǣ (K ē). OE *hǣlan hēlan* (Gothic *hailjan*) [1].

o > œ > e. ds. Nth *doehter*, WS *dehter* to OE *dohtor* [2].

ō > œ̄ > ē. ONth *sōēca* WS *sēcan* (Gothic *sokjan*) [3].

u > y (> K e). WS, A *wynn* (K *wenn*) : OS *wunnia*.

ū > ȳ (> K ē). WS, A *tȳnan* K *tēnan* to OE *tūn* [4].

ea > EWS ie (> i/y), non-WS e. EWS *hliehhan*, non-WS *hlehhan* (< *xlæoxxjan* = Gothic *hlahjan*).

ēa > EWS īe (> ī/ȳ), non-WS ē. EWS *hīeran*, non-WS *hēran* : Gothic *hausjan*.

io (broken i < PrGmc *i*, + *i, j*) > EWS ie (> i/y). EWS *hierde* (< PrE *xiurdi* = OHG *hirti*) [5].

īo (< PrGmc *iu* + *i, j*) > EWS īe (> ī/ȳ). EWS *dīepe* = OS *diupi* [6].[7]

---

[1] In its later developments this is called ǣ₂.

[2] This is a rare case, for a PrGmc o did not normally exist in a syllable followed by *i* or *j* (p. 86). The phonologically regular form would have been PrGmc *duxtri* > OE *dyhter*, but *doxtri* was substituted after the stem-vowel of the nominative singular and other cases. Normally, we have in such cases the alternation o ∽ y (< *u*, by *i*-umlaut, as below) :—OE *gold* ∽ *gylden, fox* ∽ *fyxen*.

[3] Northumbrian retains *oe* throughout the Old English period. Mercian has e/oe, ōē/ē in IX c., by 1000 only e, ē. West Saxon has e/oe in VIII c., in X c. only e ; still occasionally ōē in late IX c., before 1000 only ē. Kentish has almost invariable *oe* in early IX c., but before 1000 only ě. Thus, except in Northumbria, œ̆ is lost everywhere by 1000.

[4] In Old Frisian, ǔ > y̌ > ě as in Kentish (p. 93).

[5] No umlaut occurs in non-West-Saxon, which has *hiorde*. The corresponding non-umlauted forms have WS *eo* (*heord*).

[6] No umlaut occurs in non-WS, which has *dīope*; the corresponding non-umlauted forms have *ēo* in WS e.g. *dēop*. In Alfredian West Saxon, a few forms retain *īo* (or *ēo*) beside those with *īe*, as *stīoran*. " *Double* " *umlaut* occurs in words of pattern " vowel—*u*—*i* " :—OE *gǣdeling* = OS *gaduling* ; OE *hǣrfest* < PrGmc *xaruƀist-* ; VPs *festen* WS *fæsten* = OS *fastunnia* Gothic *fastubni*. The explanation of the change is, presumably, that medial *u* > *y* > *i* and it is this *i* which causes the umlaut. Medial o (> œ > e) or a (> æ > e) does not yield this *i* and so umlaut does not occur in inflected inf. *farenne* (< *faranjai*).

[7] The effects of *i*-umlaut are important for OE grammar and etymology. Umlauted vowels appear, for instance, in :—(i) *ja*-nouns and *ja/jō*-adjectives : *esne* = Gothic *asneis* ; *grēne* = OS *grōni* ; (ii) *jō*-nouns : *hell* = Gothic *halja* ; (iii) OE *i*-nouns : *hete* (: Gothic *hatis*) ; (iv) Weak verbs of Class I : *erian* = Gothic *arjan* ; (v) various derivatives with *i*- or *j*-suffixes : OE *gylden* = Gothic *gulpeins* ; (vi) certain parts of the paradigms of consonant-stems : ds. nap. *fēt*, to *fōt* ; (vii) the comparison parts of many adjectives and adverbs : *hīerra, hīehst* (Gothic *hauhists*) to *hēah* ; (viii) 2nd, 3rd sg. pres. of strong verbs *stentst, stent* (Gothic *standis, standiþ*).

OLD ENGLISH DEVELOPMENTS BEFORE 1100

BACK-MUTATION [1]

From the eighth century, the short vowels *i e æ* were often diphthongised when a single consonant separated them from a back vowel in the next syllable. Whether or not the change takes place depends upon (i) the nature of the vowel of the first syllable (*i, e* or *æ*); (ii) the nature of the intervening consonant :—(1) liquids and labials *f l p r*, (2) dentals and nasals *d s t þ m n*, (3) gutturals *c g*; (iii) the nature of the vowel of the second syllable :—(1) *u*, or (2) *o* or *a*; (iv) the dialect. In addition, a preceding *w* has an effect.[2][3][4] The permuting of all these different factors naturally renders the results of back-umlaut somewhat complicated ; they are dealt with in a suitable manner in my *Tables* (Table E).

INFLUENCE OF PALATAL CONSONANTS

1. *Anglian Smoothing*. In Anglian, probably in the course of VII and VIII c., the diphthongs *ĕa ĕo ĭo* (of any origin) lose their second element before *c g h* (or *x = hs/cs*), or any of the groups *rc rg rh lh* (*lc lg* appear not to occur in any of the words affected). Thus A *ĕa* (= *ǣa*) *ĕo ĭo* > *ǣ ĕ ĭ* :—sg. pret. A *sæh* EWS *seah* ; A *sēc* EWS *sēoc* (: Ic *sjúkr*) ; imp. sg. A *līh* : EWS *lēoh*.[5][6][7]

2. *Palatal Umlaut*. Before *t, s* or *þ*, and when no back vowel stood in the next syllable, PrE *h* was fronted at different times in each dialect and caused palatal umlaut :—

(i) PrE *eux+, iux+* > EWS *i(e)h+* :—EWS *cni(e)ht* (< *kneuht* < WG *knext-*) beside nap. *cneohtas*. Levelling occurs in both

---

[1] Cf. Old Norse breaking, p. 94.

[2] In Mercian and early Kentish *a > æ, æ > e* (*deg, dægas* : WS *dæg, dagas*); hence, in general, back-umlaut of *æ* can only take place in these two dialects and, if it occurs, Mercian and Kentish *ea* will correspond to WS *a*.

[3] The problem afforded by the development of *wæ* under conditions of this kind has not yet been solved.

[4] In general, back-umlaut does not take place before two consonants, though there are exceptions (e.g. WS *sweostor* < *swestur*, Ru[2] *seolla* = WS *sellan*).

[5] The earliest glosses have *ǣ*, but *ǣ* normally > *ē* ; *æ* remained only before *h*, becoming *e* elsewhere (with *i*-umlaut, > *e* also before *h*).

[6] The term "Anglian Smoothing" is due to Henry Sweet.

[7] This development annuls (*a*) some of the long diphthongs representing West Germanic diphthongs ; (*b*) some *l*- and *r*-breakings ; (*c*) all *h*-breakings ; (*d*) some results of back-mutation.

directions. A similar change occurred in Old Kentish by X c. :—
IX c. Kentish Charter [1] *mid reohte* KGl 169 *unrihthemere*.

(ii) Probably in all areas, but exemplified with differing thorough-
ness in the surviving texts, $\breve{e}+$ (of any origin) $> \breve{i}+$ (mostly later
than 900, and examples in the case of long vowels are rare) :—
KGl 36 3rd sg. pres. *genihsumiað* ($< e < $ PrE y); KGl 1151 3rd sg.
pres. *hlihð* ($<$ PrE *æo* and *i*-umlaut); Royal Gloss (c. 1000)
cniht; Ru[1] *līht* (once) beside *lēht lēoht*. Yet exceptions are common :—VPs *reht*; St Chad gp. *pehta* ' Picts '; Royal Gloss *reht-
wisnisse*, etc. ; and no Old Northumbrian texts show the change.
It probably occurred in Mercia and Northumbria in the transition-
period—hence A. Wisse, MNth, MScots *riht* (but fairly frequently
re(g)ht in northern Middle English too, indicating that the change
was not universal).

(iii) WS $\bar{e}o+$ ($< \bar{i}o$ $\bar{e}o$), K $\bar{i}o+$ remained throughout the Old
English period,[2] but $> i$ before the Middle English period :—WS
lēoht OK *līoht* EME *liht* (Orm *lihht*).[3] [4]

3. *Late Old English " Smoothing ".* LWS *ĕa* is monophthongised
after fronted *c g sc* and before *c g h*, which were still velar in the
i-umlaut period but which had presumably acquired front quality.
This change resembles Anglian Smoothing in its effects.
Examples :—LWS sg. pret. *seh* $<$ EWS *seah*; LWS *ēge* $<$ EWS
ēage; LWS *celc* $<$ EWS *cealc*; LWS *sceft* $<$ EWS *sceaft*. A few
instances occur as early as Alfredian MSS. (Orosius sg. pret. *mehte*).

Similarly, OK *ĕa* $> \breve{e}$ before *c g h*, but the evidence is incomplete
for the Old English period :—KGl 954 *smēgan*, 1035 *ðeh* but 1119
hēah, etc.[5]

4. *WS ĭe ȳ.* Before fronted *c g h*, singly or in combination, and in
certain cases before *n*, EWS *ĭe* $\breve{y} > \breve{i}$ (c. 900). A few *i*-forms appear
as early as Alfredian MSS. :—WS *niht, drihten, līg, cin(in)g* $<$ earlier
nieht, dryhten, līeg, cyning.

---

[1] Sweet, ii, 188.

[2] That $\bar{e}o + > i$ (not e) $+$ shows that palatal umlaut was still operative *after*
the late Old English shortenings occurred.

[3] $e > i$ occasionally before other palatals :—KGl *wig, slicc* ($=$ WS *weg, slecg*);
hence KathGr *rikenin* (OE *recenian*), Ayen *nhicke* ($<$ OE *hnecca*).

[4] Possible OK examples include KGl 323 3rd sg. pres. *oferwrīhð* but other explana-
tions have been offered.

[5] From this and (i), the relationship sg. pret. WS K *seh* $=$ A *sæh* will be observed.

5. *After* s. After *s* there occur three minor phenomena which suggest that it had a distinct palatal quality :—

(i) EWS *sio-* > WS [*sie-*] > *si-/sy-* :—pl. pres. *syndon* < *siendon* < *siondon* ; *sylfor* < **sielfor* < *siolfor* (Alfredian MSS. have forms with *ie io i y*).

(ii) PrE **sel-* [> WS **siel-*] > *sil-/syl-* in post-Alfredian West Saxon, and in parts of Anglian :—OE *sillan/syllan* (A. Wisse *sullen*) < EWS *sellan* ; OE *syllic* (A. Wisse *sullich*) < EWS *sel(d)lic* ; Mercian charter of 840 [1] imp. sg. *sile* [2].

(iii) OE *secg-* > LOE *sicg-/sycg-* —suggested by Middle English occurrences of *suggen* (< LOE **sycgan* beside EWS *secgan*).

INFLUENCE OF W [3]

Characteristic effects of a neighbouring *w* (rarely, other labials) can be observed in the following changes, which occurred at the periods and in the dialects indicated in the course of the Primitive English and Old English periods (the latter, mostly late) :—

1. PrGmc o^u materialises as *u* instead of the expected *o* [4] in labial surroundings in many OE words :—*wulf* (= OHG *wolf*), *wull* (: OHG *wolla*).

2. *Diphthongisation before w.* (i) PrE *e, i* + *w* > OE *eow, iow* when no *i* follows in the next syllable :—gs. OE *cneowes* < PrGmc **knewas-* ; OE *peowian* = Gothic *ga-þiwan*. This change resembles breaking, and seems to have been early and general (though less regular in Northumbrian). (ii) LWS *ēw, ǣw* > *ēow, ēaw* :—3rd sg. pres. *flēwð* > *flēowð* ; *brǣw* > *brēaw*.

3. *Rounding.* (i) OE *ni-* (*ne-*) + *wi-* > *ny-* (K *ne-*) in IX c. :—1st sg. pres. *nylle* (< *ni wille*), K *nelle* ; KGl 454 *netenes* < **ni-witen-ness*. (ii) In Lindisfarne and the Durham Ritual, *wĕ* > *wŏ* in most cases : *woeg*, pl. pret. *wōēron*. (iii) PrWS *ie* after *w* (and occasionally after *f*) > WS *y* :—EWS *wyrsa, fyrr* ; (iv) In late West Saxon (and occasionally elsewhere, e.g. parts of Mercia) *i* > *y* in labial surroundings :—LWS *wyllan, cyrice, fyrst* < EWS

---

[1] Sweet, *OET*, p. 454.

[2] The lengthening-group *ld* prevents this change (*séld, séldum*).

[3] For the influence of *w* on a preceding *ǣ*, see p. 106 ; for the development of *wi- we-* in back-mutation conditions, see Table E of my *Tables* and, for the part played by *w* in the development of new diphthongs, see p. 117.

[4] Cf. Table A of my *Tables*.

E

willan, cirice, first (= OHG *frist*). The Middle English distribution
of *u i e* forms (p. 127) for these and other words confirm this change.

4. *Velarisation.* (i) PrE *we* before *r* + consonant > Nth *wo*
LWS *wu* :—ONth *sword, worðia,* LWS *swurd, wurðian.* Middle
English evidence suggests that LWS *wu* spread to certain other
areas (later annals of the Peterborough Chronicle have *wu* ; Orm
wurrþenn but *swerd,* etc.). (ii) WS *wyr* > LWS *wur* (post-Aelfric—
he died c. 1020), whence it spread to other areas (except Kent,
where no *y* existed) :—LWS *wurm* Orm *wurrm* : Ayen *werm.* (iii)
WS *wor* > LWS (XI c.) *wur* :—LWS *wurd, wurms* [1].

5. *Shift of Accent.* In late OE, *ĕow* > *ęŏw,* sometimes *ŏw* (beside
retained *ĕow*-forms) : LOE **fower* (beside general OE *feower, fēower*) ;
hence A. Wisse *fowr,* Orm *fowwerr, fowwre* ; ME *yowe* (beside *ewe*)
< OE *eowu.*

CHANGES IN QUANTITY
(1) *Lengthening*

(i) At an early period, final short vowels in monosyllables were
lengthened :—OE *hwā* (Gothic *hvas*) ; OE *þū, nū, iū* (Gothic *þu,
nu, ju*).

(ii) Probably in the course of VII c., medial *h* was lost-between
vowels and in other voiced surroundings (especially in the combinations *lh, rh, h* + *l, r, m, n*). A preceding short vowel or diphthong
received compensatory lengthening :—PrE **sehan* > *sēon* (but 2nd,
3rd sg. pres. *siehst, siehþ*) ; OE *mearh,* gs. *mēares* ; OE *lǣne* (= OS
lêhni).

(iii) (*a*) In late Old English, *g* was frequently lost before *d ð n*
with lengthening of a preceding vowel :—LOE *mǣden* < *mægden* ;
LOE *tīðian* < *tigðian* ; LOE *þēnian* < *þegnian.* (*β*) -*igi*- -*ige*- > *ī* :—
LOE 3rd sg. pres. *līþ* < *ligeþ* ; *īl* (Corpus 765 *iil*). (*γ*) -*ig* (at end of
word or syllable) > *ī* :—LOE *ǣnī* < *ǣnig* ; asm. *ǣnine* < *ǣnigne.*
(This leads to reciprocal spellings with *ig* for etymological *ī* as nap.
hig, bigspell).

(iv) The most significant lengthening occurred before consonant
groups consisting of *l, m, n, r* + homorganic voiced consonant (most
commonly, *mb, nd, ng, ld, rd* ; less commonly, *rl, rn* ; and *rð, rs*

---

[1] These three changes caused widespread orthographical confusion (*weo wy wo
wu* being regarded as synonymous by the scribes) and false spellings such as
swyrd and *weorm* become frequent in Late West Saxon manuscripts.

before vowels). This change is shared' with Old Frisian.
Examples [1]:—*climban, séndan, láng* ; A *áld* ; *éorþe*, nap. *éarsas*,
etc. (all with short stem-vowel in the cognate languages). The
lengthening process seems to have begun in IX c. (or even earlier),
but no doubt extended over a long period of time with marked
dialectal differences. In many cases these vowels were again
shortened in early Middle English (p. 129).[2]

(2) *Shortening*

(*a*) *Early Period.* (i) Before groups of three consonants (cf.
last section, (iv)) :—OE nap. *bræmblas* (*b* intrusive, cf. OS *brâmal*
(*-busk*)) ; *næddre* (OE geminated form, < *nædre*, p. 98). (ii) Before
double consonant groups in the first syllable of words of three or
more syllables, or (later) of dissyllabic compounds :—OE *samcucu*
(OHG *sâmi-quëc*), *bledsian* (< PrGmc *blōđisōjan*), *ceapman* (> ME
chapman) < *cēap-man*. (iii) Sporadically, before intervocalic
geminates :—OE *siđđan* (< *sīđ* + *đan*) > *siođđan* (the shortening
must have preceded back-mutation).

(*b*) *Late period.* (i) Probably in X and XI c., shortening occurred
before all double consonant-groups except those mentioned under
Lengthening (iv), above :—sg. pret. *brohte, demde* ; *softe*, etc.—
except that shortening normally did not occur before *st* (*læsta*)
and before voiced consonant + *l, r* (*æfre*, gdsf. napm. *ōpre*, etc.).
(ii) Long vowels before single consonants in trisyllabic words were
sometimes shortened in late Old English, sometimes in the transi-
tional period, thus producing doublets :—LOE *haligdæg* > ME
halidai beside OE *hāligdæg* > EME *hǫlidai* > ME *holidai* (p. 31).

DIPHTHONGS [3]
ĕo ĭo

These are kept apart throughout the Old English period in
Northumbrian [4]. In Mercia (pre-VPs [5]) and post-Alfredian West
Saxon they fall together as *ĕo*. In the early Kentish Charters

---

[1] Usually marked with an acute accent, not the macron, in text-books.
[2] Lengthening did not take place (*a*) when a third consonant followed, as OE
cild, nap. *cildru*, (*b*) in trisyllabic words—hence Orm *allderrmann* beside *ald*,
(*c*) in weakly-stressed words—*and*, sg. pret. *wolde*, etc.
[3] Cf. Table on p. 108.
[4] Sometimes etymological *ĕo* appears as *ĕa* in Lind and Rit.
[5] There are here a few graphic remains of *ĭo*.

(mostly IX c.) *eo io*, *ēo īo* are, for the most part (but by no means regularly) retained, and there are some instances of *ĭa* [1]. The Kentish Glosses show that by X c., OK *ēo īo* have fallen together as *īo*, OK *eo io* as *eo*.

ĕa

This is retained in all dialects until c. 1000 (see next section) and in Kentish it remains considerably longer. In Ru[2] " etymological " *ĕa* frequently appears as *ĕo* (see Table *B* of my *Tables*).

ĭe

This diphthong is exclusively West Saxon—it results from palatal diphthongisation and *i*-umlaut (p. 109). It is presumably already monophthongal in Alfred (to judge from reverse spellings such as *iedel* = *ĭdel*, *þieng* = *þing*), yet it is mostly *written* in the etymologically correct places in Alfredian MSS. After *w f*, *ĭe* > *ẏ̆* before Alfred, and before palatals, > *ĭ* c. 900 (p. 112). In the remaining places its normal representative in literary West Saxon is *ẏ̆* by 1000, and its subsequent history is that of *ẏ̆* of other origins (p. 127).

ISOLATIVE CHANGES BEFORE 1100

1. Except in Kentish [2], all diphthongs, short and long, lost their second element, if they had not already done so :—

OE *ĕa* > *ǣ̆* (c. 1000, see below).

OE *ĕo* > *œ̆* (XI c.)—which remained in the West Midlands till Middle English times (p. 127), but gave *ę̆* in the North and the East Midlands during XII c.

OE *ĭe* > *ẏ̆/ĭ* (above).

Evidence for these changes is provided, for instance, by reverse spellings in XI c. MSS. e.g. *æ* for *ēa* in a Mercian Charter of 1038 [3] in *beæstan*, *dæcane* for earlier *beēastan*, *dēacone*.

2. By 1100, OE *å* is everywhere *a* except in the West Midlands, where *o* is general :—Orm *mann* : A. Wisse *mon* ; with lengthening (p. 114), Orm *land* : A. Wisse *lónd*.

3. New diphthongs were beginning to emerge as palatal *g* and

---

[1] A. Campbell, *JEGP* xxxvii, 149.

[2] For some remarks on Kentish developments in Middle English, see p. 128.

[3] Sweet, ii, 213.

back *g* weakened between vowels, before consonants, and when final, and began to merge with a preceding vowel :—*wcg* > *wei* ; gs. *dæg-es* > *daį-es* ; nap. *dagas* > *dau̯-es* (ME *dawcs*). These diphthongising processes were in general not completed before the early Middle English period, except that diphthongisation had certainly occurred (i) with *g* in final position after front vowels and before consonants :—*dei* (Kentish Charters), *grēi* (Epinal Glossary) = WS *græg*. In XI c. Aelfric MSS., *ig i* is sometimes written for final *g* or *g* before consonant (*weig*, 3rd sg. pres. *mæig, seið*) ; (ii) with *w* in such words (analogised on oblique cases) as *snāw, bræw, briw, dēaw* (earlier *snā, bræ*, etc.) and 3rd sg. pres. *cnæwð, flēwð* (pre-consonantal).

4. Most unstressed vowels had fallen together as [ə].

THE VOWEL-PHONEMES OF LATE OLD ENGLISH (C. 1100)

As a result of the changes enumerated in this section, Late Old English is left with the following phonemes :—

ə[1]	a	(å)	æ[2]	e	i	o	œ	u	y
ā			ǣ[3]	ē	ī	ō	ōē	ū	ȳ
			æi	ei[4][5]					

CONSONANTS

Various consonantal modifications in Primitive and West Germanic have already been mentioned (p. 96 ff.). To these may be added two changes which are of some consequence for Old English.

1. WG *j* before *i*, and *w* before *u* or *i*, are lost in unstress : 2nd, 3rd sg. pres. WG **narjis, *narjiþ* (: Gothic *nasjis, nasjiþ*) > **naris, *nariþ* > OE *neres(t, nereþ* ; WG **mādwu* > PrE **mǣdu* > OE *mǣd*[6] (gs. *mǣdwe*) ; WG **saiwi-* (Gothic *saiws*) > PrE **sā(w)i*

---

[1] Only in unstressed syllables (see above).

[2] It is possible that by 1100 *æ* had already changed to *a* (p. 126).

[3] Of double origin :—(i) the product of PrGmc *ē₁* (only WS, p. 106) which, in the next section is called *ǣ₁* ; (ii) the product of WG *ai* with *i*-umlaut which is henceforward called *ǣ₂* (some grammars oddly reverse these).

[4] The rare diphthongal phonemes *āu, ǣu*, etc., mentioned in 3 (ii) of the last section should perhaps be added here.

[5] Old Kentish had no *ȳ̆*-phoneme (it had there given *ĕ̈*, c. 900) ; on the other hand it still had the ancient breaking- and back-mutation-diphthongs *eo, ĭo, ĕa* (p. 116), here omitted from the Table.

[6] In Primitive English, final unstressed *u* is retained after short vowels (as *sunu* = Gothic *sunus*), lost after long vowels (*flōd* = Gothic *flodus*).

> OE *sǣ*. This change explains differences between the infinitive and that of 2nd, 3rd sg. pres. in the First Weak Conjugation :— *nerian—nerest, nereþ* (not **neriest, *nerieþ*) ; *fremman* (with West Germanic gemination)—*fremest, fremeþ* (without it). Moreover these developments, together with the fact that final *w* became vocalic *u* (p. 102), explain, for instance, the different endings in the OE paradigm of *wō*-nouns : *beadu* (< WG **badwu* < PrGmc **badwō*), ds. *beadwe* (< PrGmc **badwai*). (An exhaustive treatment of these matters would, of course, go far beyond the scope of this book).

2. PrGmc *x* (a voiceless spirant) became aspirated *h*, which, in Primitive English, survives in all positions :—OE *hēr*, PrE **seohan* (> OE *sēon*) ; OE *seolh*.

ANGLO-FRISIAN DEVELOPMENTS

1. WG *hs* > AFr *ks* (written *x*). The same development is found in Norse :—OE *feax* OFr *fax* Ic *fax* (but OHG *fahs* OS *fahs*). As shown by the example, it apparently occurred after the period of breaking (p. 107), but before the migration to Britain.

2. *Anglo-Frisian Palatalisation.* WG *k, ʒ* were palatalised in Anglo-Frisian in the following circumstances [1] :—

(i) Initially before an original front vowel [2] :—OE *cinn* OFr *szin(-bakka)*: Gothic *kinnus* ; WS *giefan* OFr *jeva* : Gothic *giban*— but OE *cyssan* (< **kussjan*) OFr *kessa*, OE *gōd* OFr *gôd*.

(ii) Medially between original front vowels, or between a back vowel and *i/j* (i.e. in *i*-umlaut conditions) :—WS *lǣce* OFr *lêtza* : Gothic *lekeis* ; OE *secgan* OFr *sedza* : OS *seggian* ; OE *drencan* OFr *drentza* : Gothic *dragkjan* ; OE *seng(e)an* (< PrGmc **sangjan-*) ; WS *bīegan* A *bēgan* OFr *bêia* : Gothic *-baugjan*—but OE *līcian* (< PrGmc **līkōjan-*), OE *tunge* OFr *tunge*.

(iii) At the end of a word or of a syllable, WG *k* is palatalised after *ĭ*, WG *ʒ* after all original front vowels :—OE *ic, dīc* ; OE *dæg* OFr *dei* ; OE *mægden* OFr *meiden* ; OE *weg* OFr *wei*. Here

---

[1] Note that, when palatalised, WG *k* > OE [tš] (written *c*), but OFr [ts] (written *tz ts sz*) ; similarly WG *-ʒʒj-* > OE [dž] (written *cg*), but OFr [dz] (written *dz ds dsz sz*) ; and WG *-nki-* > OE [ntš] (written *nc*), but OFr [nts] (written *nts ntz*).

[2] This excludes, of course, front vowels which arose later by *i*-umlaut (p. 109), as those of OE *cēlan* OFr *kêla* (OHG *kuolen*), but includes the Anglo-Frisian fronted sounds from WG *a* and *ā* (pp. 105–6).

there also fall for mention words where *c* is final in Old English but was not so in West Germanic but where palatalisation occurs before an original *i/j* :—OE *benc* (< PrGmc **banki-*), OE *nap. bēc* (< PrGmc *np. *bokiz*) ; examples of unpalatalised *k*, *ʒ* :— OE *bæc* OFr *bek*, OE *āc* OFr *êk*, OE *panc* OFr *thânk*, OE *dāg*, OE *lang* OFr *lâng*.[1] [2]

3. There is some evidence that WG medial *pl* > AFr *tl dl ðl* under various conditions. Dialect differences in the literary period tend to obscure the position, but, broadly speaking, West Saxon and Kentish have *tl* in forms with syllabic *l* (as *setl* beside OS *sedal*) but *dl* after long vowels (*ādl*, WS *næðdl* OK *nēdl* beside Gothic *nepla*). Anglian seems to have had *pl* throughout (and the *p* would have become voiced in the normal way). In the literary period, Epinal 796 is ds. *naeðlae* (but Corpus 66 is ns. *nētl*) ; the Vespasian Psalter normally has *ðl* (ap. *aðle*), except where there has been metathesis (below) ; Northumbrian alternates between *dl* and *ðl* (*ādl* ∽ *āðl*). In West Mercian *ðl* > *ld* by metathesis :—VPs, St Chad *scld* (WS *setl* ONth *seðel*) ; St. Chad *bold* (WS *botl*)[3].[4]

DEVELOPMENTS IN OLD ENGLISH BEFORE 1100

For the most part, the consonant-phonemes of West Germanic remain unaltered in their transmission through the Old English period, though their distribution is considerably modified. The most significant developments are the voicing of the voiceless spirants *f p s* in voiced surroundings (p. 99) and the emergence of a new phoneme, palatal [š] *sc*. An account of these and other selected changes now follows.

1. "*Later*" *Gemination.* In late Old English (there are a few instances in Alfred) the consonant is often geminated (p. 98) and the vowel shortened in the group "long vowel + *d* or *t* + *r* " :—

---

[1] The alternation [k] ∽ [tš] [g] ∽ [j] in nominal and verbal paradigms produced a pattern of irregularity : cf., for instance, OE *ceorfan* ∽ sg. pret. *carf* (A), pl. pret. *curfon*, ppart. *corfen*—which gives ME *kerven* (> MnE *carve*) ; and OE *cēosan*, sg. pret. *cēas* ∽ pl. pret. *curon*, ppart. *coren*—which gives ME *chēsen/chōsen* (> MnE *choose*).

[2] The extent of the influence of Old Norse *g* (unpalatalised) on native as well as loan-words cannot be precisely estimated but may have been considerable.

[3] *p* is lost before *l* in one word :—Gothic *mapljan* : OE *mæplan/-mǣlan*—but Scandinavian influence (: Ic *mæla*) is not impossible.

[4] Cf. *pl* > *hl* in High and Low German (p. 100).

nǣdre > *nǣddre*, gs. *ātres* > *attres* (then nas. *attor* by analogy, cf. Orm *atterr*) ; but ungeminated forms also survive.

2. By contrast, etymological geminates are often simplified, especially (i) at the end of a word or of a syllable :—*eal* (beside gsmn. *ealles*), sg. pret. *cyste* (to *cyssan*) ; (ii) in compounds :— *eorlic* (for *eorl-lic*) ; (iii) in unstressed syllables :—*bliccetan* (for *bliccettan*).

3. Initially, the phoneme *p* enormously increased in frequency through the influx of Latin words e.g. OE *pēa, pund.*

4. Voiced consonants (i) usually became unvoiced when in contact with unvoiced ones :—OE *strencþ* < WG **strangiþu* ; (ii) frequently became unvoiced in final unstress (especially in Kentish and Northumbrian) :—KGl 214 *lamp*, 256 *ðinc* ; Corpus 805 *haelsent*, Lind *hēafut*, Ruthwell Cross *k̄yniŋc*[1].

5. Assimilation, dissimilation, simplification of consonant-groups, metathesis, etc. are common. A few instances are given at p. 103 and some others below ; these may be amplified by consulting the standard handbooks. A striking feature of West Saxon is the consonantal reduction in 2nd, 3rd sg. pres. of strong verbs e.g. *-ndist -ndiþ* > *-ntst, -nt* as *bintst, bint* to *bindan* ; *-dist -diþ* > *-tst -tt* as *būtst, būtt* to *bīdan.*

6. I here give some remarks on changes affecting particular consonants.

WG f þ s

(i) At a very early period, PrE *f þ s* became voiced in voiced surroundings (but they were written *f þ/ð s*) :—OE *scōfl, brōþor, bōsm.* By reason of this change the products of WG medial *f* and WG *ƀ* fell together :—

WG *f* : OE nap. *wulfas* (Gothic np. *wulfos*) ;

WG *ƀ* : OE *giefan* (Gothic *giban*).

The earliest texts write occasional *b* for WG *ƀ* (*obaer, hebuc* Epinal). The use of *u* for the voiced spirant *ƀ* of either origin begins in XI c. MSS. but is not common before early Middle English.

(ii) Initial *þ* may have had voicing in pronominal forms (p. 100) as early as Late Old English.

(iii) PrGmc *lþ* > WG *lð* > OE *ld* :—OE *wilde* : Gothic *wilþeis* Ic *villr* [2].

---

[1] Cf. Middle English unvoicing, p. 136.

[2] Words like OE *hǣlþ(u, fȳlþ(u* are not " exceptions " but have suffix PrGmc *-iþō-*.

WG x

(i) Before *l n r*, initial *h* begins to drop at the end of the Old English period (Lind *lāf* for *hlāf*, *nesc* for *hnesc*, *ræfn* for *hræfn*) ; in EME, Orm has *h*-less forms only (*laferrd*, *rinǧenn*) except *rhof* v. 8142 (OE *hrōf*), *lhude* (OE adv. *hlūde*).

(ii) Medial *h* was frequently lost with compensatory lengthening of a preceding short vowel (examples at p. 114).

WG ʒ g

(i) From the evidence of the alliterative poetry it is normally assumed that the voiced spirant WG ʒ initially before a consonant or before a back vowel (*a*) remained a voiced spirant in Primitive English and is hence free to alliterate with fronted ʒ (as in the first line of Beowulf) ; (*b*) became a voiced stop in the course of X c. For instance, in the Battle of Maldon (c. 1000), the two *g*s no longer alliterate together [1].

(ii) For AFr fronted ʒ, see p. 118.

(iii) Medial and final ʒ were frequently lost in Old English (examples at p. 102), and in some circumstances formed diphthongs with preceding front vowels (examples at p. 117). In late Old English, final ʒ after a back vowel became unvoiced to *h* :—LOE *genōh* (OS *gi-nôg*), LOE *sorh* (OS *sor(a)ga* OHG *s(w)orga*).

WG sk

(i) Initially, WG *sk* was patalalised in all Old English dialects, but earlier before front vowels than before back ones. The palatalisation before back vowels may, in the South, have been as late as X c. OE words with initial *sc* contrast sharply with Norse loanwords which have *sk* (p. 35). For the effects of *sc* on surrounding vowels, see p. 109.[2]

(ii) Medially before a back vowel and finally after one, PrE *sk* sometimes remained and, in early West Saxon, was often metathesised to *ks* (written *x*) : WS *āxian* < *āscian* (= OHG *eiscôn*) ; WS *tūx* < *tūsc*.

---

[1] This is another instance of the " phonematologisation of a phonetic difference " (p. 105).

[2] It is possible that a few words with WG *skr* may not have undergone palatalisation ; thus MnE *scream* seems to require the postulation of an OE *scrǣman* ; contrast, however, MnE *shrine*, *shroud*, *shrive*, etc.

WG w j

(i) Initially and medially WG *w* is normally retained in Old English but is lost (*a*) before *u* :—*sund* (< **swund* to *swimman*) ; *cucu* beside *cwucu*—in absolute initial position only *uton* beside *wuton* ; (*b*) in various compounds :—as. *ealne weg* > *ealneg* ; *fulluht* (< **full-wuht*) ; 1st, 3rd sg. pres. *nyle* < *ne wile* (p. 113), etc.

(ii) For loss of *w* before *u* in unstress in Primitive Germanic, see p. 117.

(iii) WG initial *j* fell together with PrE fronted *g* in Primitive English (p. 118) and is usually written *g ge* (*i gi* before *u*) :—OE *gēar* : Gothic *jer* ; OE *gēo gīo iū* : Gothic *ju* (p. 114) [1].

(iv) WG medial *j* remained (written *i g*) after *r* preceded by a short vowel :—*nerian*, ds. *herge* but *settan* (< PrGmc **satjan-*)— see p. 102.

(v) (*a*) The PrGmc geminates *jj ww*, which hardened into stops in North and East Germanic, remained in West Germanic as semi-vowels. In Primitive English the first element of each became vocalic (*i u*) and combined with the preceding short vowel to form a diphthong (or long vowel) :—WG **wai-i̯a-* > OE *wǣg* (= Ic *veggr*) ; PrGmc **fri-i̯ō-* > OE *Frīg* [2] (= Ic *Frigg*) ; WG **dau-u̯a-* > OE *dēaw* (= Ic *dǫgg*). (*b*) A small group of words with PrGmc *awj iwj* show special developments. They undergo, in turn, (1) West Germanic gemination, giving *awwj iwwj* ; (2) diphthongisation, as in (*a*) above, giving *auu̯j iuu̯j* ; (3) *i*-umlaut (in Primitive English), the *j* dropping in the forms with original *i* but remaining (with loss of *w*) in those with original *a*. Examples :—(*a*) *awwj* in :— WG **hau-u̯ja-*, PrGmc **au-u̯jō-* > WS *hīeg, īeg* A *hēg, ēg* ; (*β*) *iwwj* in :—WG **niu-u̯ja/ō-*, **xiu-u̯ja-* > WS *nīwe, hīw*, A *nīowe, hīow*.

MIDDLE ENGLISH
1100–1500

No space can here be spared for a description of those events which led to the emergence of " Standard " English from a type of Middle English predominantly East Midland in type, that is, from

---

[1] F. Holthausen, *Altenglisches etymologisches wörterbuch*, conveniently lists the words with WG *j* and those with WG *ȝ* separately.

[2] Whence MnE *Friday*.

the direct descendant of the obscure East Mercian dialect of Anglo-Saxon, but any general history of the English Language sets out the appropriate material. The significance of this development for the study of English Etymology will be readily appreciated, and the paramount importance of the *Anglian* developments mentioned in the preceding sections made plain.

ORTHOGRAPHY

Middle English orthography, especially in the early period, is a hybrid and, in any apparatus for English Etymology, some commentary on it is desirable. This becomes apparent, for instance, when we see that the statement " OE *y* > ME *u* " has nothing to do with change of sound, whereas, on the other hand, the statement " WMerc *ea* > A. Wisse *ea* " has. The explanation of these apparent nonsensities is to be found in the intimate blend of native and French orthographical conventions in most Middle English manuscripts. Thus the Ancrene Wisse group of texts (and some others) normally retain the native diphthongal graphs *ea eo* despite the fact that they now represent the monophthongs [æ] and [œ] respectively (p. 116) and also employ these graphs in French words (*leattre, demeori*). On the other hand, because OE *y* has the same sound as OFrench *u*, Anglo-French scribes now write *u* for [y] [y :] of various origins in native, Norse and French words : A. Wisse *sunne* (< OE *synn*), *stutten* (N lw. : Ic *stytta*), *hurten* (lwf. OFrench *hurter*). The symbol *y* becomes a mere variant of *i*, useful in the vicinity of minims.

There are a few other orthographical features which require brief comment [1].

VOWELS

1. *u* is often written *o* in the vicinity of minims (ME *sone* < OE *sunu*) [2].

2. From mid-XIII c., *ū* is frequently written *ou* (as in Old French)

---

[1] It must be emphasised that conventions vary greatly from place to place and also within particular works. Anything approaching modern consistency is only to be found in the three great early Middle English monuments, the Ormulum, the Ancrene Wisse (certain MSS.) and the Ayenbite of Inwyt (from each of which I have freely taken examples for this Section).

[2] ME *o* also = OE *o* (ME, OE *horn, fōt*) so, in certain positions, *o* can represent two phonemes.

—ME *hous* < OE *hūs*—but this in no way implies an early change of pronunciation towards MnE [au].

3. After Orm, *æ* is rarely used, and this makes it difficult to ascertain whether a long *ē* was open or close in XIII and XIV c.

CONSONANTS

The conventions here are mostly self-evident (e.g. ME *quen* < OE *cwēn*—with French *qu*) and therefore, in the main, they are of no great significance for Etymology. But the development of symbols revealing the distribution of the phonemes [k]/[tš], [g]/[j], [sk]/[š]—something the Anglo-Saxon alphabet could not do—is of primary importance.

The main consonantal orthographic features are :—

1. Whereas Old English wrote *ʒ* for any type of *g*, Middle English has (i) the continental-type "g" (like the modern printed letter) for the back stop ; (ii) *ʒ* (called *yogh*), later *y*, for palatal *g* (OE *ʒer* : ME *ʒer*, later *yer*) ; (iii) *ʒh gh* (also *ʒ*) for the medial voiced spirant (nap. OE *daʒas* : ME *daʒhes daghes daʒes*) until it developed in the normal way to *w* (p. 129)—later ME *dawes* ; (iv) the fricative [dž] (as in OE *secgan*) is represented in Middle English by *gg dg*, where it occurs initially (in French loan-words) by *i* (*iustice*), rarely *g* (Orm *gyn*). Orm in fact invented a " water-tight " system of his own for the various *g*-sounds and this, like his consonant-doubling, is a gift of the first magnitude to the etymologist [1].

2. Whereas Old English wrote *c* for each of the products of WG *k*, Middle English uses (i) *ch* for [tš] (ME *chesen* < OE *cēosan*) ; (ii) *c* for [k] before back vowels (ppart. *coren*) ; (iii) *k* before *i*-umlauted front vowels (ME *kene* < OE *cēne*) and before *n* (ME *kniht* < OE *cniht*) ; (iv) *cch*, later *tch*, for medial [tš] (*tæchen*) ; (v) *ck kk* for medial back geminated [k] (*lockes lokkes* [of hair]). Similarly, Middle English has *sch ssh sh* representing OE *sc* (*shyrt*) and *sk* representing (mostly) Old Norse *sk* (*skyrt*).

3. The OE groups *ht ʒt* are now written *ht ʒt ʒht cht*, etc. An interesting graphemic phenomenon is seen in the occasional equation of French *st* (as in OFrench 3rd sg. pres. *gist*) and ME *ht ʒt* by Anglo-French scribes, hence ME *brist* ' bright ', *knist* ' knight ', etc.

4. Middle English developed separate symbols for the voiced

---

[1] Any text that uses *ʒ* and *g* in the functions just described is " Middle English " (that is, neither " Old English " nor " Modern English ").

and unvoiced materialisations of the phoneme /f/ whereas Old English did not have these, cf. OE *findan* : *yfel* as against ME *finden* : *yuel uuel* (but Orm *findenn*, *ifell*). Some manuscripts have positional preference for a round-bottomed *u* or a pointed *v*, but this is a purely palaeographical matter ; either-shaped letter *may* be used for either the consonant [v] or the vowel [u].

5. Middle English, like Old and Modern English, did not have separate symbols for voiced and unvoiced *þ*. The gradual disuse, first of *ð*, then of *þ*, and their replacement by *th* in all positions, are purely palaeographical matters ; there is no tendency to reserve *ð*, *þ* or *th* for either the voiced or the unvoiced sound.

6. A few orthographical habits evidenced in Middle English are baffling—for instance, the use of *ȝ* for *þ* [1] (especially in XV c. MSS.)— but these normally have no significance for Etymology. Special cases are afforded by :—(i) the pseudo-archaic *Ye* of *Ye Olde Tea Shoppe* and the like, which arose because the letters *þ* and *y* had become indistinguishable [2] ; and (ii) a few words like the personal name *Menzies* (where *z* is in origin a late debased form of *ȝ*, i.e. a type of *g*).

VOWELS AND DIPHTHONGS

Except for their parts in various combinative changes (see immediately below), quantitative changes (p. 128 ff.) and new diphthongising processes (p. 129 ff.), many of the vowels of accented syllables remain unaltered in each dialect in Middle English. The main developments are :—

1. OE *a e i o u ē ī ō ū* normally remain in Middle English. Examples :—ME *asse* (OE *assa*) ; OE, ME *nest* ; OE, ME *þing* ; OE, ME ppart. *holpen* ; OE, ME *ful(l* (but see p. 123 for graphic *o* for *u*) ; OE, ME *fēt*, pl. ; OE, ME *wīf* ; ME *bōk* (OE *bōc*) ; ME *hūs hous* (OE *hūs*).

The following changes, all combinative save the first, should be noted :—

(i) OE *e o* became opened to *ę ǫ* soon after 1200 ; when lengthened in Old English (p. 114) they give *ę̄ ǭ* as against *ę̄ ǭ* when lengthened

---

[1] In manuscripts where this occurs and where (as commonly) two minims can be contextually read as either *n* or *u*, two minims preceded by *ȝy* and followed by *e* can be read either as *ȝyue* ' give ' or as *þyne* ' thine ' !

[2] Those who have had occasion to consult XIV c. MSS. will be aware of the uncertainty of such graphs as *yyᴍe*.

in Middle English (p. 128). This loss of tenseness is of great consequence in the development of new diphthongs (p. 129 ff.).

(ii) OA *e* > WMids *œ* (written *eo*) between *w* and *r*, *l* :—KathGr *tweolf* (< OE *twelf*), *weorre* (lwf. OFrench *werre*). Sporadic instances occur in association with other labials :—KathGr *speonse* (lwf. OFrench *espense*). This *œ*, like *œ* under isolative conditions, later gave *e* (p. 127).

(iii) OE *e* > ME *i* in a large and somewhat ill-defined group of words in many dialects. A few of these words (especially those showing the change before η + consonant) survive into Modern English. Types :—(*a*) between *g*, *ʒ* or *r* and a dental, and before *l* :—*ridel(es)* (OA *rēdels*) PPl, Trevisa ; *togider* (OA *togedere*) Ayen, Chaucer ; sg. pret. *fill* (OE *fĕoll*) Hav, Ayen, Chaucer, etc. ; (*b*) before covered *n* (especially in the North) :—*find* (OE *fĕond*) ; *strinth* (OE *strengþ*)—there are instances in various northern works ; (*c*) before palatals, especially *ηg*, *ηc* : *Inglish Ingland* (OE *englisc Englaland*) first recorded in CM ; *flingen* (N lw. : Ic *flengja*) Arthur and Merlin ; *singen* (OE *seng(e)an*) ; *link* (OE *hlenca*) ; *sik* (OE *sēoc*—now with shortening in the compounds), etc.

(iv) In the West Midlands (but later than KathGr [1]) *ong* (< *óng*, p. 114) > *ung* (cf. *eng* > *ing*, above) :—*tonge* (OE *tunge*) rhymes with *stronge* (to OE *strang*), *longe* (to OE *lang*) Gawain vv. 32, 6. A few instances are found elsewhere (e.g. in Norfolk and Suffolk). From this development Modern English has *among* (OE *on-gemang*), *-monger* (OE *mangere*)—and note the rhymes *young* : *wrong* (Otway), *flung* : *song* (Dryden).

(v) North of the Humber *ǭ* > *ū*, c. 1300, thus *bōk* (OE *bōc*) > *bŭk*, later *buik*.

2. OE *æ* (of any origin) > ME *a* before or about 1100. This affects each word of the *fæt*-type (p. 105) in the areas where Second Fronting did not occur in Old English (i.e. Northumbrian, East Mercian and West Saxon). Further, for instance, OE *næddre* (shortened *ǣ₁*, p. 115) > ME *(n)adder* ; sg. pret. OA *sæh* (p. 111) > ME *sah* ; nap. WMerc *dægas* (p. 105) > ME *daʒhes* ; OE (Essex) **sændan* (p. 109) > ME *sanden*.[2]

---

[1] d'Ardenne, p. 188.

[2] This *a* gradually penetrated to the areas where Second Fronting had occurred so that even they eventually had the type ME *fat* (as against OK and WMerc *fet*)—but later than KathGr and Ayen, respectively.

3. OE $\breve{\alpha}$ ($<$ $\breve{e}o$, p. 116) $>$ $\breve{e}$ everywhere save in the West Midlands, the South-West and Kent in XII c., in the first two of these areas not till the end of XIV c. (before then written eo, or, through Anglo-French influence, o ue u, etc.).[1] Thus *herte*, earlier *heorte horte huerte hurte* (OE *heorte*) ; *dẹp*, earlier *deop duep dup* (OE *dēop*).

4. OE $\breve{\bar{y}}$ appears as (i) $\breve{i}$ in the East Midlands, the North and a limited area in the South-West ; (ii) $\breve{e}$ in Kent and adjacent areas of the South-East—this is, in fact, an Old English change (c. 900)—see p. 110 ; (iii) $\breve{\bar{y}}$ (written u, p. 123) in the West Midlands. Thus :— Orm *sinne* Ayen *zenne* KathGr *sunne* (OE *synn*), Orm *fir* Ayen *uer* KathGr *fur* (OE *fȳr*)[2][3].

5. OE $\bar{a}$ gives (i) $\bar{a}$ in all dialects north of the Humber, later $\bar{e}$ (XIV c.) and (ii) $\bar{\rho}$ in all dialects south of the Humber after 1200 (post-Orm, KathGr)[4][5][6]. Thus Northern *rāp* (*raip rayp*) Orm *rap* Southern *rọp* (Chaucer *rope*) $<$ OE *rāp*.

6. OE $\bar{æ}_1$ ($<$ PrGmc $\bar{e}_1$—only WS) appears as (i) $\bar{e}$ in the Middle English area which corresponds to the West Saxon one ; in addition, some words in ME texts from the West and East Midlands have $\bar{e}$ instead of $\bar{e}$ (below) indicating that in certain conditions this phoneme supplanted $\bar{e}$ in the Old Anglian areas ; (ii) $\bar{e}$, elsewhere.

---

[1] For the Kentish position, see p. 116.

[2] In the West Midlands, before the beginning of XIII c., this $\ddot{u}$ when before [tš]—and probably when before [dž]—gave u (written u o). Evidence for this is found in La₃, RGl, Trevisa and the alliterative poetry of the West Midlands. The following forms have spread to the standard language and survived :—*muchel* (OE *mycel*) $>$ MnE *much* ; *swuch* (OE *swylc*) $>$ MnE *such* ; *thrusche* (OE *prysce*) ; *cudgel* (OE *cycgel*) ; *clucchen* (OE *clyccan*). Similarly, WMids u ($<$ OE y), α ($<$ OE eo) frequently give u in labial surroundings (after labials and s, [tš] or before r, or combinations of these) :—*churche* (LOE *cyrice*) ; *schutte*(*n* (OE *scyttan*) ; *burden* (OE *byrpen*) ; *churl* (OE *ceorl*).

[3] There are a few words with dialectal e in Modern English :—*bury* (OE *byrgan*), *merry* (OE *myrge*), etc.

[4] Early French loan-words show $\bar{a}$ (*dāme*, *rāge*) and ME a is lengthened to $\bar{a}$ not $\bar{\rho}$ (p. 128). It follows that $\bar{a}$ $>$ $\bar{\rho}$ before both the borrowing and the change.

[5] In parts of the Midlands in XIII c., ρ after a consonant $+$ w gave $\bar{\rho}$:—*twọ* (OE nanf. *twā*) ; *swọpen* (OE *swāpan*) ; *whọ* (OE *hwā*). Somewhat later (first evidence in Bokenham, born c. 1392) this occurred also in the suffix -*họde* (OE *hād*), as *childhọde*.

[6] Different developments can be observed in the place-name element *Weald* (WS, OK *wéald* with breaking and lengthening before *ld* to ME $\bar{e}$) and *wold* (OA *wáld*, unbroken, with Midland $ọ$).

Thus (normal development) WS $s\bar{\ae}d$ > Southern ME $s\dot{e}d$; OA, OK $s\bar{e}d$ > ME (Midlands and South-East) $s\dot{e}d$ [1].

7. OE $\bar{\ae}_2$ (< WG ai, by i-umlaut) appears as (i) $\bar{\dot{e}}$ in all ME dialects except Kentish and, towards the end of XV c., this $\bar{\dot{e}}$ > $\bar{e}$; $\bar{\dot{e}}$ in Kent (already in Old English, p. 110). Thus OE $h\bar{\ae}lan$ > ME (except K) $h\bar{\dot{e}}len$ (Orm $h\alpha lenn$) ; OK $h\bar{e}lan$ > MK $h\bar{\dot{e}}len$ (Ayen $hele$)[2][3][4].

8. I may note here that the Middle Kentish diphthongs are difficult and refer the reader to standard treatments such as that in Luick, and J. K. Wallenberg, *The vocabulary of Dan Michel's Ayenbite of Inwyt* (pp. 305–14).

LENGTHENING IN OPEN SYLLABLES

Old English has in common with Modern English the property that the quantity of a vowel does not depend on the nature of the syllable in which it stands. By contrast, from XIII c. (earlier in the North), all short vowels standing in open syllables of dissyllabic words were lengthened in Middle English (earlier and more generally in the case of $a\ e\ o$ than in that of $i\ u$). Detail :—(i) $a\ e\ o$ > $\bar{a}\ \bar{\dot{e}}\ \bar{\dot{o}}$: $n\bar{a}me$ (OE $nama$), $esc\bar{a}pen$ (lwf. OFrench $escaper$), $b\bar{\dot{e}}ren$ (OE $beran$), $pr\bar{\dot{o}}te$ (OE $prote$) ; (ii) $i\ u$ > $\bar{\dot{e}}\ \bar{\dot{o}}$: $w\bar{\dot{e}}ke$ (OE $wicu$), $d\bar{\dot{o}}re$ (OE $duru$). The second change occurred first in Northern dialects in XIV c. and gradually spread southward but it is by no means universal (thus MnE ppart. *driven*, ppart. *written, love, come*, etc.). Other MnE

---

[1] The problems afforded by the spread of $\bar{\dot{e}}$ into the Anglian areas still await elucidation ; no doubt various analogies account for some of the instances and d'Ardenne, p. 191, has pointed out that a group of identical west-saxonisms exist both in Orm and KathGr (Orm $d\alpha dbote$, KathGr $deadbote$), beside $dede$ in each text ; sg. pret. Orm $b\alpha h$, $fl\alpha h$ KathGr $beah$, $fleah$ beside heh in each.

[2] α (for this, for α_1 or for $\bar{\dot{e}}$ of other origin) is seldom written after Orm, being replaced by e.

[3] Other sources of ME $\bar{\dot{e}}$ are OE $\bar{e}a$ (p. 116) and e lengthened in open syllables (below).

[4] $\bar{a}$-forms are found in part of the South-East Midlands (Essex and adjacent counties) in XIII c. for the products of both α_1 and α_2 :—$d\bar{a}de$, $cl\bar{a}ne$, $str\bar{a}t$. Some of these forms are found in XIII c. London documents, others have survived in place-names as *Whipsnade* Beds. (OE $sn\bar{\ae}d$), *Saybridge* Essex (OE $s\bar{\ae}$). A similar development for OE $\bar{a}$ with i-umlaut has already been mentioned (p. 109). Evidence for it is found in documents from and the place-names of Essex, Kent, Sussex, Surrey, the Isle of Wight, Hertfordshire and Bedfordshire :—Vices and Virtues $sanden$, Ayen $dane$ (OE $denu$) ; *Thanet* (*Tanatos* in Bede, c. 732).

words developed from lengthened forms include *weevil, beetle, evil, peel, creek,* Elizabethan *weet* ' to know '.[1] [2]

SHORTENING

Many of the vowels lengthened in Old English before consonant-groups (p. 114) became shortened again in the course of the Middle English period. Chronological indications are elusive but it is generally believed that, at the end of XIV c., lengthened vowels remained only as follows :—

i, o + *mb* : *clīmbe(n, cǭmb* ;

e (not all words), *i, u* + *nd* : *fēnd, fīnde(n, wūnd (wound)* sb. any vowel + *ld* : *chīld, fḛld, ǭld.*[3]

FORMATION OF NEW DIPHTHONGS

The diphthongising processes which began in Old English (p. 117) continue and develop greatly in the Middle English period. A very large number of words is now affected. The largest group contains words with original front *g*, back *g* or *w*, singly between vowels. As in Old English, front *g* vocalised to *i*, back *g* and *w* to *u* ; diphthongs resulted when these merged with preceding vowels. The stages of diphthongisation may be represented as follows :—

OE *ege* : OE *e-ge* [i.e. *e-i̯e*] > EME *ei̯-i̯ə* > *ei̯-ə* : Orm *eʒʒe*.

OE *clawu* : OE *a-wu* [i.e. *a-u̯u*] > EME *au̯-u̯ə* > *au̯-ə* : Orm pl. *clawwess.*

OE *dragan* : OE *a-ga* > EME *a-ʒə* [Orm *draʒhenn*] > ME *a-u̯ə* > *au̯-u̯ə* > *au̯-ə* [Hav *drawen*].

The development " vowel + back *g* > vowel + *w* > diphthong " is thus slower than that of " vowel + *w* > diphthong "—and this difference, together with the fact that diphthongisation occurred earlier after short vowels than after long, is the basis of the division

---

[1] The alternation of lengthened and unlengthened forms in nominal paradigms may be observed in the Modern English products :—ME *sādel* : gs. *sadeles* (MnE *saddle*) ; ME *crādel* (> MnE *cradle*) : gs. *cradeles* ; ME *staf* (> MnE *staff*) : gs. *stāves* (MnE *stave*).

[2] For the purposes of this sound-change, the group *st* apparently " counts as " one consonant—thus ME *rǫsten* (lwf. OFrench *rostir*) ; and a few other common consonant-groups do the same, as consonant + liquid or nasal (e.g. ME *wḛsle* < OE *wesle* ' weasel ').

[3] Our main source of information about quantity in early Middle English is the Ormulum ; the lengthening processes outlined on p. 114 are mostly preserved in it except, for instance, in the groups *nd ng* (*stanndenn, senndenn, brinnǵenn*).

into Groups A and B below. The dividing line is the date of the
Ormulum, assumed to be c. 1200.

Group A. Pre-1200 Diphthongisation

(i) After short vowels.

OE $e + ʒ$ [1] $> ei$:—gs., ds. *weies, weie* (OE *weʒes, weʒe*).

OE $æ + ʒ > ai$:—gs., ds. *daies, daie* (OE *dæʒes, dæʒe*), in OE
æ-area (p. 105).

OE $y + ʒ > üi, ī, ei$ respectively in ME *ü-, i-, e*-areas (p. 127) :—
rüie rīe reie (OE *ryʒe*).

OE $a + w > au$:—*clawe* (OE *clawu*).

OE $eo + w > eu ou$:—*strew(i)en strow(i)en* (OE *streowian*).

The groups OE $i + ʒ, u + w > ī, ū$, respectively :—ME *tīle*
(OE *tiʒele*), ME *foul fowl* (OE *fugol*).

(ii) After long vowels.

OE $ē + ʒ > ei$:—*tweien* (OE *twēʒen*).

OE $ǣ + ʒ > ei$:—*clei* (OE *clǣg*).

OE $ȳ + ʒ > üi, ī, ei$ (p. 127) :—*drüie drīe dreie* (OE *drȳʒe*).

OE $ō + w > ou$:—*flowen* (OE *flōwan*).

OE $ā + w > ou$ in the South, *au* in the North [2] :—*knowen knawen*
(OE *cnāwan*).

OE $ēo + w >$ EMids *eu*, WMids *œu* :—*rewen ruwen* (OE *hrēowan*).

OE $ēo + w$ (with shift of stress) $> ou$:—*trowen* (OE
trēowian).

The OE group $ī + ʒ > ī$:—*Frīdæig* (Chronicle, a. 1129).[3] [4]

Group B. Thirteenth-Century Diphthongisation

(i) Vowel $+ w$.

ME $ī + w > iu$:—*sniwen* (OE *snīwan*).

EMids $ē$ ($<$ OE *ēo*) $+ w > eu$:—sg. pret. EMids *knewe* (OE *cnēow*).

WMids $ǣ$ ($<$ OE *ēo*) $+ w > œu$, later *eu* :—sg. pret. WMids *knuwe
knewe* (OE *cnēow*).

---

[1] In these lists $ʒ$ is used for OE front *g*, and *g* for OE back *g*.

[2] p. 127.

[3] At this point EME *e o* gained open quality (p. 125), becoming *ę ǫ*. Hence
ęi ęi fell together as *ęi* and *ǫu ǫu* as *ǫu*. In a few words containing a labial or *j*,
ǫu may have given *ū* almost at once, e.g. *fǫur, yǫu*.

[4] *ęi* of any origin became *ai* by the end of XIII c.—hence MnE *way, day,
twain, clay*, etc.

ME $\bar{e}$ (< OE $\bar{æ}$ $\bar{e}a$) + w > eu :—*hewen* (OE *hēawan*).

MK $\bar{e}$ (< WG ai, by i-umlaut) + w > eu :—Ayen *lewed* (OK *lēwede*).

MK ie (< OK $\bar{i}o$, cf. p. 128) + w > iu (written *ew eu*) :—Ayen *trewe* (OK *trīowe*).

MK ea + w > eu (? eu or ϱu) : Ayen *ssewy sseawy* (OE *scēawian*).[1]

(ii) Front vowel + back g.

ME e + g > ei :—*pleien* (OE *plegan*).

ME $\bar{e}$ + g > ei :—*neien* (OE *hnǣgan*).

ME $\bar{e}$ + g > ei :—*eie* (OE $\bar{e}(a)ge$).

Midlands $\bar{e}$ (< smoothed $\bar{e}o$, p. 111) > ei :—*lеien* (OE $l\bar{e}(o)gan$).

The groups $\bar{i}$ + g > $\bar{i}$:—*nī(e)n* (OE *nigon*), *stīe* (OE *stīgan*)—Orm has *niȝhenn, stiȝhenn* [2].

(iii) Back vowel + back g.

ME o + g > ϱu : *bowe* (OE *boga*).

ME $\bar{\varrho}$ + g > ϱu :—*bowes* (OE *bōgas*), pl.

ME $\bar{\varrho}$ (< $\bar{a}$) + g > ϱu : *owen*, North *awe(n* (OE *āgan*).

ME a + g > au :—*drawe(n* (OE *dragan*).

The groups $\bar{u}$ + g > $\bar{u}$:—*sów(e* (OE *sugu*), *būen bówen* (OE *būgan*) [3][4][5][6].

Group C. Other Types of Middle English Diphthongisation

(i) Diphthongisation before [ç] and [x].

South of the Humber, in the course of XIII c., a glide-vowel, i, developed between $\breve{e}$ and a following [ç], and a glide-vowel, u, between $\breve{a}$ $\breve{o}$ and a following [x]. Examples :—

ME e + h > eih :—*eighte* (OE *eahta*).

ME $\bar{e}$ + h > eih :—*heigh* (OE $h\bar{e}(a)h$).

ME a + h > auh :—sg. pret. *taughte* (OE *tǽhte*).

ME o + h > ϱuh :—*douhter* (OE *dohtor*).

---

[1] The products of $\bar{i}$ + w and $\bar{e}o$ + w (that is, iu, eu) fell together as iu (written, indifferently, *iw ew iu eu*) c. 1400.

[2] There is a divergent development in the North, for which see Luick § 401.2.

[3] After w, ϱu may already have become $\bar{u}$:—*wówen* (OE *wōgian*).

[4] In the North, $\bar{o}$ + g, o + [x] > $\bar{u}u$ (just as $\bar{o}$ in isolation gave $\bar{u}$). This later gave iu (written *eu ew*) :—nap. *plewes* (OE *plōgas*) to *pleuch* (OE *plōh*).

[5] Vowel + g did not diphthongise in Kent until after 1340 (Ayen *laȝe, ǫȝe,* etc.).

[6] For the later development of these diphthongs, see p. 133.

ME $\bar{\varrho} + h > \varrho uh$:—*dough* (OE *dāg*).

ME $\bar{\varrho} + h > \varrho uh$:—*bough* (OE *bōg*).[1] [2]

(ii) Diphthongisation before [š] and $n(c)t$ $n(c)þ$ $n(g)d$.

(*a*) In certain areas, in the course of XIII c., [aš] [eš] > [aiš] [eiš] :—*waischen* (OE *wascan*), *freisˑh* (OE *fersc*). This is a limited, minor change. Instances of *ai ei* graphs are found, for instance, in the Jesus MS. of the Owl and the Nightingale, in MS. E of Cursor Mundi, Havelok, Oxford MSS. of Wyclif and Peacock, etc. No example survives into Modern English, though Lyly has *threisch* ' to thresh '.

(*b*) Diphthongisation occurred sporadically (mostly in the West, not in the North) before $n(c)t$ $n(c)þ$ $n(g)d$:—*leinten* (OE *lencten*), *streinþe* (OE *strengþ(u*), sg. pret. *dreinte* (OE *drencte*). Examples are found in the Lambeth Homilies, Ancrene Riwle, Laȝamon, Shillingford, etc.

(iii) Diphthongisation or loss of *v*.

In many areas, in Middle English, *v* before certain consonants [3] either (*a*) gave *u* and then formed a diphthong with a preceding vowel (frequently before *k g l*, sometimes before other consonants) :— nap. EME *hav(e)kes* (OE *heafocas*) > *hawkes* (thence sg. *hawk*), similarly *awkward* (N lw (: Ic *ǫfugr*) + OE *-weard*), *Cowley* Oxon. (OE *Cufan* + *lēah* ' glade of Cufa ') ; or (*b*) was lost, with lengthening of the preceding vowel (most commonly before *n*, *r* or dental) :— EME gs., ds. *lovrdes lovrde, lōrdes lōrde* (thence nas. *lord*) ; similarly, *hḗd* (OE *hēafod*), *lādie* (OE *hlǣfdige*), *Daventry* ['deintri] < OE **Dafan* + *trēo* ' tree of **Dafa* ' [4].

(iv) Diphthongisation of $(h)\bar{\varrho}$ $(h)\bar{\varrho}$, $\bar{\varrho}$ $\bar{\varrho}$.

In late XIV c., first in the South-West and then in other areas,

---

[1] ME $i + h$, $u + h$ naturally gave *īh*, *ūh* :—*knīght* (OE *cniht*), *drought* (EME *druȝt* < OE *drŭhþu*).

[2] Except after *a* (and sporadically after *ā*) diphthongisation did not normally occur in the North :—thus pret. *raughte*, but *hēgh*, *doghter*, *dāgh* (beside *daugh*), *bōgh*, etc.

[3] Normally these have been brought together by reason of the syncope of a medial unstressed vowel.

[4] This change seldom occurs in Southern Middle English before *l m n* but is common enough in these positions in the North (especially after a back vowel) :— Northern *crawle(n* (N lw. : Ic *krafla*), *auntir(e* (lwf. OFrench *aventure*) ; note also *pǫure* (> *póure*, p. 133) beside *pǫre* (< *pǫvre*, lwf. OFrench *pǫvre*).

initial $\bar{\varrho}$ $\bar{\varrho}$ (and these after h) gave $\mu\bar{o}$ (written wo-, who-) :—$w\bar{\varrho}n$ (OE $\bar{a}n$), $wh\bar{\varrho}le$ (OE $h\bar{a}l$), $wh\bar{\varrho}re$ (OE $h\bar{o}re$). Modern English retains the pronunciation only in one, but the spelling in $whole$, etc. (cf. also Spenser's $whot$ ' hot ').

Similarly $\bar{\varrho}$ $\bar{\varrho}$ > $\mu\bar{e}$ (written $\zeta e\ ye$), which accounts for the XVII c. by-forms $yerth$ ' earth ', $yerb$ ' herb '. This is by no means a purely Middle English phenomenon, for examples can be found both in Old English and in many Modern English dialects.

LATER DEVELOPMENT OF MIDDLE ENGLISH DIPHTHONGS

1. ME ϱi (of any origin) except before [ç] > ai by the end of XIII c. Thus, MnE way (EME $w\varrho i$), day (EME dai), $play$ (EME $pl\varrho ien$). These were joined by ϱi before [ç] in XV c. (usually written $eigh$) :—MnE $eight$, $weight$, $sleight$, $height$ (with stem-vowel of $high$), $neighbour$, etc.

2. ME ϱi, except before [ç], > $\bar{\imath}$ (from the end of XIII c., but probably there was variation from place to place) :—EME ϱie > ME $\bar{\imath}e$ ' eye '. Similarly ME pl. $b\bar{\varrho}ies$ $b\bar{\imath}es$ ' rings ', $dr\bar{\imath}en$, MnE tie, verb ; fly, verb ; die, verb (N lw. : OSw $d\bar{\varrho}ja$) ; dye, verb ; fly [the insect]. These were joined by ϱi before [ç] probably by the end of XIV c. :—ME $h\varrho igh$ > $h\bar{\imath}e$; similarly, MnE $nigh$, $thigh$ (but $flea$ < OE $fl\bar{e}(a)h$).

3. In late XIV c., ME ϱu > iu, thus falling together with the product of $\bar{\imath}$ + w (both written, indifferently, iw ew after 1400) :— pret. $knew$, $sniwen$; similarly MnE new, $true$ (original ϱu) ; yew, $Tuesday$, $steward$ (original iu).

4. (i) ME ϱu (< OE $\bar{e}ow$ with shift of stress), after labials and [j] (written ζ y) > $\bar{u}$ (p. 131) ; (ii) ϱu (< $\bar{o}$ + w) > ϱu (p. 133) — and remained diphthongal in Middle English ($flowen$, $blowen$, $glowen$, etc.) ; (iii) $\bar{\varrho}uh$ (< $\bar{\varrho}$ + h) > $\bar{u}$ in LME ($b\check{o}ugh$, $pl\check{o}ugh$, $en\check{o}w$) ; (iv) whether ϱu (< ϱu < $\bar{\varrho}$ + g) remained diphthongal throughout Middle English or became $\bar{u}$ is disputed ($bowes$, pl. ; $plowes$ pl., pl. pret. $drowen$) ; but the levelling influence of $\bar{u}$ in the other parts of the paradigm (as in (iii)) must have been powerful.

5. ME ϱu > au, but less generally. There is evidence in XIV c. Kentish (Ayen $snaw$, $zaule$) and in the North-West Midlands (Gawain 394 $trawpe$ < OE $tr\bar{e}owp$). Traces of the change are found before

[x] in the Modern English period, as *daughter* (OE *dohtor*). But the normal development here is for ME *ǫu* to remain (above).

6. In Middle Scots and Northern English of XIV c., the diphthongs *ai oi ui* > *ā ō ū* :—*rāse* (N lw. : Ic *reisa*) ; sg. pres. *mā* (EME *mai*) ; *vōs* (lwf. OFrench *vois*) ; *punt* (lwf. AN *puint*). As a consequence words with etymological *ā ō*, etc. were often written with *ai, oi*, etc. as *hail* ' whole ', *moyne* ' moon '.

7. In the course of XIV c. many diphthongs in French loan-words were monophthongised to a long vowel. Thus (i) *u*-diphthongs were monophthongised (*a*) before labials :—*sāfe* (lwf. OFrench *sauf*) ; *săvage* (lwf. OFrench *sauvage*) ; *rẹ̄me* (lwf. OFrench *reaume*) ; *trīfle* (*ī* < [iu] < OFrench *ū* of *trüfle*) ; (*b*) before [(t)š] [(d)ž] :—*sāge* (lwf. OFrench *sauge*) ; *Bẹ̄cham* (lwf. OFrench *Beauchamp*) ; *sōdiour sōdier* (lwf. OFrench *soudier*). (ii) *i*-diphthongs were monophthongised (*a*) before [š] and [š]-combinations :—*cash(e* (lwf. OFrench *caisse*) ; *busshel* (lwf. OFrench *buissiel boissiel*) ; *cusshin* (lwf. OFrench *cuissin*) ; (*b*) before *s*-groups :—*mastre* (lwf. OFrench *maistre*) ; *buste* (lwf. OFrench *buiste boiste*)—there are but few certain instances. In Norse loan-words :—*bask* (: Ic *beiskr*, Orm *beӡӡsc*) ; *frāstc(n* (: Ic *freista*).

8. About the year 1400, ME *ai* (< ON *æi* = Ic *ei*) before *k* > *ẹ̄* :— *wẹ̄k* (: Ic *veikr*), **blẹ̄k* ' bleak ' (: Ic *bleikr*).

er > ar

From about mid-XIV c. there is evidence, from all areas, of the change *er* + consonant > *ar* + consonant, though the process was probably not completed in the South before XV c. :—*farre* (OE *feorr*), *harte* (OE *heorte*), *starve* (OE *steorfan*), *sarve* (OFrench *servir*). The *e*-spelling (especially in French loan-words and in place-names) was often retained. Out of this situation there come (i) words with *ar* (the largest group) :—*far, heart*, etc. (above) ; (ii) words with *er* preserved in spelling and pronunciation :—*serve, deserve, certain* ; (iii) words with *er* preserved only in the spelling (and dialectally in the pronunciation) :—*Derby, Hertford, clerk, sergeant* ; (iv) doublets :— *person/parson* ; *university/'varsity* [1].

CONSONANTS

The Old English consonantal phonemes remain unaltered in number

---

[1] The present-day comparative stability of these groups is of very recent date. Eighteenth-century novels have plenty of forms such as *fartile, desart*, etc.

in Middle English but a great number of combinative changes
disturb their distribution. I give here an account of the more
important of these.

1. Initial *s* before vowels and *w*, and initial *f* before vowels and
l, *r* (probably also in other voiced surroundings) became voiced
south of the Thames [1] very early in Middle English, at least before
the influx of French loan-words. The same change may have occurred
to initial voiceless *þ* but this cannot be proved because of the
absence of separate graphs for voiced and voiceless *þ*. The new voiced
sounds are clearly seen in the Ayenbite :—*zenne, zuift, uoluelle*
' fulfil ', *uless* ' flesh ', *urend*. French loan-words there have *f, s* :
sauf, substance, folie, flour ' flower ', *frut* [2] [3].

2. Old English aspirated *hw* is for the most part retained in
Southern Middle English (written *wh*) [4]. ONth spirantal [xw]
appears in Northern Middle English texts as *qu qw quh qwh* (Gawain
quen ' when ', *queþer* ' whether ') and there are numerous reverse
spellings (Gawain 877 pl. *whyssynes* ' cushions ' for *qu-* (OFrench
cuissin)). The spirantal graphs also appear in Middle English
texts from the East Midlands (Bestiary *qual* ' whale ').

In the final position, there are occasional early instances (from
c. 1300), especially in the West, of [x] > [x^w] > *f* :—*thurf* (OE
þurh), *dwerf* (OE *dweorg*).

3. *ð* followed immediately by *m, n, l, r* > *d* (usually in inflected
forms, thence introduced into the nominative singular) :—OE ds.
byrþne (ns. *byrþen*) > ME **bürdne*, etc. (whence nas. *burden birden
berden*). Similarly *rudder* (OE *rōþor*), *fiddle* (OE *fiþele*). Doublets
are common :—*fadom/fathom, burden/burthen*, etc.

In XV c., the reverse process occurred when *d* > *ð* before syllabic
r :—*weather* (OE *weder*), *thither* (OE *þider*), *mother* (OE *mōdor*), etc.

---

[1] The extent of the area is uncertain for not all texts have the conveniently
consistent orthography of the Ayenbite. The modern dialects of Kent, Sussex
and Surrey, for instance, no longer retain the voiced sounds (influence of London
speech ?) but the South-West counties (Devon, Somerset, etc.) usually do.

[2] Modern English retains *v* in *vat, vane, vixen* (as against *fox*) from this dialectal
development.

[3] Finally, *-es* became voiced to *-ez -iz* before the loss of final *-e* in XV c. (how
long before is uncertain because *ez iz* are not commonly written before XV c.
MSS.). In words like *once* (OE *ānes*), *else* (OE *elles*), etc., syncope of *e* occurred
earlier and a voiceless *s* results.

[4] Numerous *w*-spellings are no doubt to be explained as due to Anglo-Norman
scribal influence.

4. Voicing of the voiceless spirants *f* and *s* and of [tš] when in unstress occurred during the course of the Middle English period (there is hardly any evidence before XV c.) :—*active* (lwf. OFrench *actif*) ; *knowlege* (< *knowleche*, OE *cnāw-lǣc*) ; *cabage* (lwf. OFrench *caboche*). Note also the doublets *plaintive/plaintiff, of/off*.

In the case of *s* this change is most common in nominal endings (examples at p. 135) and in low-stressed *is, has, does, was, his,* and is not found at all in suffixes :—*goodness, palace, mistress* (yet *Mrs.*).

5. Unvoicing of final consonants is found sporadically in most areas but is very common in the West Midlands (especially, *t* for *d*) :— KathGr *hundret, heauet, grunt-wal,* etc. ; Gawain *bront* ' sword ', *lortschyp, ʒonke pynk* ' young lady ', etc.

6. *sc* > *s* in unstress (mostly Northern) :—ME *Inglis, outlandis, worsip, peris* ; sg. pres. *sal,* pret. *sulde.*

LOSS OF CONSONANTS

b, finally after *m,* c. 1300 (first in the North) :—*lam(b, dum(b* (the latter can now rhyme with *buhsum*). There is at least one similar Old English instance :—OE *ācumba* > *ācuma.*

j before *i* (XIV c.) :—*icchen* (OE *gyccan*), *if* (OE *gif*). The OE prefix *ʒe-* gives *i-* or is lost—Orm has *is'anedd* (v. 1969), *ʒehatenn, unnʒerim,* but otherwise no trace. Note ME *handiwerk* ' handi-work ' (< OE *hand-geweorc*).

k medially in the preterite and past participle of *māken* and in the latter form of *tāken* :—*māde, mād* (whence new infinitive *mā*) ; ppart. *tān* (whence *tā*). As an auxiliary in low stress sg. pret. *macode* > **maʒde* > *maude* (e.g. Hav 436).

l before [tš], finally :—*which* (OE *hwilc*), *s(w)uch* (OE *swylc*). Contrast ME *belchen* ' to belch ', *milce* ' milch '.

n finally as part of an inflexion :—OE *sittan* > ME *sitten* > *sitte.* Also in articles, prepositions and pronouns (in some areas, before 1200) :—*mī(n, a(n, o(n, i(n,* etc.

w initially before *l* weakened in the course of the Middle English period and was lost (Chaucer MSS. still have *wlatsom*). Medially, *w* is frequently lost before *u* :—*suche* (OE *swylc*). Other types of *w*-loss may be observed in the following examples :—*pong* (OE *pwong*), *sō* (OE *swā*), *goddot* ' God knows ' (OE *God wāt*), *ichot* ' I know ' (RGl), *ichulle* ' I will ' (KathGr), *Cantoreburi* (OE *Cantwarabyrig*), *ōse* ' ooze ' (OE *wāse*).

VARIOUS CONDITIONAL CHANGES

Metathesis :—OE *þurh* > ME *þruh* ' through ' ; AR *nēld* (OE *nǣdl nēðl*)[1] ; ME *wordle* (OE *weorold*) Ayen, LambHom, etc.

Sandhi-Forms :—(i) *forr þe nánness* (Orm) (MnE *for the nonce*), cf. OE *for þǣm ānum* ; *atte nale* (Chaucer) ; *nĕke-name* ' nick-name ' (< OE **ēac-nama*) PromptP ; EME *lest(e* < OE *þȳ lǣs þe* ; (ii) ME *addre* < *a naddre* (OE *næddre*) ; ME *apron* (lwf. OFrench *naperon*), ME *umpire* (lwf. OFrench *nonper*).

Assimilation :—*at þēre* > *atter(e* in *Atterbury* Oxon. ; OE *sūþfolc* > MnE *Suffolk* ; OE **lēofman᷄* > ME *lemman*. Orm almost invariably writes *t* for *þ* when it follows *d* or *t* :—*annd tatt, þatt ḡodd tatt*.

Dissimilation :—*hþ* > *kþ* : 3rd sg. pres. *zicþ* Ayen ; *hf* > *kf* : *hekfere* (OE *hēah-fore*) PromptP ; *hþ* > *ht* (mostly XIV c.) :—OE *drūhþ(u, gesihþ(u* > ME *drŏught, sight* ; *lh* > *lk* : OE *eolh* > ME *elk* (first occurrence, 1486).

Inorganic Consonants :—(i) final : ME *hēst* ' behest ' Laȝ AR, etc. (OE *hǣs*) ; *aȝenest* Laȝ (< OE *ongegn* + adverbial *-es*) ; (ii) medial :—EME *empti* AR (< OE *ǣmettig*) ; EME *glistnen* (< OE *glisnian*). Especially in the groups *ml, mr, nl, nr, lr* :—ME *þunder* (OE gs. *þunres*) ; ME *alper- alder-* followed by superl. (OE gp. *ealra*) ; ME *thimbel* (OE gs. *þȳmles*).

MODERN ENGLISH
1500–

[It is with great regret that I have decided that I cannot carry on the History of English Language beyond 1500 in the present book. And I must first point out that my failing to do so will not be as great a handicap to the English etymologist as might at first sight appear ; for, as the Reader will already have realised, the spelling-system of present-day English is, essentially, of Middle English age. It is thus certainly true to say that a knowledge of Middle English phonology is greatly more important to the English etymologist than is a knowledge of Modern English phonology.

But the reason for my not presenting here a Modern English Phonology is quite other. It does seem that Dr. E. J. Dobson's recent great work, *English pronunciation, 1500–1700*, will entirely

---

[1] Note that *neel*, *needle* (monosyllabic) occur in Shakespeare.

revolutionise the views on Modern English hitherto accepted as standard. It is, however, still far too early for this work to have been digested and assessed by the few scholars competent to do this. Under these circumstances I feel it would be wrong—and also most unfair to Dr. Dobson—to force a summary of his book upon the Reader here. Furthermore, that lack of space which has already precluded me from discussing the major changes of Old English would certainly operate even more gravely in the present context.

The Reader interested in Modern English must, then, read Dr. Dobson's work for himself, comparing it with the relevant sections of Luick—an experience which he will find profitable, if traumatic.]

(ix) A note on Morphology

All Indoeuropean words are of the form **PRSE** where :—
   P denotes any number (including zero) of prefixes ;
   R denotes the root ;
   S denotes any number (including zero) of suffixes ;
   E denotes *one* ending, or *no* ending.[1]

Thus, IndE *dom-en-o-s* (> Latin *dominus*) is RS_1S_2E, with root (**R**) *dom-*, two suffixes (S_1 and S_2) *-en-* and *-o-*, and ending (**E**) *-s*. The main outline of the function of a prefix (MnE *happy* : *un-happy*) is well-known ; the root has a general meaning which is made more precise by the suffix(es)—thus *dom-* means, roughly, ' a dwelling-place ', *dom-en-o-* ' he who rules a *dom-* ' ; the ending indicates the syntactical rôle of the word—thus *-s* is " nominative singular ". Further examples :—**R** : 2nd sg. imp. Latin *ī* (< **ei* ; root **ei-*) ; **RS** : 2nd sg. imp. Greek φέρε (< **bher-e*) ; **RE** : Latin as. *pedem* (< **ped-m̥*) ; **RSE** : 3rd sg. pres. Skt *bhárati* ' to bear ' (< **bher- -ti*). An Indoeuropean " word " may now be defined [2] : it is all save the fourth part of the form [P]R[S][E] [3] ; thus *dom-en-o-* and **ped-* are " words ". It is then clear that the conventional use of the term *stem* (*of the word*) lies very close to the concept that I have called *word*, for in **PRSE** it is **RS** that is the stem. Stems are classified

---

[1] Notationally, the form $[P_1P_2 \ldots P_m]R[S_1S_2 \ldots S_n][E]$ (square brackets [ ] indicate the possibility of absence) would thus be more correct.

[2] Cf. my remarks at p. 26.

[3] Save in the rare case (Latin 2nd sg. imp. *ī*) where the form is only **R** and then **R** is the word.

by the suffix, if there is only one suffix, by the last suffix if there is more than one ; thus IndE *u̯l̥k̯ʷ-o- (> Gothic *wulfs*) and Latin *dominus* (< IndE *dom-en-o-s*) are both " o-stems " [1] [2]. Nearly all Indoeuropean words are either nomina (noun-adjectives) or verbs [3] and these great classes are sub-divided by stem into declensions and conjugations respectively. Thus the Latin Second Declension (*lupus*) and the Gothic First Declension (*wulfs*) comprise the o-stems, the Latin First (*mensa*) and the Gothic Second (*giba*) the ā-stems [4]; the Germanic Second Weak Conjugation comprises verbs with suffixes -ā- or -ā-i̯e- and thus corresponds to the Latin First Conjugation.

When I have said—as has already been adumbrated on p. 104— that, in many languages (and especially in Germanic) the development of the vowels (and a little that of the consonants) is altered by their being in unstress, the " ideal " state [5] of the present section will become clear : it should deal with the suffixes, the endings and the phonology of the unstressed syllables. In Germanic, these subjects are somewhat interwoven ; thus, in discussing the morphology of the o-stems, it is convenient to treat the suffix and the ending as one unit (as when we say that IndE -o-m of Latin as. *lupum* vanishes in Gothic as. *wulf*); again, at least in teaching, it is useful to present the development of the unstressed vowels in Germanic as a corollary to the morphology. For the Etymology of English—as for all Etymology—knowledge of the relevant suffixes is of paramount importance ; the history of the

---

[1] Suffixes, too, may of course show ablaut : Greek as. πατέρα, εὐ-πάτορα ; ns. πατήρ, εὐ-πάτωρ ; gp. πατρῶν (Homeric). Hence, for instance, the naming of the o-declension as the " e/o-declension ".

[2] Convention varies as to the citing of words ; nouns are sometimes given in the stem-form, sometimes in that of the nominative singular (thus, in this book, Sanskrit nouns are normally given in stem-form, Latin nouns—as invariably—in that of the nominative singular e.g. Skt *aśva-* ' horse ' = Latin *equus* (p. 88)) ; Sanskrit verbs are usually given as 3rd sg. pres., Greek verbs as 1st sg. pres., Latin and Germanic verbs almost invariably as the infinitive, while in Balto-Slavonic it is usual to vary between the Sanskrit and Greek methods of citation (and often to give both forms).

[3] Many of the remaining words (e.g. adverbs and prepositions) are, by origin, nominal cases ; the pronouns have nominal flexion with certain additional endings.

[4] The nomenclature is confusingly affected by sound-change ; thus IndE o > OBg *a*, IndE *ā* > PrGmc *ō*, so that the IndE o-stems are often called " a-stems " in Slavonic, and the IndE ā-stems, " ō-stems " in Germanic.

[5] Cf., p. 70.

endings and the phonology of the unstressed syllables is, in this case, considerably less important, especially for Modern English Etymology. But, in any case, all three subjects are extremely large and cannot at all be dealt with in this book. They have, however, been exhaustively studied. For the suffixes, the student may be referred to the relevant sections of K. Brugmann, *Kurze vergleichende grammatik der indogermanischen sprachen* ; the same, *Grundriss der vergleichenden grammatik der indogermanischen sprachen* ; and, above all, to the recent new part of J. Wackernagel, *Altindische grammatik* ; for Germanic, we have the excellent work of F. Kluge, *Nominale stammbildungslehre der altgermanischen dialekte* [1]. The morphology is covered by the relevant sections of Brugmann's two great works ; the best general accounts of Germanic morphology are still those to be found in W. Streitberg, *Urgermanische grammatik* and R. C. Boer, *Oergermaansch handboek* (where also the phonology of the unstressed syllables is well set out). For the simpler morphology of later English it will probably be sufficient to refer to H. C. Wyld, *The historical study of the mother tongue.*

---

[1] If the suffix is found in English, reference to the *New English Dictionary* (which enters suffixes as head-words) is very profitable.

CHAPTER THREE

SELECTED ENGLISH ETYMOLOGIES

ALE. The following sets of words are obviously related :—

1) OPR *alu* ' mete '[1] Lith *alùs* ' home-brewed beer ' Lettish *alus* ' beer '.

2) Finnish *olut* ' beer ' Aunus *olud* ' do.' Veps *олид олиź* ' do.' Vatya *olut* ' do.' Estonian *olut* ' do.'.

3) Russian Church Slavonic *olъ* ' σίκερα ' Russian d. *olovina* ' dregs ' Slovene *ọl* ' beer ' S-Cr *olovina* ' a kind of beer ' MnBg *olovina lovina* ' do.'.

4) Ossete *æluton ilæton* ' boiled beer ' Georgian *aludi ludi* ' do.'.

5) OE *ealu* (ds. *ealoþ*) (> MnE **ale**) Ic *ǫl* (cf. *ǫlðr*) MnNorw *øl* OSw *øl* MnSw *öl* ODanish *øl* MnDanish *øl* OS *alo(-fat)* MDutch *āle*.

This word for ' beer ' is normally brought into connection with Latin *alūmen*, etc. It has frequently been suggested that the Balto-Slavonic and Baltic Fennic words are borrowed from Germanic, but the word has here been gravely misconstrued. There is, in fact, nothing against the view that the Baltic, Slavonic and Germanic forms are related and show no inter-borrowing ; the Baltic Fennic forms are, however, borrowings from Baltic, with Baltic Fennic *o* for Baltic *a* as in Finnish *lohi* ' salmon ' Baltic lw. : Lith *lašis* ' do.'. Finnish *olut*, etc. does however entitle us to suppose that a final *-t* once existed in the word in Baltic (cf. OE ds. *ealoþ*), since lost (OPR *alu*). For the germanist, perhaps the main interest of the Caucasian words is that they appear to be borrowings of a lost Gothic **aluþ*[2].

BELIEF < EME *bile(a)ue* < OE *ge-lēafa* (with altered prefix[3]) = OHG *giloubo* (> MHG *g(e)loube* > MnHG *glaube*) OS *gilôbo* MDutch *gelôve* (> MnDutch *geloof*) < PrGmc **galaubōn-*[4].

---

[1] i.e. MnHG *met*.   [2] See further, A. S. C. Ross, *TPS* 1954, pp. 111-5.
[3] Cf. MnE *besiege*, lwf. OFrench *asegier* (> MnFrench *assiéger*).
[4] The corresponding verb *believe* is from EME *bileven* < OA *gelēfan* (= WS

BUDGET [1], lwf. MnFrench *bougette*, diminutive to Latin *bulga* ' leather bag ' (ba. ME *bulge* ' wallet, purse ' [2]). From the frequent use of the word *budget* as a pedlar's or tinker's bag [3] came the—at first—derogatory connotation of the phrase *to open the budget* as in a pamphlet entitled *The Budget opened* which appeared in 1733, in which Sir Robert Walpole, about to present his Excise Bill, is compared to a mountebank opening his wallet of quack medicines and conjuring tricks.

CHEESE < OA *cēse* (< PrE **cēasi* (*i*-umlaut) < **kǣsi* < WG *kāsi*, lwf. (before V c.) Latin *cāseus* [4] (ba. OHG *kâsi* (> MHG *kæse* > MnHG *käse*) OS *kâsi kêsi* MDutch *kâse* (> MnDutch *kaas*) ; OIrish *cáise* ' cheese ' OCornish *cōs* ' do.' Welsh *caws* ' do.' OBreton *cos(-mid)* ' serum ') = OBg *kvasъ* ' sour drink ' Prākrīt *chāsī* ' butter-milk '. If this medial *s* is from IndE dental + *s* [5], then further cognates would be Skt *kváthati* ' to boil' Gothic *hapo*, *hapjan*. IndE **ku̯āt(h)*- is an extension of **ku̯ā-* [6] in, for instance, OE *hwǣg* (> MnE *whey*) MLG *heie hoie* MnDutch *hui* [7].

COBLE. This word is used for two different kinds of boats :—(1) ' a short, flat-bottomed rowing-boat, used in salmon-fishing and for crossing ferries, etc. ' [Scotland] ; (2) ' an open or deckless fishing-boat used principally on the north-east coast, with sharp bows, flat, sloping stern and without a heel ' [Scotland, Northumberland, Durham, Yorkshire and East Anglia] [8]. NED s.v. *Coble* plausibly suggests that this is a British loan-word ; cf. Welsh *ceubal ceubol*

---

geliefan) = OHG *gilouben* (> MnHG *glauben*), etc. < PrGmc **galaubjan-*. The differentiation of the consonant as between the MnE noun and verb (*belief* ∽ *believe*)—we should expect **beleave* noun ∽ *believe* verb, identical in sound—occurred in XVI c., apparently on the model of pairs such as *grief* (lwf. OFrench *grief*) ∽ *grieve* (lwf. OFrench *grever*).

[1] First occurrence 1432.

[2] By XVIII c. the sense ' protuberance ' had developed, hence MnE *bulge*, etc.

[3] E.g. *Winter's Tale* IV.iii.20 (First Folio Facsimile, ed. J. Dover Wilson).

[4] > Sp *queso* It *cacio*.

[5] So H. Pedersen, *Indogermanische Forschungen* v, 37.

[6] Petersson, *Indogermanische Forschungen* xxiii, 388.

[7] The original Germanic word for " cheese " is PrGmc **jūsta-* (> Ic *ostr* MnSw *ost* MnDanish *ost* — MnE d. *oast*, N lw.), ba. Finnish *juusto* ' cheese ': Latin *jūs* (> OFrench *jus* (> MnFrench *jus*, ba. MnE *juice*) Lith *jūšė* ' thin soup ' OBg *jucha* ' soup ' (MnHG *jauche* is a Slavonic loan) Skt *yūṣ yūṣán-* ' soup '.

[8] J. Wright, *The English Dialect dictionary*, s.v. *coble* sb[1].

Breton *caubal*, both meaning ' some kind of boat '. Two glosses in the Lindisfarne Gospels are of interest here : at J 6, 22 ' nauicula ' is glossed *floege l lyttel scipp* and, at Mt 8, 23, ' in nauicula ' is glossed *in lytlum scipe l in cuople*. *Floege* is a Scandinavian loan-word and it may reasonably be suggested that it is used in this passage in the sense of the corresponding MnNorw word *åfløy* ' river-ferry-boat '. This further suggests that *in* . . . *cuople* also means ' in a ferry-boat ' ; if we emend *cuople* to **couple*, this **coupel* could well be the PrBritish parent of Welsh *ceubol*. And we know that, in Old Welsh, one of the meanings of the word was certainly ' river-ferry-boat ' ; in the Laws " three things . . . defend a person from a summons to pleadings " ; one of them is *llif yn auon heb pont aheb keubal* ' flood in a river without bridge and without *keubal* ' [1]. In the Book of Llandâf we read [2] of a place " coupalua super ripam taf " ; *coupalua* is *coupal* + *ma* ' place ' so that this was a place for ferrying across the river (the name still survives as a place-name in Wales e.g. *Cabalva* Breconshire).

The Celtic word (Welsh *ceubol*, etc.) is, in all probability, a borrowing from Latin ; cf. Latin *caupulus caupillus caupilus* ' little boat ' (> Prov *caupol* Sp *copano*). But there seems to be no Indo-european etymology for this Latin word. It may possibly be of Semitic origin ; cf. Arabic *quff-at-un* ' tarred basket used at Basrah as a boat ' ; (a picture of the modern *guffa* as used on the Tigris will be found in Meissner, *Babylonien und Assyrien* i, 251 and, at p. 179 of L. W. King's *History of Babylon*, a bas-relief in the British Museum showing its Assyrian prototype is depicted). In order to explain Latin *caup-*, we should have to assume that the word reached Latin, not directly from Arabic, but via East Syriac, which has a *p* in such positions—hence **qup* ; and, further, that Semitic *qu* (with back *q*) was heard, by lautersatz, as [kau], which is, phonetically, very plausible.[3]

CROSS, together with its derivatives *cross*, verb and adj., is, ultimately, from Latin *crux*, as. *crucem*, in several forms :—

1) OE *cros*, lwf. OIrish *cros* ' cross ', or N lw. (: Ic *kross*, lwf. Latin *crux*), the dominant, surviving form.

---

[1] A. W. Wade-Evans, *Welsh medieval Law*, pp. 138, 280.
[2] Edition of J. G. Evans and J. Rhys, p. 151.
[3] See further, A. S. C. Ross, *LSE* iv, 77–8 and *TPS* 1940, pp. 41–2.

2) LOE *crūc*, lwf. Latin as. *crucem* (ba. OHG *krûzi* (> MHG *kriuze* > MnHG *kreuz*) OS *krûce(-wika)* MDutch *crûce* (> MnDutch *kruis*) OFr *kriôze*). This LOE form descends as ME *cruche* ' cross, sign of the Cross ' and survives in MnE *Crouchmas* ' festival of the Invention of the Cross, observed on May 3 ' ; MnE *Crutched*, *Crouched* (or *Crossed*) *Friars*, a minor order of friars so called from their bearing or wearing a cross.

3) ME, EMnE *crois croix* (lwf. OFrench *crois* < Latin as. *crucem*). Derivatives include ME, EMnE *croise(n* (lwf. OFrench *cruisier croisier*) (*a*) ' to mark with the sign of the Cross ', (*b*) ' to crucify ' ; EMnE *croisee* (lwf. OFrench *croisée*) ' crusade '.

4) The later Norse form to Ic *kross* MnNorw *kross* (MnSw *kors* MnDanish *kors*) is found, for instance, in Scotch and Northern proper names (*Corserig, Corstorphine*) and dialects.

It has been suggested [1] that Latin *crux* is a Punic (i.e. Phoenician) loan-word. If it is not, then its Indoeuropean cognates would include OHG *hrucki* (> MnHG *rücken*) OS *hruggi(-bên)* OE *hrycg* (> MnE *ridge*) < PrGmc *xruʒja-* (IndE *kru-k-*) and ablaut variants would then be Ic *hrúga* ' heap ' MIrish *crúach* ' pile, hillock ' Welsh *crûg* ' heap, barrow ' Cornish *cruc* ' hill ' Breton *krug* ' hillock ' < IndE *krō-k-* ; (Lith *kriauklas* ' rib ' Skt *kruñcati* ' to bend, curve ' < IndE *kreu-k-*).

CUD. Old English has three main forms : *cwidu, cweodu, c(w)udu*, all of which survive into later English, the first as MnE *quid*, the second as ME *quẹde*, the third as MnE *cud*. The word also exists in High German : OHG *kuti* MHG *küt(e* MnHG *kitt kitte küt kütt kütte köt köte* ; there are also a variety of forms in Plattdeutsch, mostly with *tt* (thus presumably High German loan-words) but there is also a form *köde*, apparently with unshifted *d* (cf. p. 98 ff.) [2]. All the Germanic forms may safely, despite the difficulties of the phonology, be derived from a PrGmc *kweđu- < IndE *gʷetu- > Skt *játu-* ' lacquer, gum ' ; cf. Latin *bitūmen* (Oscan-Umbrian loan)—further Latin *betulla betula* (Gaulish loan) MIrish *beith* ' buxus ' Welsh *bedw(en)* ' poplar ' Cornish *bedewen* ' do.' Breton *bezvenn* ' birch ' [3].

---

[1] So A. Ernout and A. Meillet, *Dictionnaire étymologique de la langue latine* s.v.

[2] MnSw *kitt* MnDanish *kit* Polish *kit* ' putty ' Czech *kyt* ' do.' Estonian *kitt* ' do.' are all loan-words from High German.

[3] See further A. S. C. Ross, *TPS* 1954, pp. 94–6.

DEVIL < OE *dīofol dēofol* < PrE **diubul*, an early continental loan-word from Latin *diabolus* Greek διάβολος. This word was adopted into each of the Germanic languages (with lautersatz *iu* for *ia* in West Germanic) : Gothic *diabaúlus* OHG *tiufal* (> MHG *tiuvel* > MnHG *teufel*) OS *diubal* MDutch *dûvel* (> MnDutch *duivel*) OFr *diôvel* Ic *djǫfull* MnSw *djävul* MnDanish *djævel*. The use of Greek διάβολος in the meaning ' Satan ' is a specific application of the same word in the meaning ' accuser, slanderer ' (to διαβάλλω ' to slander ').[1] [2]

DIAMOND < ME *diama(u)nt*, lwf. OFrench *diamant* = Prov *diaman* ' diamond ' Sp *diamante* Port *diamante* It *diamante* < LLatin **adiamantem*, an alteration of Latin *adamas* (as. *adamantem*) or of its secondary form *adimantem* (> OFrench *aïmant*, ba. Ayen *aymont*), apparently under the influence of Greek διά. Latin *adamas* ' (i) the hardest metal, adamant ' ; (ii) ' diamond ' (cf. Greek ἀδάμας ' the unconquerable ; the hardest metal [i.e. probably, steel] ; diamond ') developed the sense ' loadstone ' in late Latin. In all languages where it was adopted OFrench *diamant* became restricted to the precious stone. In English *adamant* was in use in both the senses ' loadstone ' and ' diamond ' as late as XVII c.[3]

DOUGH < OE *dāg* = Gothic *daigs* Ic *deig* MnSw *deg* MnDanish *dej* OHG *teic* (> MHG *teic* > MnHG *teig*) MLG *dêch* MDutch *dêch* (> MnDutch *deeg*) < PrGmc **đaiʒa-* to IndE **dheiĝh-* ' to smear, knead, mould ' as in Gothic *digan* Latin *fingo, figulus, figūra* Oscan ap. *feíhúss* ' wall ' Greek τεῖχος Russian *dezha* Skt *deha-* (m. and n.) ' body ' Av *pairi-daēza-* ' enclosure '[4] " Tocharian A " *tseke* ' carving '[5] [6].

---

[1] The Hebrew of the Old Testament has *ṣāṭān*, in the Vulgate *diabolus* is normal.

[2] OE *dēo-* of *dēofol* should have given MnE [di:]- (thus the word should have rhymed with *evil*) but there was shortening at an early date to *de-* (hence the modern pronunciation), sometimes to *di-* (hence MnE dial. *divvle*).

[3] See further *NED* s.v. *Adamant*.

[4] Iranian loan :— Greek παράδεισος, ba. Latin *paradīsus*, ba. OFrench *paradis*, ba. E *paradise*.

[5] The same root appears in OE *hlǣfdige* (> MnE *lady*), originally ' loaf-kneader '.

[6] MnE (*plum-*)*duff* is the same word with final [f] instead of zero. .

F

EVIL < ME *ifel* (> *ēvel* in the open syllable [1]) < OE *yfel* = Gothic *ubils* OHG *ubil* (> MHG *übel* > MnHG *übel*) OS *ubil* MDutch *evel* (> MnDutch *euvel*) OFr *evel* < PrGmc **ubila/ō-* < IndE **upélo/ā-* (: OIrish *fel* ' bad ') or to IndE **upó-* ' under ' (Skt *úpa* ' to, at, with, etc.' Greek *ὑπό* Latin *s-ub* OIrish *fo* ' under ' Gothic *uf*, etc.) + IndE suffix *-elo-* [2].

FLAN FLAWN is a borrowing of OFrench *flaon* (> MnFrench *flan*) existing elsewhere in Romance :—OLombard *fiaon* ' kind of Easter-cake ' Abruzzi d. *fiadonę felatonę* ' do.' "altunterengadinisch" *fladun* (*da meil*) ' honey-comb ' Prov *flauzon* ' kind of cake with curd-filling ' Catalan *flahó* ' do.' (ba. Sp *flaon* [3]), representing LLatin as. *fladōnem* (ba. ME *flathon*) ; this is of Germanic origin : MnNorw *flade flae* MnSw d. *flada flade* OHG *flado* (> MHG *vlade* > MnHG *flade*) OS *flaðo* MLG *vlāde* MDutch *vlāde* (> MnDutch *vlade vla*) MnE *flathe* < PrGmc **fladu-* = Skt *pŗthú-* ' wide, broad, spacious ' Av *pərəθu-* ' do.' Greek *πλατύς*.

FURROW < OE *furh* [4] = OHG *furh* (> MHG *vurch* > MnHG *furche*) MLG *vore* MnDutch *voor* Ic *for* MnNorw *for* MnSw *fåra* MnDanish *fure* < PrGmc **furx-* < IndE **pṛk̂-* (cf. Latin *porca* Arm *herk* ' newly-ploughed land ' OIrish (*et-*)*rech* ' furrow ' Welsh *rhŷch* ' do.' OBreton *rec* ' sulco ')[5].

GINGER [6] < ME *ginger* [7], lwf. OFrench *gimgibre*, etc. (> MnFrench *gingembre* [8]) ; ba. OHG *gingibero gingiber* ∞ *ingúber* (> MHG *gingebere* ∞ *ingeber, ingewer* (> MnHG *ingwer*, dial. *ginfer*

---

[1] p. 128.

[2] The word is not found in Scandinavian where the corresponding word is Ic *illr*, etc. (ba. ME *ill* > MnE *ill*) of disputed origin.

[3] ba. " logudoresisch " *fraone* ' do.' Calabrian *fragune* ' do.'.

[4] Cf. also the derivative *furlong*.

[5] This group is now usually linked with the derivatives of IndE **perk̂-* ' to root up ', as Latin *porcus* Greek *πόρκος* Lith *pra-paršas* ' grave ', also PrGmc **farxa-* > OE *fearh* (> MnE *farrow*) OHG *farah*, diminutive *farhili* (> MHG *verhelīn* > MnHG *ferkel*), etc.

[6] Unless otherwise stated the meaning of any word cited is ' ginger ' or ' some kind of ginger ' (cf. the " meaning-rules " on p. 37).

[7] ba. MIrish *sinnsar* MnIrish *gingsear* Scots Gaelic *dinnsear* Welsh *sinsir*.

[8] ba. Breton *gingemmbre*.

imber [1])) MLG *gingeber* ∞ *ingever* [2] (> Plattdeutsch *gemware* ∞ *engeber*) MDutch *gengber*, etc. (> MnDutch *gember*) Frisian *gingber-wirtel*)) [3] < Latin *zingiberi zingiber* (> It *zenzero* [4], etc.

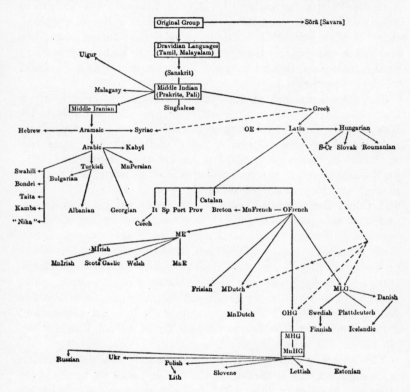

Sp *jengibre* Port *gengivre* Prov *gengibre*, etc. Catalan *gingibre* ; ba. OE *gingifer gingifere* and Hungarian *gyömbér*, etc.[5]) lwf. Greek ζιγγίβερις (> MnGreek ζεγγίβερις) lwf. Pali *singivera-* lwf. [Originating Group]—see below. Skt *śṛngávera-* (> Prakrit *siṃgabera-* Singhalese *iṅguru*) is by analogy with Skt *śṛnga-* ' horn '—

---

[1] ba. Russian *inbir'* Ukr *imber* Polish *imbier imbir* (ba. Lith *imberas*) Slovene *imber* ; Lettish *ingwers* ; Estonian *ingver*.

[2] ba. MnSw *ingefära* (ba. Finnish *inkivääri*) MnDanish *ingefær* (ba. MnIc *ingifer*).

[3] These Germanic forms have, in part, been influenced by Latin.

[4] ba. Czech *zázvor*.

[5] ba. Slovak *d'umbier* S-Cr *dùmbir* ; Roumanian *ghimber*.

an analogy natural enough in view of the horny, wrinkled appearance of the ginger-rhizome. It is from Middle Indian that the Middle Iranian forms derive [1] e.g. Pahlavi *sngypyl* and Sogdian *snkrpyl*. Arm *sngrvēl* is a borrowing of a Middle Iranian form, so also is Aramaic *zanghĕbhīl* ; this latter form is borrowed as Syriac *zenīghber*, etc.[2] Hebrew *zanghĕbhūl* [3] Arabic *zanjabīl* (ba. Turkish *zencefil* [4] ; MnPersian *zanjabīl* ; Georgian *ǰanǰapʻili* ; Kabyl *skenjebbir* ; Swahili *tangawizi* Bondei *sangaizi* Taita *tangaisi* Kamba *tangaisi* " Nika " *tanga(w)izi*).

The second element of the type Pali *singivera-* is certainly a Dravidian word meaning ' root ' : Tamil *vēr* Malayalam *vēr* Kanarese *bēr* Tuḷu *bēru* Telugu *vēru*. The first element, too, *singi-*, is a loan-word from Dravidian (cf. Tamil *iñji* Malayalam *iñci* < *cingi or *śingi or *singi), or just possibly, Munda (cf. Sōrā [or Savara] *siŋ(er)*). It seems probable that the word for " ginger ", in some such form as the proto-Tamil one given above, reached India and China from South-East Asia, for many of the languages of and near this part of the world have similar-sounding words for " ginger ". To this " originating group " (as I have called it above) there belong, for instance, Manipurī *śiṅ* Khasi *s'iṅ* Burmese *khyaṅ* (pronounced [džin]) Shān *khiṅ* Siamese *khiṅ* Chinese (Mandarin) *kiang* (< *ḳiang*)[5] Palaung *śi-āṅg* Khmer *khñi* Annamite *gừ'ng* Luśēi *sə̀'-tʻiṅ* Haka *aĭ-tiṅ* Thādo *tiṅ* Khyang *(ă-)tʻēn* Minbu *tʻēṅ* Lakher *ia-śaṅ* Shendu *ă-tsain* Khami *kɟ-sīn* Rengmā *gă-sen* Gārō *e'-tśiṅ* Dīmāsā *ha-dźiṅ* Tipura *hăĭ-tśiṅ* Morān *hăĭ-teṅ* Rawang *luṅ-ziṅ* Lhōtā *-saṅ, -sāṅ* Rong *hiṅ* [6].

The above etymology [7] is so complicated that diagrammatic representation may be useful ; in the diagram only the names of the languages are given ; lines with arrows on them —————→ denote borrowing, lines without arrows ————— simple descent, dotted lines with arrows - - - - - - -→ " extra influencing ".

---

[1] As do also (i) Uigur *singir*, (ii) Malagasy *śakavīru*.

[2] Many of the Syriac forms are influenced by Greek.

[3] Hence the modern surname *Zangwill*.

[4] ba. Albanian *zenxhefill* MnBg *zhindzhifil*.

[5] ba. Japanese *kiō* (*kiau*)—hence, perhaps, with " nigori ", *shō-ga* ' green ginger ' (cf. *shō* ' to live ; raw, natural, fresh ') and *hoshi-ga* ' dried ginger ' (cf. *hoshi-gaki* ' dried persimmon ' to *kaki* ' persimmon ').

[6] Very many of these forms are due to the kindness of Dr. R. Shafer.

[7] See further A. S. C. Ross, *Ginger*, pp. 15-22.

HEAD. There are several developments and subsidiary points which require notice :—

1) MnE *head* < OE *hēafod* [1], a common-Germanic word :—OFr *hâved hâfd hâud* OS *hôbid* (> MLG *hôvet*) MDutch *hôvet* (> MnDutch *hoofd*) OHG *houbit* (> MHG *houbet* > MnHG *haupt*) MnSw *huvud* Gothic *haubiþ* < PrGmc *xaubuda-, *xaubida- < IndE *kauput-, *kaupet-.

2) The correspondence with Latin *caput* is now generally explained by assuming a second stem represented by OE *hafud-* Ic *hǫfuð* MnDanish *hoved* beside Latin *caput* Skt *kapucchala-* ' hair at the back of the head ' < IndE *kaput-. Forms with -*l*-suffix include OE *hafola* Skt *kapāla-* ' skull '.

3) Beside IndE *kap- there existed a second root, *keup-, represented, for instance, by Greek κύπελλον ' drinking-vessel ' Latin *cūpa* ' tun, cask ' [2]; OE *hȳf* (> MnE *hive*) ; Ic *húfr* ' ship's hull '.

HENGEST [3] = OE *hengest* ' stallion ' = OHG *hengist* (> MHG *heng(e)st* > MnHG *hengst*) MLG *hengest hingest* MDutch *henxt* (> MnDutch *hengst*) OFr *hangst hengst* < PrGmc *xangist- ; Ic *hestr* MnNorw *hest* OSw *hæster* MnSw *häst* ODanish *hæst* MnDanish *hest* < PrGmc *xanxist-. *xanxist-, *xangist- are superlatives to Lith *šankùs* ' clever ' < IndE *k̑ənku- [4]; the basic meaning is ' jump ', cf. Lith *šankínti* ' to make a horse jump ', *šokti* ' to jump, dance ' Greek κηκίω.

HIDE ' skin [of an animal] ' < OE *hȳd* = Ic *húð* MnSw *hud* MnDanish *hud* OHG *hût* (> MHG *hût* > MnHG *haut*) OS *hûd* MDutch *hût* (> MnDutch *huid*) OFr *hêd* < PrGmc *xūdi- to IndE *keut-, as in Latin *cutis* Greek κύτος Lith *kiautaî* pl. ' husks ', *kutỹs* ' bag, pouch ' Welsh *cwd* ' scrotum '; IndE *s-keut- [5] appears in Latin *scūtum* Greek σκῦτος [6].

---

[1] With loss of medial [v].

[2] A semantic development ' cup ' > ' head ' (cf. MnFrench *tête* < Latin *testa* ' pot, vessel ') is shown in MnHG *kopf* ' head ' < MHG *kopf* ' do.' < OHG *kopf* ' cup ', lwf. Latin *cuppa* (ba. OE *cuppe* (> MnE *cup*), Ic *koppr*), a by-form of *cūpa*.

[3] The famous Anglo-Saxon personal name.

[4] Without, respectively, with Verner's Law.

[5] Of the two words homonymous with the one discussed, *hide* ' a measure of land ' (< OE *hīd* < *hīgid* to *hīg- hīw-* ' household, family ') is not etymologically related, whereas *hide*, verb, (< OE *hȳdan* < PrGmc *xūdjan-) probably is.

[6] Cf. p. 77.

LAST. There are several different homonyms of different etymology :—

(1) noun, ' shoe-maker's last ' < OE *lāst* ' footstep '[1], *læst(e* ' shoe-maker's last ' = Gothic *laists* Ic *leistr* MnSw *läst* MnDanish *læst* OHG *leist* (> MHG *leist* > MnHG *leist*) < PrGmc **laisti-*, to IndE **leis-* + suffix *-ti-* ; the same root appears in OHG (*wagan-*) *leisa* OS (*wagan-*) *lêsa* MHG *leise* MnHG *geleise*.

(2) noun, ' measure of weight (varying according to type of goods and locality) as a ' *last* of herrings ' < OE *hlæst* ' load, burden '[2] = OHG *hlast* (> MHG *last* > MnHG *last*) MLG *last* MDutch *last* (> MnDutch *last*) OFr *hlêst* < IndE **kləd(h)sto-, kləd(h)sti-*.

(3) noun, obsolete, from Anglo-Latin *lastum*, *lestum* (Doomsday Book *lest*) ' an administrative district (or the corresponding assembly) in Kent '—thus exactly equivalent in sense to OE *læþ* (> MnE *lathe*).

(4) adj., adv. and noun, ' following all others ' < OE *latost*, sup. of OE *læt* adj., *late* adv.

(5) verb, < OE *læstan* (related to (1) above) = Gothic *laistjan* OHG *leisten* (> MHG *leisten* > MnHG *leisten*) OS *lêstian* OFr *lâsta lêsta* < PrGmc **laistjan-*[3].

LEW[4] ' warm ' < OE (*ge*)*hlēow* = (1) Ic *hlær hlýr* < PrGmc **xlēwja/ō-* ; (2) OHG *lâo*, gsmn. *lâwes* (> MHG *lâ*, gsmn. *lâwes* > MnHG *lau*) MLG *law* MDutch *laeu* (> MnDutch *lauw*) EMnDanish *laa* < PrGmc **xlēwa/ō-*. PrGmc **xlewa-* in ON *HlewagastiR* (on the Gallehus Horn)[5] Ic *hlé* MnSw *lä* MnDanish *læ* OS *hleo* (> MLG *lê* (ba. MnHG *lee*)) MnDutch *lij* OFr *hlî* OE *hlēo(w* (> MnE *lee*, reinforced in form and in the nautical sense by Scandinavian influence (: Ic *hlé*)). Non-Germanic cognates include Latin *calor, caleo, calidus* Skt *śarád-* ' autumn ' Lith *šìlti* ' to become warm ' Welsh *clyd* ' warm '[6].

---

[1] This sense survives in English until 1500 (*NED* s.v.).

[2] Last recorded by *NED* s.v. *Last*, sb.², in a general sense in 1399.

[3] Obsolete homonyms include *last* noun ' vice, fault ' (recorded c. 1175–1380) (N lw. : Ic *lǫstr* < PrGmc **laxstu-*) and the corresponding verb meaning ' to blaspheme, blame ' (: Ic *lasta*) recorded in a small group of texts of XIII c.

[4] A dialect word.   [5] Finnish *levo* ' roof ' is an Old Norse loan.

[6] The relationship between *lew* and *luke(warm)* is disputed ; it has been assumed that [k] of Ayen *lheuc* (> MnE *luke-*) is an adjectival diminutive suffix added to the descendant of OE *hlēow*, or, again, that MnE *luke-* is related to MnDutch *leuk* (this last view is, however, rejected by *NED* s.v. *Luke* a.).

LOOSE < ME *lōs*, N lw. (: Ic *lauss* MnSw *lös* MnDanish *løs* ' unfixed, unrestrained ') = OE *lēas* ' false, feigned, untrue ' (this sense is restricted to Old English among the Germanic languages [1]) MnE *leasing* and also suffix *-less* ; OFr *lás* OS *lôs* OHG *lôs* (> MHG *lôs* > MnHG *los*) Gothic *laus* < PrGmc **lausa/ō-* (ablaut variants IndE **leus-* : OE *for-lēosan* (> MnE *lose*), etc. ; IndE **lus-* : MnDutch *los* ' loose ') ; IndE **leus-* is an extension of **leu-* found, for instance, in Greek λύω Latin *soluo* (< **se-luō*), *luo* Skt *lunáti* ' to cut, sever '.

MONEY < ME *moneie*, lwf. OFrench *moneie monoie monnoie* (> MnFrench *monnaie*) < Latin *monēta*, originally the epithet of a goddess (in classical times regarded as identical with Juno) in whose temple at Rome money was coined ; by transference, ' a place for coining money, a mint '. Latin *monēta* is represented in the Romance languages by It *moneta* Prov *moneda* ' coin, money ' Catalan *moneda* ' do.' Sp *moneda* Port *moeda*. When it was adopted from Vulgar Latin into Germanic the word underwent the normal shift of stress to **múnīta*, whence OE *mynet* (> MnE *mint*) OHG *muniza* (> MnHG *münze*) OS *munita* (> MLG *munte monte*) MnDutch *munt* OFr *menote mente* [2].

MORGANATIC is to be explained from an old Germanic marriage-custom. From the first element of the Germanic word attested by OE *morgen-giefu* ' morning-gift, a gift (of money or property) made by the husband to the wife on the morning after the consummation of the marriage ', the Latin phrase *matrimonium ad morganaticam* was formed (whence the head-word), with reference to a marriage in which the wife (and any children) have no claim to any posses sions or dignities of her husband except the morning-gift.[3]

MOSS < OE *mos* ' bog ' = OHG *mos* ' bog, moss ' (> MHG *mos* ' do.' > MnHG *moos* ' do.') MnDanish *mos* ' moss ' MLG *mos* ' moss ' [4]

---

[1] See J. R. R. Tolkien, " Middle English ' Losenger ' ", *Bibliothèque de la Faculté de Philosophie et Lettres de l'Université de Liège*, Fascicule CXXIX.

[2] MnE *monetary* (first recorded early XIX c.) is a direct borrowing of Latin *monētārius*.

[3] OE *morgen* (> MnE *morn(ing)*— *-ing* on the model of *evening*) = OHG *morgan* (> MHG *morgen* MnHG *morgen*) OS *morgan* MnDutch *morgen* ; Ic *morginn* MnSw *morgon* MnDanish *morgen* ; Gothic *maúrgins*, etc.

[4] ba. MnFrench *mousse* ' moss '.

MDutch *mos* ' bog, moss ' < PrGmc **mosa-* ; cf. Ic *mosi* ' bog, moss ' MnDanish *mose* ' bog ' < PrGmc **mosan-*. The Germanic ablaut **meosa-* appears in OE *mēos* (> MnE dial. *meese*) OHG *mios* (> MHG *mies*) ; cf. also OIc *mýrr* (MnE *mire*, N lw.). Cf., further, OBg *mъchъ* ' moss ' Lith *mūsai* ' mould ' Latin *muscus* ' moss '.

MOUSE < OE *mūs* (pl. *mȳs* > MnE *mice*) = Ic *mús* MnSw *mus* MnDanish *mus* OHG *mûs* (> MHG *mûs* > MnHG *maus*) OS *mûs* MnDutch *muis* Latin *mūs* Greek *μῦς* Skt *mūṣ-* ' mouse ' Albanian *mī* ' do.' OBg *myšь* ' do.' (cf. also MnPersian *mūš* ' do.' Arm *mukn* ' do.') < IndE **mūs-* (root-stem). OHG *mûs* (> MHG *mûs*) OE *mūs* have an additional sense viz. ' muscle ', apparently from the resemblance of certain muscles to the form of a mouse or from the fact that flexing a muscle can give the appearance of something running under the skin ; cf., here, Greek *μῦς* ' muscle ', *μυών* ' cluster of muscles ' Latin *musculus* OBg *myšьca* ' βραχίων ' Arm *mukn* ' muscle ' Skt *muškά-* ' testicle ' (see **MUSK**, below) [1] [2].

MUSK ' odoriferous, reddish-brown substance, secreted in a gland or sac by the male musk-deer ' [3], lwf. OFrench *musc* [4] = Prov *musc* ' musk ' Sp *musco* It *musco muschio* < LLatin *muscus* [5] *mosc(h)us* ; cf. LGreek *μόσχος μόσκος* lwf. Persian *mušk* ' beaver's cod, etc.' (cf. Skt *muškά-* ' testicle ', above).[6]

OOZE < OE *wāse* = Ic *veisa*, < PrGmc **waesōn-*. With these words it is possible to relate OS *Wisura* ' the Weser ' and, further, Latin *uīrus* Greek *ἰός* MIrish *fī* ' poison, poisonous ' Skt *viṣá-* ' poison ' *viṣ-* ' faeces ' *veṣati* ' to melt ' Av *vaēsa-* ' rotting ' " Tocharian A " *wäs* ' poison '. PrGmc **wīsk-* in OE *wīsc(e* ' piece

---

[1] MnE *muscle* (first recorded in 1533) MnHG *muskel* MnDutch *muskel* MnSw *muskel* MnDanish *muskel* are all comparatively recent adoptions of Latin *musculus* (> MnFrench *muscle* It *muscolo*, etc.).

[2] MnE *mussel* (cf. MnHG *muschel* MnDutch *mossel*, etc.) < OE *muscle*, lwf. monastic LLatin *muscula* (> OFrench *mouscle* > MnFrench *moule*) < Latin *musculus*.

[3] So *NED* (first recorded 1398).

[4] First recorded XIV c.

[5] In Tertullian (c. 160–c. 240 A.D.).

[6] LLatin *moschus* ba. EMnHG *moschus* (first recorded XVII c.), MnDanish *moskus muskus*.

of marshy meadow ' (> MnE dial. *wish*) ; cf., also, (without *k*)
OHG *wisa* (> MHG *wise* > MnHG *wiese*) [1].

OYSTER lwf. OFrench *oistre* (*h*)*uistre* (> MnFrench *huître*) = Sp
ostra Port *ostra* (cf. It *ostrica*) < Latin *ostrea ostreum*, lwf. Greek
ὄστρεον. The shell-fish was originally named from its shell, as is
shown by Greek ὄστρακον ' the hard shell of testacea, as snails,
tortoises, etc. ; potsherd ' ὀστέον ' bone ' Skt *ásthi* ' do.' Av
ast- asti- ' do.' Latin *os* (cf., also, Welsh *asgwrn* ' do.') < IndE
*ost(h)-.[2]

READY [3] < OE *geræde* + ME suffix *-iȝ -y* < PrGmc **raiđja/ō-*
to IndE **rei-dh-*. The Germanic cognates (some with altered prefix)
include Gothic *garaiþs* Ic (*g*)*reiðr* (ME *graiþ greith*, N lw.) OHG
reiti MHG *bereite gereit*(*e* MnHG *bereit* MDutch *bereit gerêt* (>
MnDutch *bereid gereed*) OFr *rêde* ; cf., further, Lettish *raids* ' ready '
MIrish *réid* (< **reidhi-*) ' level, smooth ' (originally ' navigable ')
Welsh *rhwydd* ' free, easy ; ready ' (originally ' ready for a
journey ').

ROOT < LOE *rōt*, N lw. (: Ic *rót* MnNorw *rot* MnSw *rot* MnDanish
rod). Germanic cognates of the Norse words are doubtful : thus,
MnNorthFr *rôt rut* Plattdeutsch *rut* could be Norse loan-words.
Outside Germanic we have, however, OIrish *frén* ' root ' (< **urdno-*)
Cornish *grueiten* ' do.' Welsh *gwrysgen* (< **urdskā-*) ' branch '
Latin *rādix* (< **urād-*), *rāmus* (< **urādmo-*), *radius* Greek ῥάδιξ,
ῥάδαμνος all to IndE **u(e)rād-* ∽ **uerьd-*. Closely-related words
are :— (1) Gothic *waúrts* OE *wyrt* (> MnE *wort*) OS *wurt* OHG *wurz*
(> MHG *wurz* > MnHG *wurz*) Ic *urt* MnNorw *urt* MnDanish *urt*,
OSw *yrt* < PrGmc **wurti-* < IndE **urdi-* and (2) the different
(though in some languages homonymous) words for ' brewer's

---

[1] By XV c. ME *wǫse* (< OE *wāse*, above) fell together with the descendant of
OE *wōs* ' sap, juice ', the semantic meeting-point no doubt being the notion of
' moisture '. The loss of *w*, which occurred in XVI c., is exceptional.

[2] The Latin word made its way into most of the Germanic languages as OE
ostre Ic *ostra* MnNorw *ostra* MnSw *ostron* MnDanish *østers* MDutch *oester* (>
MnDutch *oester*) [MnHG *auster*, lwf. XVI c. LG *úster*].

[3] First recorded c. 1200. ·

wort ', as MHG *würze* (> MnHG *würze*) beside Ic *virtr* OHG *wirz* (> MHG *wirz*) OE *wiert* > *wyrt* (> MnE *wort*) < PrGmc **wirti-* < IndE **u̯erdi-*.

SHIP < OE *scip* = Gothic *skip* Ic *skip* OHG *skif skëf* (> MHG *schif schëf* > MnHG *schiff*) OS *skip* (> MLG *schip schep*) MDutch *scip scep* (> MnDutch *schip*) OFr *skip* < PrGmc **skipa-*, possibly related to Lettish *škibīt* ' to hew, cut '.[1][2]

SHOP < OE *sceoppa* ' gazophylacium ' (ἅπ. λεγ., WS Gospels L 21, 1) = OHG *skopf scof* ' porch, vestibule ' (> MHG *schopf(e* ' porch, vestibule, barn ' > MnHG dial. *schopf* ' barn, shed, shippen ') < PrGmc **skoppan-*. As closely-related forms we have OE *scypen* ' cattle-shed ' (> MnE (mainly Northern dialects) *shippen* ' do.') MLG *schoppen, schuppen*[3] ' do.' < PrGmc **skuppinjō-*. The Germanic stem was borrowed into Old French as *eschope escope* (> MnFrench *échoppe*) ' booth, cobbler's stall '[4].

SNOW < OE *snāw* = Gothic *snaiws* Ic *snjór* MnNorw *snjo* MnSw *snö* MnDanish *sne* OHG *snêo* (> MHG *snê* > MnHG *schnee*) OS *snêo* (> MLG *snê*) MDutch *snê* (> MnDutch *sneeuw*) OFr *snê* < PrGmc **snaewa-* < IndE **snoig^ₓho-*. The corresponding verb is old : OE *snīwan* OIc ppart. *snifenn* OHG *snîwan* MDutch *snûwen*[5] < PrGmc **snīwan-* < IndE **sneig^ₓheti*. Non-Germanic " snow "-words include Lith *sniēgas* ' snow ' Lettish *snìegs* ' do.' OBg *sněgъ* ' do.' Russian *sneg* OPR *snaygis* (< **snoig^ₓhi-*) ' sne ' Greek as. νίφα Latin *nix* (as. *niuem*) Welsh *nyf* ' snow ' OIrish *snige* ' drop, rain '. For the old verb, cf. Av *snaēžaiti* ' it snows ' Greek νείφει

---

[1] OHG *skif* ba. It *schifo* OFrench *eschif* (ba. MnE *skiff*, first recorded 1575). MnE *equip* (first recorded 1523) lwf. French *équiper* (< earlier *esquiper*, N lw. : Ic *skipa* ' to man (a vessel), fit up, arrange ' to Ic *skip*).

[2] The word " ship " was originally confined to Northern Europe. The principal Indoeuropean word was *nāus : Latin *nāuis* Greek ναῦς Skt *nắu-* Arm *nav* OIc *nór* (cf. also OHG *nacho* OS *nako* OE *naca*, etc.).

[3] ba. MnHG *schuppen*.

[4] The homonym MnFrench *échoppe* ' burin, graving-tool ' is etymologically unconnected ; it is an XVIII c. alteration of *eschople* < OFrench *eschalpre* < Latin *scalprum* ' cutting-instrument, chisel, etc.' (its diminutive *scalpellum* is the source of MnE *scalpel*).

[5] MnE *snow*, verb, is a reformate on the noun.

Latin *niuit* Lith *snìgti* ' do.' MIrish *snigid* ' it rains, snows ' Latin *ninguit* Lith *sniñga* ' it snows '.[1]

SPOON < OE *spōn* ' chip, shaving ' (the MnE sense is adopted from Norse) = Ic *spónn spánn* ' chip, shaving ; spoon ' MnNorw *spôn* ' chip, spoon ' MnSw *spån* ' chip ' MnDanish *spaan* ' do.'[2] OHG *spán* ' chip, splinter ' (> MHG *spán* ' do.' > MnHG *span* ' do.') MLG *spôn* ' chip ; wooden spatula ' (as MLG *botter-spôn*) MDutch *spaen* ' long thin piece of wood, wooden spoon ' (> MnDutch *spaan* ' chip ') < PrGmc *spēnu-[3] [4].

TALENT < OE *talente* = OHG *talenta* (> MnHG *talent*), both being adoptions of Latin *talentum* (pl. -*a*), lwf. Greek *τάλαντον* ' balance, weight ; (particular) sum of money '. In form, ME *talent* was reinforced by OFrench *talent* ' will, desire, appetite ' and took this sense as well as retaining the older, monetary sense. The modern sense ' mental endowment, natural ability '[5] (also in German, French, Italian and other languages) is, of course, from the Parable of the Talents (Mt 25, 14–30).

THROW < OE *prāwan* ' to turn, twist '[6] = OHG *drâen* (> MHG *dræjen dræhen* > MnHG *drehen*) OS *thrâian* (> MLG *dreien*) MDutch *draeyen* (> MnDutch *draaien*) < PrGmc *prējan-* to IndE *ter-* in Greek *τρῆμα*, *τείρω* Latin *tero* OBg *trěti* ' to rub ' Lith *trinù* ' to rub, file, saw ' OIrish *tarathar* ' borer, drill ' Welsh *taradr* ' auger ' ; there are, further, many words formed on this base (and its ablauts) in Germanic e.g. MnE *trite* (lwf. Latin ppart. *trītus* to *tero*) ; MnE dial. *tharm* ' intestine ' < OE *pearm* = OHG

---

[1] On " snow ", see further R. L. Turner, *Bulletin of the School of Oriental and African Studies* xviii, 449–52 ; xix, 375 ; E. Benveniste, *Μνημης Χαριν Gedenkschrift Paul Kretschmer*, pp. 35–9 ; A. S. C. Ross, *Neuphilologische Mitteilungen* lviii, 144–7.

[2] *span-new*, N lw. (: Ic *spán-nýr*).

[3] Finnish *paanu* ' roof-shingle ', N lw.

[4] There is another Germanic word for ' spoon ': OHG *leffil* (> MHG *leffel* > MnHG *löffel*) OS *lepil* MnDutch *lepel* ; cf. OE *læpeldre* ' dish ' < PrGmc *lap- < IndE *lab-* in OHG *laffan* OE *lapian* (> MnE *lap*, verb) MnSw *lapa* MnIc *lepja* ; Latin *lambo* Greek *λάμπω* OBg *lobъzati* ' to kiss ' Arm *lap'el* ' to lick '.

[5] First recorded c. 1430.

[6] On the semantic change, see *NED* s.v. *Throw* vb.

darm (> MHG *darm* > MnHG *darm*) Ic *parmr* MnSw *tarm* MnDanish
tarm < PrGmc **parma-* ; MnE *thread* < OE *prǽd* = OHG *drât*
(> MHG *drât* > MnHG *draht*) Ic *práðr* MnSw *trâd* MnDanish
traad < PrGmc **prēdu-*.

THUNDER < ME *pŏnder* [1] *pŏner* < OE *punor* = OFr *thuner* OS
thuner MDutch *donder* (> MnDutch *donder*) OHG *donar* (> MHG
doner > MnHG *donner*) Ic *þórr* (< **ponṛ*) < PrGmc **ponara-*,
ultimately from IndE **ten-* (**ton- *tṇ-*) ' to stretch, resound ',
attested, for instance, by Latin *tonāre* (> Roumanian *tuna* ' to
thunder ' It *tonare* MnFrench *tonner* Prov *tronar* ' do.' Catalan
tronar ' do.' Sp *tronar*) Skt *tanayitnú-* ' thundering ' MnPersian
tundar ' thunder '.

The Germanic weather-god *Thunor* or *Thor* replaces Jove in the
name of the fifth day of the week ; thus LLatin *dies Iouis* (> It
giovedì MnFrench *jeudi*) is equivalent to OE *punresdæg*, later
þórsdæg (N lw. : Ic *þórsdagr*), *pūrsdæg* (N lw. : OSw *pūrsdagher*)[2] ;
cf. MDutch *donresdach* (> MnDutch *donderdag*) OHG *donares-tag*
(> MnHG *donnerstag*) OFr *thunresdei* < PrGmc **ponaras ðaʒa-* [3].

WALRUS. The European words for this beast are of exceptional
difficulty and have recently been subjected to a most exhaustive
study by Professor V. Kiparsky [4]. I attempt here the briefest
of summaries, referring the reader interested to the work itself.
The ultimate origin of the word appears to be in Lappish : Kola
Lappish *morša* ' walrus ' Inari Lappish *muršša* ' do.', a word which
imitates the sound made by the animal. This Lappish word was
borrowed into Finnish as **morsa *mursa morsu mursu norsa norsu
nursa nursu* and into Karelian as *muržu *moržu* ; the *n*-forms are
probably due to the influence of Lappish *nuorroš* ' a kind of seal ' [5].
The Karelian form was borrowed, not earlier than XII c., into
Russian as *morzh* ; this form, written *morſſ*, first appears in *Tractatus
de duabus Sarmatiis*, the work of the Polish scholar, Matias Miecho-

---

[1] For the *d* see p. 32.
[2] It is possible that *pūrsdæg* may be, not a Danish loan-word, but a form showing
the assimilation *nr* > *r*.
[3] OE *punor* is represented in a number of place-names e.g. *Thunderfield* Surrey
(written *punresfeld*, c. 880) ; *Thursley* Surrey (written *thoresle*, a. 1296).
[4] *L'histoire du morse* (*Suomalaisen Tiedeakatemian Toimituksia* B. LXXIII.iii).
[5] From 1856 *norsu* has been used in the sense ' elephant ' in Finnish.

wita, which was published in 1517 ; and this written form spread, in various guises, with the translations of Miechowita's book—so that we have German *morſs*, French *mors*, Italian *morsf* (and even *morff*). The word *morse* however entered the English language *before* the publication of Miechowita's book, namely in the year 1480, for in *The Chronicles of England* (printed by Caxton in that year) there is a passage (Chapter CCLVII) which deals with the events of 1456, which is relevant : " This yere were taken iiij grete fisshes bitwene Eerethe [1] and London, that one was called *mors marine . . .*". It seems that the only possible route by which this word could have reached the English of this date is via Basque whalers in British service who had heard the word from the Lapps. *Morse* (later *Sea-Morse*) was used in English until XVIII c., when it was supplanted by *walrus*. The word *walrus*—cf. also MnHG *walross* MnNorw *kvalross* MnSw *valross* MnDanish *valros*—is the result of a " metathesis " in the compound *ross* + *hval* which must have happened not later than XII c. because it is attested in OFrench *galerous* of that date. It is suggested that this change of order originated in Belgium where French- and Dutch-speaking people lived together and were used to the opposed word-order of French and Germanic compounds (cf., for instance, MnFrench *homme-poisson* = MnHG *fisch-mann*, MnFrench *poisson-homme* = MnHG *mann-fisch*). The second element of *rosshval* (also *rosmhval rostmhval rosthval russhval hrosshval*) is the word " whale " (PrGmc **xwala-*) ; the first part was at one time supposed to mean ' red ' but Kiparsky rejects this view ; the earliest occurrence of the form is in Ohthere's Voyage, where one of the two Anglo-Saxon texts has dp. *horschwælum* [2] ; Kiparsky supposes this *horsc* (i.e. [horš]) to be a distortion of the original Lappish word, *morša* etc. In the Norwegian dialects we have forms such as *rosmal rosmul rosmer rosmar* (from earlier *rosmhval*) ; in 1551, Olaus Magnus created a latinized *rosmarus* which, since the time of Linnæus, has become the scientific name of the animal.[3] [4]

---

[1] i.e. *Erith.*

[2] See my *Terfinnas and Beormas of Ohthere*, p. 20.

[3] OFrench *rohal* < **roshal* < *rosshvalr* ; we have also OFrench *rohart roal*, the latter form being borrowed into English as ME *ruwal rewell(-bone)*, *ruel*, etc. ' ivory '.

[4] In Icelandic there are curious forms such as *rostung rostingr*, which are difficult to explain ; they appear to contain this same *ros-* < *hross-* < **horš-* < *morš-*.

WINTER < OE *winter* = Gothic *wintrus* Ic *vetr* (gs. *vetrar*) OHG *wintar* (> MHG *winter* > MnHG *winter*) OS *wintar* (> MLG *winter* [1]) MDutch *winter* (> MnDutch *winter*) OFr *winter* < PrGmc **wintru-*. The ultimate origin is disputed : the word may represent a nasalised form to IndE **u̯ed-* as in MnE *wet water otter*, or perhaps it may be from IndE **u̯ind-* ' white [time] '—cf. Gaulish *Uindo-magus* OIrish *find* ' white ' Welsh *gwyn* ' do.' [2].

WOOD < OE *wudu* = Ic *viðr* MnNorw *vid* OSw *viper* (> MnSw *ved*) ODanish *with* (> MnDanish *ved*) OHG *witu* (> MHG *wite* > MnHG d. (*krane-*)*wett*) OS *widu* (> MLG *wēde*) MDutch (*tal-*)*wēde* OFr *widu*(-*bên*) ; OIrish *fid* ' tree ' Welsh *gwydd* ' do.' MCornish *gueyth* ' do.' Breton *gwez* ' do.' (cf. also Gaulish *Uidu-casses*) < IndE **u̯idhu-*, which is usually taken as essentially the same as Skt *vidhú-* ' isolated ' Lith *vidùs* ' the inside ' Lettish *vidus* ' middle ' OPR *widus* ' noet ' [3].

WORM < OE *wyrm* ' serpent ; worm [4] ' = OHG *wurm* (> MHG *wurm* > MnHG *wurm*) OS *wurm* (> MLG *worm*) MDutch *worm* (> MnDutch *worm*) OFr *wirm* < PrGmc **wurmi-* ; Ic *ormr* MnNorw *orm* MnSw *orm* MnDanish *orm* < PrGmc **worma-* [5]—each of these normally has the primary sense ' serpent '— < IndE **u̯r̥mi-*, **u̯r̥mo-*. Outside Germanic we have : Latin *uermis* (< **uormis*) Greek *ρόμος* OPR *wormyan urminan* ' rot '.[6] IndE **kʷr̥mi-* (of similar sense—but it is difficult to see how it can be connected with IndE **u̯r̥mi-* above) is also widely evidenced : Skt *kr̥mi-* ' worm ' MnPersian

---

[1] ba. MnSw *vinter* MnDanish *vinter*.

[2] In most other Indoeuropean languages another word for " winter " appears, IndE **ĝheim-* ∽ **ĝhim-* ∽ **ĝhi̯em-* : Latin *hiems* Greek *χειμών* Hittite *gimmant-* Skt *hemantá-* Albanian *dimɛn* OBg *zima* Av *zyà* Lith *žēmà* MIrish *gam* OWelsh *gaem* (> MnWelsh *gaeaf*). Traces of this root are also to be found in Germanic, as Salic Law *ingismus*, etc. ' yearling beast ' (see W. L. van Helten *PBB* xxv, 268 ff.) MnIc *gimbur* ' ewe before the first lambing ' MnSw *gimmer* ' do.' MnNorw *gimber gimre* ' young ewe ' (MnE d. *gimmer*, N lw.).

[3] i.e. MnHG *naht*.

[4] The latter sense is rare in Anglo-Saxon save in combination (*seoloc-wyrm*) and is normally expressed by OE *maþa* = Gothic *maþa* OHG *mado* (> MnHG *made* ' maggot ') OS *maðo* ; cf. Ic *maðkr* (ME *maþek* (> EMnE *maddock*, MnE dial. *mawk*) is a Scandinavian loan-word).

[5] The declension of Gothic *waúrms* is uncertain.

[6] From the colour of worms ; cf. OE *wurma* ' murex ' OFr *worma* ' purple '— and MnE *vermilion*.

kirm ' do.' Albanian *krimp* ' do.' OBg *čьrvь* ' do.'[1] Lith *kirmis*
' do.' Lettish *cefme* ' do.' MIrish *cruim* ' do.' Welsh *pryf* ' do.'[2].

YAD YAUD, etc.[3]. This word is plentifully attested in the Northern
dialects ; I have noted the following written forms : *yad yaud yade
yaid* (Scotland) and *yaud yawd yode yoad yowd yod yāad* (Northern
Counties). The chief meanings are ' (old) mare ' (Scotland, Cumber-
land, Yorkshire) and ' (old) horse ' (Yorkshire and North Lancashire) ; in Northumberland the sense ' work-horse, *or* -mare ' is
also found—and, in this area too, the word is applied to women in
bait-yauds ' women who gather bait for fishermen ' ; the specific
sense ' riding-horse ' appears in Yorkshire and North Lancashire ;
a connotation of inferiority—thus ' nag, jade ' is often present in
Yorkshire ; the word is sometimes applied as a term of abuse to
women in much the same sense as standard English *jade*—sometimes, too, to other female animals than horses ; in Cleveland,
the word is recorded applied as a term of abuse to a man.

Save for *yaid* (on which see below), all the forms listed above can
safely be considered as being descended from ME *ʒald*. This word
is rare and Northern.   In the Morte Arthure, the opprobrious
epithet *ʒaldsons* is applied to the Saracens at v. 3809. The word is
apparently first recorded as the first element of a Yorkshire place-
name, *Yaldesik*, occurring in a charter of 1307 which is an inspeximus
of an earlier one.[4]   The word is recorded several times in Middle
Scots and one occurrence in Dunbar is especially interesting—in the
Petition of the Gray Horse, Auld Dunbar. In the poem, the poet likens
himself to an old horse, worn out by long service ; it is Christmas
time and he petitions King James IV for a Christmas present.
The poem[5] is in stanzas and each stanza ends with the refrain

> Schir, lat it never in toune be tald
> That I suld be ane Yuillis yald.

The expression *Yule's yaud* is attested in late XVIII c. Scots and
Yeel's jade survived until XX c. These expressions mean ' a person

---

[1] Cf. also OBg *črьmьnъ* ' red '.
[2] In MnE *worm, wo* is a graphic substitution for *wu* made early in the Middle
English period (as also in *wort, worse*) ; for LOE *wur-* < EOE *wyr-*, see p. 114.
[3] A dialect word.
[4] *Calendar of Charter Rolls* iii, 95.
[5] W. M. Mackenzie, *The Poems of William Dunbar*, pp. 46 ff.

who is without a new garment at Christmas' and Dunbar's use is thus very apt—if the King does not give him a present he will be a *Yeel's jade*.

This expression is, by itself, sufficient to show that *ya(u)d* is of Scandinavian origin, as is indeed the case. For similar superstitions are well-attested in Scandinavia. Thus we have the "Christmas Cat" of Iceland for which the *locus classicus* is the following passage from Jón Árnason's *Íslenzkar þjóðsögur og æfintýri* ii, 570 [I translate]: "Nevertheless people could not enjoy Christmas festivities altogether without anxiety for . . . there was a belief that the monster which was called the 'Christmas Cat' [*jólaköttur*] was on his wanderings then. He did no harm to those who *had* some new garment to put on on Christmas Eve, but those who had got no new garment 'all put on [went into][1] the Christmas Cat'". In his book *Jul*, H. F. Feilberg records that in Sunnmøre (Norway) the "New Year's Goat" (*Nyårsbukken*) is supposed to get those who have not had new clothes for the New Year (ii, 59) and in Salten (Norway) the fabulous "Yule-Lads" (*Julesvendene*) are supposed to take those who have no new clothes for Christmas (ii, 51–2).

ME *ʒald* is undoubtedly a Scandinavian loan-word. In Norse we have OIc *ialda* and MnSw d. *jäldä*, both meaning 'mare'. The word is rare in Old Icelandic [2] but it occurs in Icelandic place-names as also in those of Norway and, less certainly, Denmark.

The Scandinavian word is undoubtedly an early loan from Finnish; the word is not actually recorded in Finnish but it exists in two languages related to Finnish viz. Lappish *al'do* 'full-grown female reindeer which has a calf of the current year' (in Polmak: 'full-grown female reindeer', in general) and Mordvin *el'de äl'd'ä jäl'd'ä* 'mare' (also applied to women as a term of abuse). The phonological problems arising in the history of this word are throughout difficult but, in brief, the Lappish and Mordvin forms entitle us to postulate a PrFinnish ns. **ältä* ∽ gs. **äldän* and this

---

[1] *fóru allir í jólaköttinn* ; *fara í* means 'to put on' but there is a pun here—for *fara í* also means 'to go into' i.e. 'be eaten by'.

[2] In view of the use of the word in Cleveland dialect as a term of abuse applied to a man, it is interesting that the Icelandic word is a nick-name in *Ásbjǫrn ialda*, a man mentioned in the Heimskringla (ed. of F. Jónsson [1911], p. 606, line 27).

would indeed appear when borrowed as OIc *ialda* ; ME *ʒald* does, on investigation, correspond well with the Scandinavian form.

I may conclude this section with a mention of two other English words. The first is the word **jade** (of a horse or a woman). This first occurs in the Canterbury Tales where, at B 4002, it rhymes with *glāde* ' to gladden '. This rhyme clearly indicates a pronunciation with *ā* and the Modern English pronunciation with [ei] is thus the direct descendant of Chaucer's form. It has sometimes been suggested [1] that *jade*, too, represents a borrowing of ON *ialda*, either direct or via Anglo-Norman. The suggestion that it is a direct borrowing, that is, a parallel form to ME *ʒald*, may at once be dismissed on the ground that Chaucer's *ā* and MnE [ei] could not possibly derive from an earlier *ald*. (We need not therefore discuss the question whether an exceptional development ME *ʒ* > MnE [dž] might be possible [2]). If ON *ialda* had been borrowed into Anglo-Norman, it would have appeared as **jaude* and, again, it would be impossible to derive Chaucer's *ā* and MnE [ei] from this form. Nor is there, in fact, any trace of such a word in Anglo-Norman or in French at all. There is thus no etymological connection between *jade* and *ya(u)d*. But the two words have influenced one another, both formally and semantically. Thus MnScots *jaud* *jad* can hardly derive from ME *jāde* ; they owe their form to *yaud* *yad*. On the other hand, the Scots form *yaid* cannot derive from ME *ʒald* ; it is clearly due to the influence of ME *jāde* [3]. Moreover, the connotation ' inferior, worn-out, old ' appears to belong to the word *jade* ; it is not present in ON *ialda* or in the Finno-Ugrian cognates of its etymon. When, therefore, this connotation is found in the English representatives of ON *ialda* (above), it may well be due to the influence of *jade*. The etymology of *jade* remains quite obscure ; it is tempting to suggest some connection with Sp *jadear* (earlier *ijadear*, cf. Latin pl. *īlia*) ' to breathe with difficulty because of tiredness ' ; cf., particularly, MnE *jade* intrans. verb, *jaded* adj. But it must be admitted that there are considerable difficulties in this etymology. If, however, it were accepted, it might perhaps be

---

[1] E.g. by H. C. Wyld, *The universal dictionary of the English Language* s.v. *jade (II)*.

[2] In connection with *jolly-boat*, *NED* (s.v.) mentions MnSw *jolle* MnDanish *jolle*.

[3] *ai* is a Middle Scots spelling for *ā*.

suggested that, originally, *jade* had no female connotation and that this arose in England under the influence of ME *ʒald*.

My second English word is one of exceptional rarity ; it is, in fact, only recorded once—it is **yolk** ‘ spayed pig ’ given as a Kentish dialect word at J. C. Morton, *A cyclopedia of Agriculture* [1855] ii, 727. Attempts to find the word among present-day Kentish farmers and those interested in Kentish dialect have met with no success. In Norse we have the Set OIc *ialkr* ‘ gelding ’ MnIc *jálkur* ‘ gelding ; nag, jade ’ MnNorw *gjelk jalk* ‘ gelding ’ MnSw dial. *jälk* ‘ stallion ’ [1]. In Orkney Norn there is a word *yaager* ‘ horse, strong man ’ ; and, in Shetland Norn, there is—to come round once more to the Christmas Cat—a word *jøl-jager* ‘ person, particularly boy, who has not had new clothes, or something else new, for Christmas ’. In his *Etymologisk ordbog over det norrøne sprog på Shetland*, s.v., J. Jakobsen suggests that *-jager* in this word is the same as Shetland *jager* ‘ pedlar ; one who buys on the Q.T. (particularly of a buyer of fish) ’. But this latter word *jager* is clearly a normal derivative of the Shetland verb *jag* ‘ to buy on the Q.T. (particularly of fish) ’ so that Jakobsen’s etymology of *jøl-jager* is highly unsatisfactory. In fact, it is certain that Orkney *yaager* and Shetland (*jøl-*)*jager* must be added to our Set OIc *ialkr*, etc.

It does seem fairly safe to assume that Kentish *yolk* is somehow connected with the Set OIc *ialkr*, etc. ; if so, there are only two possibilities : the English word may be a Scandinavian loan-word, or it may be a native English congruent. On the first hypothesis we should have to assume that the modern dialect form derived from a ME **ʒalk*, lwf. ON *ialkr*, just as ME *ʒald*, lwf. ON *ialda*. On general grounds it is improbable that a Kentish word is of Norse origin and the phonology is definitely against this suggestion, for *yolk*—presumably indicating a pronunciation [jouk]—could hardly be a Kentish development of a ME **ʒalk* ; cf. South-East Kent dialect [tɔːk] < ME *talken* (= MnFr *talken*). The suggestion that *yolk* is a Norse loan-word may thus be rejected and it must therefore be a native English congruent to OIc *ialkr*, etc.

The etymology of the words is difficult. OIc *ialkr*, etc., can clearly not be connected with OIc *ialda*, etc., if we accept the Finno-

---

[1] And with this last sense we may compare OIc *Iálkr* as one of Odin’s names— an epithet ‘ stallion ’ is far more appropriate to him than is ‘ gelding ’.

Ugrian etymology for the latter suggested above, for a -*k*-suffix-
formation in the case of a loan-word would be most unlikely.
A. Torp, *Nynorsk etymologisk ordbok* s.v. *jalk* 2, suggests that
MnNorw *jalka* ' to castrate ' is etymologically the same word as
MnNorw *jalka* ' to chew ' (hence with semantic change ' to bite '
> ' to castrate by biting ') < **jakla* (cf. MnNorw *jagla* ' to chew
laboriously at (something) '); but the native Kentish form cannot
possibly be derived from such a base, for the original *kl* must have
been preserved in English.

I suggest, then, that Torp's etymology of MnNorw *jalk* ' gelding '
be rejected and that the following etymology is to be preferred :—
OIc *ialkr*, etc. < PrGmc **elka-* < IndE **el-go-*, with " animal "
-*g*- suffix as in Ic *maðkr* OE *bulluc* (> MnE *bullock*) Skt *turaga-*
' horse ' to the root **el-* found in various animal-names e.g. Ic
elgr Wakhi *rʋš* ' Ovis Poli ' Greek *ἔλαφος* MnE *lamb*. Kentish
yolk can then be derived from a closely-parallel PrGmc **eluka-*
> OE **eoloc*; the development to *yolk* would then afford an exact
parallel to that attested by OE *eowu* > ME *ʒow* > MnE dial. [jau]
[jou] [joː], etc., beside ME *ewe* > MnE *ewe* [1].

YULE < OE *geōl*, earlier *geoh(h)ol geh(h)ol*, also *geōla* ' the name
of a mid-winter festival, then ' Christmas Day, Christmastide ' (cf.
se ǣrra geōla ' December ', *se æfterra geōla* ' January ') = OIc *iól*
pl. OSw *iūl* pl. ' a heathen feast lasting twelve days ', later ' Christmas '. In his *De temporum ratione*, Bede cites *giuli* as the name of
December and January [2]; this form is congruent to OIc *ýler* pl.
' a month beginning on the second day of the week falling within
Nov. 10–17 ' and Gothic *fruma jiuleis* ' November '.

The ultimate etymology of the word is obscure; some have
held that it derives from an IndE **i̯ekʷlo-* with alteration of the
initial consonant by dissimilation (and/or under the influence of
PrGmc **jēra-* ' year ' (> Gothic *jer*)) < IndE **kʷe-kʷl-o-* in the
sense ' year's end, turn of the year ', a reduplicated form of the
root **kʷel-*, evidenced, for instance, in Skt *cárati* ' to move ' Av
čaraiti ' to turn ' Greek *πέλω πέλομαι* ' to be in motion '; Skt

---

[1] For the words discussed in this section see further A. S. C. Ross, " *Jólaköttur,
Yuillis Yald* and similar expressions ", *Saga-Book of the Viking Society* xii, 1–18
(also *ibid.* xiii, 113–4) and *Acta Philologica Scandinavica* xiv, 1–10.

[2] C. W. Jones, *Bedae opera de temporibus*, p. 211, line 10.

cakrá- ' wheel ' Av *čaxra-* ' do.' ; " Tocharian A " *kukäl* ' waggon '
Greek κύκλος ' ring, circle ' Ic *hjól* OE *hwēol* (> MnE *wheel*).

The word *Yule* largely dropped out of current use after Middle
English times, save in Scotch and Northern dialects; in 1661
T. Blount[1] records that " In Yorkshire and our other Northern
parts . . . the common people run about the streets singing Ule,
Ule, Ule, Three Puddings in a Pule. Crack nuts and cry Ule ".
But, in XIX c., the word was revived in general use as a
" picturesque " alternative to *Christmas*.

[1] *Glossographia* s.v. *Ule*.

GLOSSARY OF LESS WELL-KNOWN
TECHNICAL TERMS

THE PURPOSE of this *Glossary* is to afford at least an indication of the meaning, as used in this book, of some terms which may not all be familiar to all its readers. If the term is explained, or if its meaning is to some extent indicated, in this book, the relevant page-number is given, in brackets, after the term—in the former case only the number is given, as (76), in the latter this is preceded by *see* or *cf.* (as, *see p.* 76). Brief indications of the meaning of the remaining terms, whether these are linguistic or not, are given in this *Glossary*.

Ablaut (26).

Acoustics (19).

Adessive case : the case which expresses *at*ness or *with*ness, as in Finnish *minulla* [adessive sg.] *on* [3rd sg. pres. of verb " to be "] ' there is . . . with me ', i.e. ' I have . . .'.

Affect, verb (32).

Affix, noun (26).

Alternate, verb (26).

Analogy (33).

Aorist : the name of a tense (as in Greek).

Aphasia (see p. 20).

Assimilation (32).

Association (of " ideas "), as of " night " with " day " (see p. 33).

Augens : an emphasising particle, as *su* of OIrish *túsu* ' toi ' (*tú* ' thou ').

Axiom : a fundamental assumption.

Back-formation : as in the case of MnE *kiss* (noun) which has been " back-formed " on *kiss* (verb), thus replacing the descendant of OE *coss* (noun).

Bipartite : having two parts.

Borrowing, noun (34).

Breaking, noun (31).

Calque, verb (34).

Centum-language (82).

Chance (see p. 27).

Class (21).

Class of classes (21).

Coding (see p. 22).

Cognate (36).

Combinative sound-change (32).

Communication theory : it is difficult to give a concise indication of the meaning of this term, except to make the obvious remark that its scope is the discussion of how information is communicated (see p. 16).

Congruent, adj. (36).

Corollary, noun : something that follows from a Main Proof.

Cybernetics : essentially, the Theory of Feed-Back Mechanisms (such as the Governor of a Steam Engine)—but see p. 17.

Decode, verb (17).

Deformation : the alteration of a word, often deliberate (as MnE *Gosh !* for *God !*).

Denominative : formed from a nomen (q.v.).

Dental, noun (75).

Derived (26).

Descend (28).

Deverbative : formed from a verb.

Diachronic (15).

Digamma (see p. 84).

Diphthong (76).

Dissimilation (32).

Distant assimilation : a translation of MnHG *fernassimilation* (see the example at p. 62).

Elliptical : showing *ellipse* (or *ellipsis*), as the compound MnE *music-master* which means ' master [who teaches] music ', with ellipse of the part in square brackets.

Enclitic, noun : an appended particle, as Latin *-que*.

Encode, verb (17).

Essential Standard Dictionary (see p. 43).

Etymological Dictionary (see p. 43).

Etymology (36).

Etymon : the proximate source of a loan-word.

Euphemism : the replacement of a tabu-word by something else, as MnE *pass away* for *die*.

Extended root : in Indoeuropean, the addition of something to a root to make what is virtually a new root.

Extension : that which is added to make an extended root.

Family (29).

Finno-Ugrian : the family to which belong Finnish, Hungarian and several other languages.

Folk-etymology : the alteration of an unfamiliar word into something more familiar, as MnE dial. *roebuck* for MnE *robot*.

Grassmann's Law (82).

Grimm's Law (88).

Guttural, noun (75).

Hearing (see p. 19).

Hypochoristic, adj. : the hypochoristic form (MnHG *koseform*) of a name (or, sometimes, other word) is the " familiar " form, as MnE *Liz* for *Elizabeth*.

Illative case : the case of " motion towards ", as in Finnish *Helsinkiin* ' to Helsinki '.

Indoeuropean (71).

Indogermanic = *Indoeuropean*.

Infix (26).

Information Theory = *Communication Theory*.

Instrumental case : the case in which the instrument of an action is put, as in OBg *tlъkomь* [' per interpretem '] *reče* [' dixit '].

Intonation : essentially, the pattern of musical pitch.

Intrusion (32).

Isolative sound-change (31).

Junggrammatisch : belonging to the late nineteenth-century school of German philologists called *Junggrammatiker*.

Labial, noun (75).

Labio-velar, noun (75).

Laryngeal Theory (cf. p. 7).

Lautersatz (35).

Learned loan : a loan-word first borrowed into the written, as distinct from the spoken language, as OE *nōn* ' noon '.

Linguistic act (17).

Linguistics (15).

Liquid, noun (see p. 78).

Loss (32).

Meaning (see p. 20).

Media, Media aspirata (75).

Metathesis (32).

Monophthongisation : the changing of a diphthong into a simple vowel.

Morphology (26).

Mutation (32).

Nasal, noun (see p. 78).

Natural number : a positive integer, as the number *five*.

Nomen (see p. 139).

Objective conjugation : a conjugation of the verb used with an object, as Hungarian *várja* [' he is awaiting '] *az embert* [' the person '] (as against *vár* ' he is waiting ').

Onomatopoeic : formed in imitation of the thing it means, as MnE *cuckoo*.

Palatal, noun (75).

Partitive case : for expressing such things as French *du pain* ' some bread '.

Pattern of Descent (28).

Perfect alphabet (25).

Philology (15).

Phonematic (see p. 24).

Phonematology (31).

Phoneme (24).

Phonology (31).

Popular Etymology (68).

Prefix (26).

Primality : primeness (of numbers), as in the phrase *the primality of five*.

Primitive (29).

Proto-form : parent form (cf. p. 35).

Reduplication : the repetition of the whole, or part, of a word, as Tahitian *parauparau* ' to chatter ' (as against *parau* ' to talk '); Gothic sg. pret. *haihait* to *haitan*.

Reform, verb : to alter by analogy (q.v.).

Related (28).

Remodel = *Reform*.

Root (138).

Rough breathing : the Greek aitch, as in ὁ *ho*.

Runic : the ancient Germanic alphabet.

Satəm-*language* (82).

School-grammar (cf. p. 25).

Semantic Change (33).

Semantics, Semasiology, Semology (33).

Set : this word is used somewhat in its mathematical sense.

" *Sound and Symbol* " (25).

Sound-Change (31).

Sound-Law (31).

Specialise : in Semantics, the narrowing of a meaning, as from OE *hund* ' any kind of dog ' to MnE *hound* ' a special kind of dog '.

Spirant, noun (see p. 84).

Standard, adj. : used of a type of language generally received, as *Standard English*.

Stop, noun (75).

Stufenwechsel (27).

Subset (21).

Suffix (26).

Svarabhakti (32).

Synchronic (15).

Tenuis, tenuis aspirata (75).

Translation-loan (34).

Translative case : the case of " becoming ", as in Finnish *hän on tullut* [' he has become '] *vanhaksi* [' old '].

Umlaut (32).

Vary (26).

Verner's Law (88).

Wanderwort : a word that has travelled widely, in company with the thing it means, as MnE *ginger* (see p. 147).

Weltsprache (8).

Word (see p. 26).